THE
MOVIE BOOK

THE
MOVIE BOOK

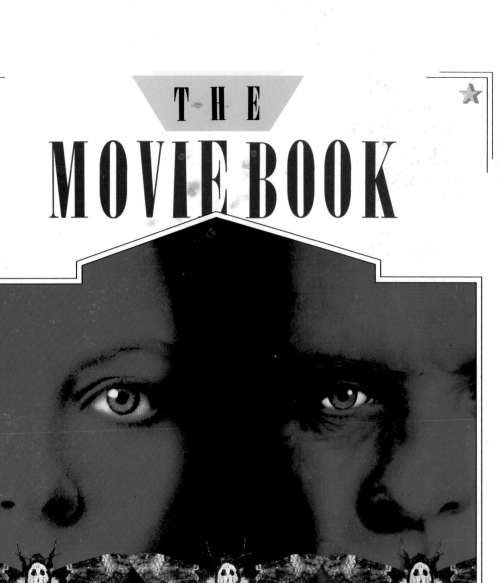

An Illustrated History of the Cinema
DON SHIACH

ULTIMATE
EDITIONS

LEFT
*Kevin Costner as Elliot Ness
in the critically acclaimed*
The Untouchables.

This edition published in 1995 by
Ultimate Editions

© Anness Publishing Limited 1992, 1993, 1995

Ultimate Editions is an imprint of
Anness Publishing Limited
Boundary Row Studios
1 Boundary Row
London SE1 8HP

This edition exclusively distributed in Canada
by Book Express, an imprint of
Raincoast Books Distribution Limited

Distributed in Australia by Reed Editions

ISBN 1-86035-022-4

Publisher: Joanna Lorenz
Project Editor: Stephen Adamson
Art Director: Peter Bridgewater
Designer: Terry Jeavons

Printed and bound in China

The publishers and author wish to thank the British Film Institute and the various private individuals
who have kindly given permission to reproduce pictures in this book, and apologise for any inadvertent omissions.
Taxi Driver and *The Way We were* (pp29, 156) reproduced courtesy of Columbia Pictures, copyright © 1976, 1973
Columbia Pictures Industries Inc. All rights reserved. *Friday 13th, Indiana Jones and the Last Crusade* and
Top Gun (pp218, 212 and 168) reproduced courtesy of Paramount Pictures, copyright © 1980, 1989, 1986
Paramount Pictures. All rights reserved.

Jacket illustrations:
Beverly Hills Cop Copyright © 1984 Paramount Pictures. All rights reserved.

CONTENTS

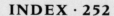

FOREWORD

THE GREAT OLD days of Hollywood, and for movies in general, may have gone forever. Certainly, the movie business has changed enormously in the last few decades, as most people now see their movies in their own homes via videos and television rather than in the cinema. But somehow the magic of the movies lives on. Each new generation falls in love with the products of old Hollywood or the British film industry at its peak, revelling in Astaire-Rogers musicals, suffering with Margaret Lockwood and James Mason, or laughing with Buster Keaton or Cary Grant. Old movies never die, they just resurface on late-night television.

If Hollywood in its heyday with its excesses and absurdities, its real achievements and its abject failures, has gone forever, it is equally true to state that the movie business constantly re-generates itself in different forms. The Holly-wood studio system has been transformed, but new stars, on both sides of the camera, are constantly being created. New markets for different types of movies are being identified and catered for. Movies are still very big business and enormous riches await those, like Steven Spielberg, who tap into the public consciousness. Movies are spectacle, they are dreams, they are a view of reality, a world of fantasy, an escape, a Utopia, a separate universe of their own – movies are several different things to many different people. They are the art of the twentieth century and of the twenty-first century as well. Movies, for good or ill, touch the lives of more people on this planet than books, music or theatre do. There is no escaping them.

This book attempts to encapsulate something of this magic of the movies. By its very nature, it has had to be a selective process; no two movie fans would agree on a list of favourite stars, most important directors or best movies. Hollywood has taken a giant share of our attention because the history of movies is largely the history of the American film industry, although that is not to deny the importance of other major film-producing nations. If you are reading this, you are almost certainly a movie fan, maybe even a movie buff. You belong to a universal club with millions of members across the globe, all in love with a technological medium that has harnessed 'the stuff of which dreams are made'. So, as Dorothy Parker once put it:

Oh, come my love and join with me,
The oldest infant industry.
Come seek the bourne of palm and pearl,
The lovely land of boy-meets-girl.

Come grace this lotus-laden shore,
The isle of Do-What's-Done-Before.
Come curb the new and watch the old win,
But where the streets are paved with Goldwyn.

INTRODUCTION

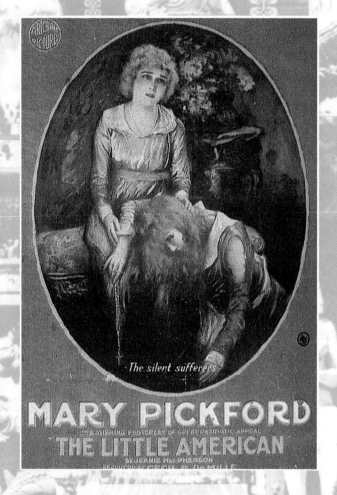

THE HUMBLE BEGINNINGS

FROM THE EDISON factory's humble kineto-scope, the amoeba of the film industry, grew the international market for film we know today. It was just a simple machine comprising a cabinet and a length of film on a spool. The customers inserted a coin, the light shone and the film was projected onto the back of the cabinet.

Movies have always been perceived as an American product, but, in fact, European inventors played crucial roles in the development of the cinematic apparatus: for example, William Friese-Green in England, Georges Demeny of France, and Anschutz and Skladanowski in Germany. In the 1890s the pioneers were French: the Lumière brothers, Gaumont and Pathé.

Kinetoscope Parlors were opened in 1894 in the principal cities of America. Perhaps it is not absolutely accurate to say that cinema began with the kinetoscope, because the essence of the cinematic experience is its communal nature (whilst retaining privacy for the individual sitting in the darkness of the cinema as he or she sees their dreams appear before them). Thus, the

RIGHT

An advert for the Lumière brothers' shows in Paris. To a turn-of-the-century audience, these Lumière extravaganzas had more than a touch of magic about them, an expectation the brothers skilfully exploited.

BELOW

A contemporary artist's impression of a kinetoscope parlour in America. Note the respectable ambience and the genteel decor that seek to reinforce the notion that such establishments are quite 'proper' for ladies and gentlemen.

cinema was really born with the invention of a projector that could throw a series of moving images onto a screen. The Latham brothers and W.K.L. Dickson invented the Panoptikon projector which took movies out of the kinetoscope cabinet and in September 1895, in Paris, the Lumière brothers showed a paying audience films that they themselves had produced in their Lyons factory.

In the States, musical theatres began to present movies as part of their variety bills. Film companies were formed – the Biograph and Vitagraph companies, for example. In 1902 the first motion picture theatre, the Electric, was opened in Los Angeles. Early cinemas were called 'nickelodeons' because you paid a nickel (five cents) to see the show. By 1907 there were approximately 3000 such nickelodeons across America. The cinema was on its way to becoming big business.

THE NARRATIVE FILM

THE PATH TO *BIRTH OF A NATION*

New York was at this time the centre of American filmmaking; Hollywood was still a suburb of Los Angeles that was kind to oranges. In 1903 the Edison factory produced a landmark in cinematic history – the first true narrative film, *The Great Train Robbery*. At the Biograph Studios in New York a few years later a young actor, Lawrence Griffith, replaced a sick director on a one-reeler, *The Adventures of Dolly*, and launched the career of D.W. Griffith, film director. If the young Griffith had had any pretensions at this stage of his career to being a 'serious artist', then he must have had to lay them aside, because between 1908 and 1913 he directed 450 motion pictures. The nickelodeons were hungry monsters with an endless appetite for fifteen- or thirty-minute features to set before an eager, mass audience. Films were cranked off the assembly line. Movies were in business already.

TOP

It's a long, long way to Dances with Wolves, *but* The Great Train Robbery *(1903) was not only the first full-length narrative film but also the first western to have them queueing round the block.*

ABOVE

The emblems of the Vitagraph and Essanay Studios.

By 1912 'proper' cinemas, as opposed to nickelodeons or halls, were fairly common and admission prices had doubled. Commensurate with this increase in admission prices was the increased length of the movies shown: one- and two-reelers of fifteen or thirty minutes had given way to four- and five-reelers. Motion pictures were moving up in the world. One of the first entrepreneurs to realise this was Adolph Zukor,

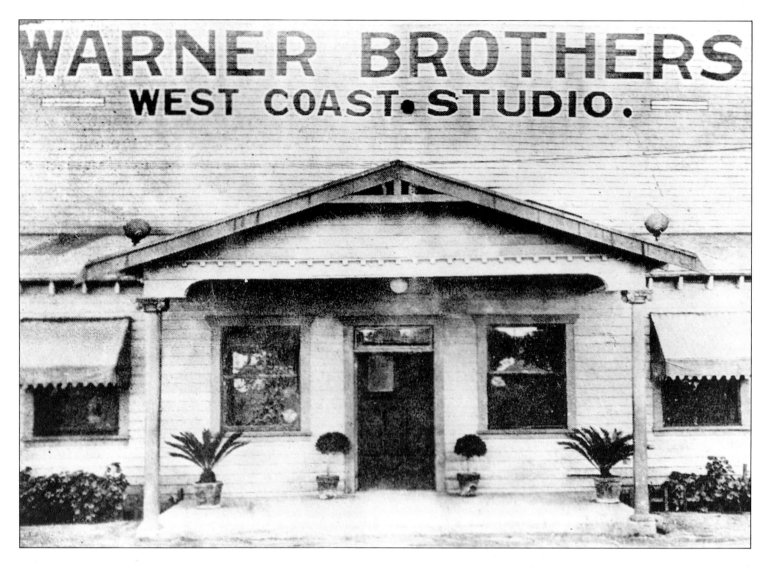

ABOVE
Yes, this was the humble beginning of the major studio, Warner Brothers. Even today, Hollywood and Los Angeles have a certain air of impermanence about them, but these premises look like they would not have survived a strong wind, let alone the mildest of Californian earth tremors.

who founded the Famous Players Film Company. Gradually, he and other entrepreneurs seduced famous stage actors away from the stage and onto the screen.

However, American films had hot competition from abroad. For example, the Italian-made *Quo Vadis*, an eight-reel epic, ran for twenty-two weeks in New York.

Hollywood began to replace New York as the centre of filmmaking. The reasons were several: independent producers went west to escape the clutches of the Motion Picture Patents Company, a trust (including the Vitagraph and Biograph companies) formed to enforce a monopoly on filmmaking patents; the suburbs round Los Angeles were relatively undeveloped and furnished excellent natural resources for filmmaking on the cheap (sun, desert, mountains, nearby urban locations); and, crucially, the area was also a source of far cheaper labour than could be found in New York.

In 1914 the Jesse Lasky Feature Play Company

was formed. Lasky's brother-in-law, Samuel Goldfish, later Goldwyn, joined the company, as did another famous Hollywood name, Cecil B. de Mille, who directed their first feature *The Squaw Man* in a barn. In the same year Paramount Pictures was formed to release the pictures of the Famous Players Company. Production, distribution and exhibition were the three battlegrounds for the early companies.

In 1915 arguably the most famous silent movie of all, *The Birth of a Nation*, was released. A twelve-reel epic about the civil war and its aftermath, the movie, directed by D.W. Griffith, was the first film to be granted 'road show' status. It was a huge box-office hit all over the world and won critical praise from sources which had hitherto scorned the movies as 'dreams for the masses'.

The Birth of a Nation also aroused great controversy and opposition, particularly from black people. With our historical perspective, we can see just how horrendously racist it was in its ideology. The Ku Klux Klan were represented heroically as the defenders of civilised values, and carpetbaggers and rapacious 'negroes' as the villains of the piece. However, Griffith's advanced film techniques – close-ups, cross-cutting, the staging of elaborate crowd and battle scenes – indicated that the cinema had made a huge technical advance.

AMERICAN DOMINATION OF THE WORLD MARKET

By the end of the First World War the American film industry had effectively established itself as the dominant cinema, although the film industries of the Soviet Union, Germany, France and Scandinavia would challenge Hollywood in the twenties in terms of the artistic use of the medium. Directors such as Fritz Lang, Sergei Eisenstein, Friedrich Murnau, Abel Gance, Jean Renoir, Mauritz Stiller and Carl Dreyer made films that very few American filmmakers could match. However, to ruthless movie executives films are pure business. Hollywood studios had the power to impose their products wherever films were shown commercially.

Their own huge domestic market gave American filmmakers an enormous advantage over other countries. Studios could make film after film in the sure knowledge that American box-office revenues alone would produce substantial profits. Foreign revenues were the icing on the cake. Exhibitors all around the world were clamouring for products to show and America produced far more films than anywhere else.

The businessmen who owned the studios realised that there were three crucial areas of the film business they had to control if they were to establish a virtual monopoly in the marketplace: production, distribution and exhibition. Of these the real money was to be made in distribution and exhibition, so all the major Hollywood studios were intent on setting up their distribution arms and buying as many cinemas in prime locations as they could. As the distributors of their own films, they could charge a substantial rental (usually between 30 and 40 per cent of box-office receipts) to cinemas not owned by themselves. As the owners of their own cinemas, they were showing their own products and all revenues came back to the parent company. Most of the early movie moguls came into film production via other business activities as diverse as theatre ownership and scrap-dealing, and they brought a hard-nosed, ruthless, market-orientated approach to the enterprise of making movies for a mass audience.

The American film industry was also very efficient at publicising its wares. The studios were adept at creating an aura of glamour and excitement round movies, and stars were the main carriers of this 'aura'. The production of glamour was aided and abetted by newspapers and magazines in all the developed countries of the world. Thus, when Douglas Fairbanks and Mary Pickford came to Europe after the end of the First World War, they were greeted by enormous numbers of people wherever they went. Movie stars were the new royalty, and a huge publicity machine, partly wielded by the Hollywood studios and partly by other media with vested interests in aiding this publicity, made sure they would retain that aura for years to come.

LEFT
A publicity still for The Birth of a Nation *(1915) – hopefully, the only film in movie history to project in its publicity the Ku Klux Klan as the heroic defenders of Christian civilisation. The movie caused a furore, but it also made Griffith's reputation as a major innovator in terms of film technique. And, yes, it made megabucks at the box-office.*

LEFT

Douglas Fairbanks in The Thief of Bagdad *(1924). Fairbanks' films were elaborately costumed affairs which took full advantage of his natural athleticism, but his star waned with the advent of sound.*

BELOW

Norma Shearer in the 1927 silent melodrama After Midnight. *Shearer's career lasted well into the sound era at MGM, possibly helped by the fact that she was married to the studio's golden boy, Irving Thalberg. Of Shearer, Lillian Hellman wrote that she had 'a face unclouded with thought'.*

BELOW RIGHT

Her acting abilities may be in dispute, but for her many fans, Greta Garbo remains the eternal goddess of the silver screen.

By the twenties movies were very big business indeed. The average movie product was unsophisticated and direct in its appeal, whether it was a Mack Sennett comedy or a melodramatic tearjerker starring Gloria Swanson or Norma Talmadge. Filmmakers went after family audiences because that was where the money was, so escapism was the order of the day. The showmen's belief was that the movies should offer harmless entertainment and not bother with 'messages'. Movies offered an escape from everyday problems; they transported you to exotic locations and embroiled you in romantic and dangerous exploits. Up there on the screen, you could watch the parting of the Red Sea (courtesy of Cecil B. De Mille), see Ramon Navarro win a chariot race in Ancient Rome, or witness the crucifixion of Christ in *King of Kings*. Spectacle, mayhem and moralising melodrama are the stuff of which dreams are made, and the movies sold dreams.

The Hollywood studios were the Dream Factories, manufacturing fantasy for the millions. Dream Factories required Dream Palaces in which these manufactured dreams could be experienced, and so exotic cinemas such as Grauman's Chinese Theater in Los Angeles, the Gra-

nada in humble Tooting in South London, or Radio City Music Hall in New York were built in the years to come to add an extra enticement to cinema-goers. Movies transported you to a different world, so it was appropriate that cinemas should have this other-worldly ambience as well.

Although movies had become established as a worldwide major entertainment form, by the mid-twenties audiences were beginning to decrease. Films such as *Ben Hur* and *The Ten Commandments* still made a fortune for their makers, but

"Mary, you mustn't!"

A Metro-Goldwyn-Mayer PICTURE

Norma Shearer in AFTER MIDNIGHT

Greta GARBO

The DESERT SONG

ABOVE

John Boles and Carlotta King starred in this 1929 version of The Desert Song. *Hollywood turned to ready-made, fairy tale operettas like this famous story to show off its new technological advance: the soundtrack.*

ABOVE RIGHT

George Raft in the 1932 Night after Night. *Raft certainly had friends in low places; he was banned from entering Britain in 1966 because of his Mafia connections.*

BELOW RIGHT

Mae West as the tart with the heart in the 1936 Klondike Annie. *West's sexual innuendoes and brazen strumpetry aroused moral outrage in many quarters. It all seems very mild nowadays, but West played her image to the hilt in the thirties – a parody of female beauty as constructed by men.*

for the run-of-the-mill product, audiences were becoming harder to find. Just as it looked as though the cinema advance might be checked the Cavalry, in the shape of Warner Brothers and Vitaphone, came riding over the horizon, bugles blowing, to the rescue. Movies with sound had already been tried in a series of Vitaphone shorts and a musical accompaniment to the John Barrymore version of *Don Juan*, but the major studios had turned their backs on it because of the cost of installing expensive equipment. But the Warner brothers – Harry, Jack, Sam and Albert – took a chance on Vitaphone because they needed a new impetus if they were going to be able to force their way into theatre ownership, which was so crucial if you wanted to become a major player on the Hollywood stage. The brothers backed *The Jazz Singer*, and it made millions. The end was nigh for silent movies and every studio in Hollywood clambered on the bandwagon that Warners had set in motion. The headstart they had in producing 'talkies' catapulted Warner Brothers to major studio status.

They talk! They sing! They have sound effects! Movie makers turned to musicals to make the most of this new technological development. During the first couple of years of the talkies, the market was saturated with all-singing, all-talking, all-dancing musical extravaganzas like *Hollywood Revue of 1929*, *Broadway Melody*, *The Desert Song*, *Show of Shows* and *The Gold Diggers of*

Broadway. Producers also turned to filming Broadway stage shows, which was easy and relatively cheap. However, the essence of movies is that they move and so audiences soon tired of these stage-bound exercises. A surfeit of musicals also led to audience indifference. And the Wall Street Crash had heralded the start of the Depression; millions of people round the world were struggling to survive and had no extra money to indulge in the purchase of movie tickets. The movie business faced a hard task in enticing Depression audiences into the cinemas.

GANGSTERS, MOLLS AND CENSORSHIP

In the early years of the thirties, Hollywood turned to sensation to attract customers back into the cinemas. Three gangster films made in 1931–2, *Little Caesar*, *Public Enemy* and *Scarface*, were successes both commercially and artistically, but aroused opposition from pressure groups in society such as the American Legion and Daughters of the American Revolution. These films portrayed the underbelly of the American Dream, a distorted Horatio Alger morality tale of success. The methods used by Edward G. Robinson, James Cagney and Paul Muni in these movies to achieve power in their gangland underworld had more than a passing resemblance to the ruthless machinations of American big business, and this did not endear them to the establishment. Law enforcers were portrayed as, at best, incompetent, at worst, as equally corrupt and this, too, irritated those who cherished the idea of the Republic as the land of opportunity for decent citizens who played it by the rules.

The other ingredient producers used to seduce customers into the cinemas was sex. Although extremely mild by present-day standards, movies such as *Rain* with Joan Crawford and *The Story of Temple Drake* with Florence Eldridge had puritans all over the country reaching for their writing pads to dash off a letter to their congressmen. Mae West's films, such as *She Done Him Wrong* and

Night After Night, also produced strong reactions. Hollywood sniffed the wind and recognised that, if they did not do something themselves, they might be faced with external censorship. In 1927 the Motion Pictures Producers and Distributors of America (MPPDA) had established a code to govern the making of motion pictures, but now this code was updated and an office known as the Production Code Administration (PCA, but commonly called the Hays' Office after William Hays, then later the Breen Office) was given the responsibility for making sure that the studios obeyed it. All scripts had to be approved by the PCA before shooting started, and when the film was completed the PCA could insist on cuts; the PCA could refuse its Seal of Approval, preventing films from being shown in any cinema that came under the jurisdiction of the MPPDA. In fact, the major studios, which controlled the MPPDA, turned this situation to their own advantage; they used the Seal of Approval system to ward off competitors and independent producers. They not only controlled which films could be shown on the major circuits, but now they had a stranglehold through their own Production Code Administration on the content of all American movies. The extreme puritanism of the PCA suited their commercial needs because they were

basically after a mass, family audience, and this was their excuse to produce anodyne, family-orientated 'harmless' movies that radiated 'down-home' values and something called 'the American Way of Life'.

Other genres that did well at the box-office in the thirties were horror films and musicals once again. A cycle of cheaply made flicks dealing with the Dracula and Frankenstein myths made stars of Bela Lugosi, Boris Karloff and Lon

The comedy duo Stan Laurel (he's the thin one) and Oliver Hardy (he's the more portly one) in Saps at Sea *(1940). Laurel graduated from British music hall, Hardy from the American equivalent, vaudeville. Although they did make appearances in films separately, they were never as effective solo as they were as a double act.*

Chaney Jnr. After its brief demise the musical underwent a rebirth with a series of Warners 'Depression' musicals directed by Busby Berkeley, the recipe for which was regimented battalions of sturdy chorus girls, Nuremberg Rally-type production numbers and opulent costumes and settings. More sophisticated were the series of Astaire-Rogers musicals with Art Deco settings and the effortless grace of the two stars. These musicals could safely be described as 'harmless entertainment', an antidote to the grimness of the decade. It was also the decade of screwball comedy and the Marx Bros. In the midst of all this escapism, some films with a populist tone emerged to confront some of the social problems of the time: Frank Capra's *Mr Deeds Comes to Town* and *Mr Smith Goes to Washington*, Fritz Lang's *Fury* and John Ford's *The Grapes of Wrath*. However, audiences continued to decline, despite the studios offering double bills to their customers and cinema-owners offering free china and other give-aways.

In Britain, the Korda brothers were establishing a production company that would rival Hollywood studios with films such as *The Private Life of Henry the Eighth* and *The Four Feathers*. Britain was often in the vanguard of technical advance, such as the introduction of colour, and Michael Powell's movie, *The Thief of Bagdad*

(1939) showed what British technicians could achieve under imaginative direction. However, as usual, most British cinema seemed to be stuck in the past. In contrast, French cinema, with talents such as Marcel Pagnol, Jean Renoir and Marcel Carné, produced memorable films such as *Marius*, *La Règle du Jeu*, *La Grande Illusion* and *Quai des Brumes*. Stalinist dictatorship had locked Soviet directors such as Eisenstein into serving the interests of the totalitarian state.

WARTIME BOOM

Colour quickly caught on in the late thirties, and on 31 December 1939 in Atlanta, Georgia, the premiere was held of the technicolor epic, *Gone with the Wind*, which would go on to be the box-office winner of all time. Once America was in the war, an economic boom followed. People had money to spend and audiences craved Hollywood's brand of escapism to help keep grim reality at bay. Musicals flourished once more, with stars such as Betty Grable, Judy Garland

LEFT
Pierre Fresnay as Boldieu, the French aristocrat, in Jean Renoir's La Grande Illusion (1937). An anti-war parable, the movie also documents the demise of the class to which Boldieu belongs.

BELOW
Clark Gable in his most famous role, Rhett Butler, romances Vivien Leigh as Scarlett O'Hara in Gone with the Wind.

LEFT
*Rita Hayworth, danced a
little, sang a little, and
smouldered alot in the
classic film noir* Gilda.

and Gene Kelly. The so-called woman's picture took off, aimed at a predominantly female audience separated from lovers and husbands: *Since You Went Away*, *Now Voyager* and *Mildred Pierce* were three of the more memorable of these melodramas. Orson Welles had managed to make *Citizen Kane* and *The Magnificent Ambersons* before RKO and Hollywood realised they had a talented rebel on their hands. Humphrey Bogart became a megastar with *The Maltese Falcon* and *Casablanca*, which did Ingrid Bergman's career no harm either. The dark days of the war also saw the emergence of a group of films that critics later dubbed '*film noir*'. The wartime shortages of

materials to build sets and the restriction on the use of lighting may have forced filmmakers to employ shadowy lighting techniques and expressionist designs, but there was also something doom-laden in the air that lasted into peacetime and permeated classic film noir movies such as *Crossfire*, *The Blue Dahlia* and *Out of the Past*. Britain, meanwhile, predictably produced morale-raising movies such as *In Which We Serve* and *The Way to the Stars*: at times, it seemed that only John Mills stood between the country and defeat. France under German occupation still managed to produce the odd masterpiece, especially *Les Enfants du Paradis*.

ABOVE
*A tough indictment of
professional boxing,* The
Harder They Fall *(1956) is*
*also remembered as the last
film Humphrey Bogart
made before dying of throat
cancer the following year.*

1946 was the absolute peak year for audience attendance in America: 90 million admissions per week across the nation. Business would never be the same again, however, and from then on the film industry contracted. In 1948 there was a great increase in the number of television sets sold in the States; television was now the cinema's greatest competitor. The Paramount Decree in the same year forced the studios to sell off their cinemas; their monopoly hold on all aspects of the film business was now to be broken. This, in tandem with the 50 per cent drop in audiences suffered by the industry in the ten years after the peak of 1946, forced the break-up of the old studio system. 'Old Hollywood' would, over the next twenty to thirty years, change into 'new Hollywood', in which the names of Louis B. Mayer, Harry Cohn and other moguls became a distant reminder of the great old days. The power of the PCA was eventually challenged by filmmakers such as

Otto Preminger with *The Moon is Blue* and *The Man with the Golden Arm*. Hollywood, with its need to offer the public films that would drag them away from their television sets, found it politic to relax censorship and allow hitherto taboo subjects to be dealt with on screen. *Cat on a Hot Tin Roof*, *Baby Doll* and *Anatomy of a Murder* were typical of these 'outspoken' movies about 'adult issues'. Hollywood also discovered that most of its audience were between sixteen and twenty-five, so James Dean, Sandra Dee and Elvis Presley starred in 'teen appeal' movies.

The fifties was the decade of pneumatic blondes, fantasy women created by men to pander to male chauvinism: Marilyn Monroe, Jayne Mansfield, Kim Novak, Diana Dors and Mamie Van Doren. Simultaneously new directors such as Sidney Lumet, John Frankenheimer and Martin Ritt learnt their craft in television studios and then transferred to the big screen. Alfred Hitchcock made some of his best films round this time,

ABOVE
Slow-talking Gary Cooper in a characteristic western role of 1952. Cooper symbolised simple, moral worth in a handsome frame.

RIGHT
Many fifties films offered buxom ladies to appeal in a guarded and measured way to the male libido. The movie magazines were equally happy to exploit the selling potential of these starlets.

including *Rear Window*, *Vertigo*, *North by Northwest* and *Psycho*. However, it was with technological innovation that Hollywood principally gambled in its attempts to win back mass audiences: CinemaScope, VistaVision, 3-D, Todd-AO, Cinerama and others. Between the years 1954 and 1956 audience figures did show some increase over the preceding years, but the attractions of wide-screen and three-dimensional effects were short-lived and audience figures began to 'dive' once again.

French cinema gained new impetus with the Nouvelle Vague (New Wave), led by directors such as François Truffaut, Jean-Luc Godard, Claude Chabrol, Louis Malle and Eric Rohmer beginning to make their mark. In the late fifties and early sixties Ingmar Bergman directed a series of outstanding films in Sweden, including *The Seventh Seal* and *Wild Strawberries*. The international success of this 'art cinema' testified to the fact that mass audiences were generally not available, except for epics such as MGM's remake of *Ben Hur* and De Mille's remake of his own *The Ten Commandments*. Italy had led the way after the war in establishing this 'art' market with the Neo-realist school of directors, pre-eminent of whom were Vittorio De Sica and Roberto Rossellini. Now, in the late fifties, a new generation of Italian directors was coming to the fore, including Michelangelo Antonioni and Federico Fellini. Something was even stirring in Britain, and movies such as *Room at the Top* and *A Taste of Honey* helped to extend the range of British films beyond war epics and genteel Ealing comedies. Japanese cinema was also making a world impact, principally through Akira Kurosawa's films *The Seven Samurai* and *Rashomon*. Eastern European cinema, particularly the Polish, Hungarian and Czechoslovakian industries, provided an outlet for covert social criticism, and directors such as Andrzej Wajda and Milos Forman became familiar names on the art-house circuit.

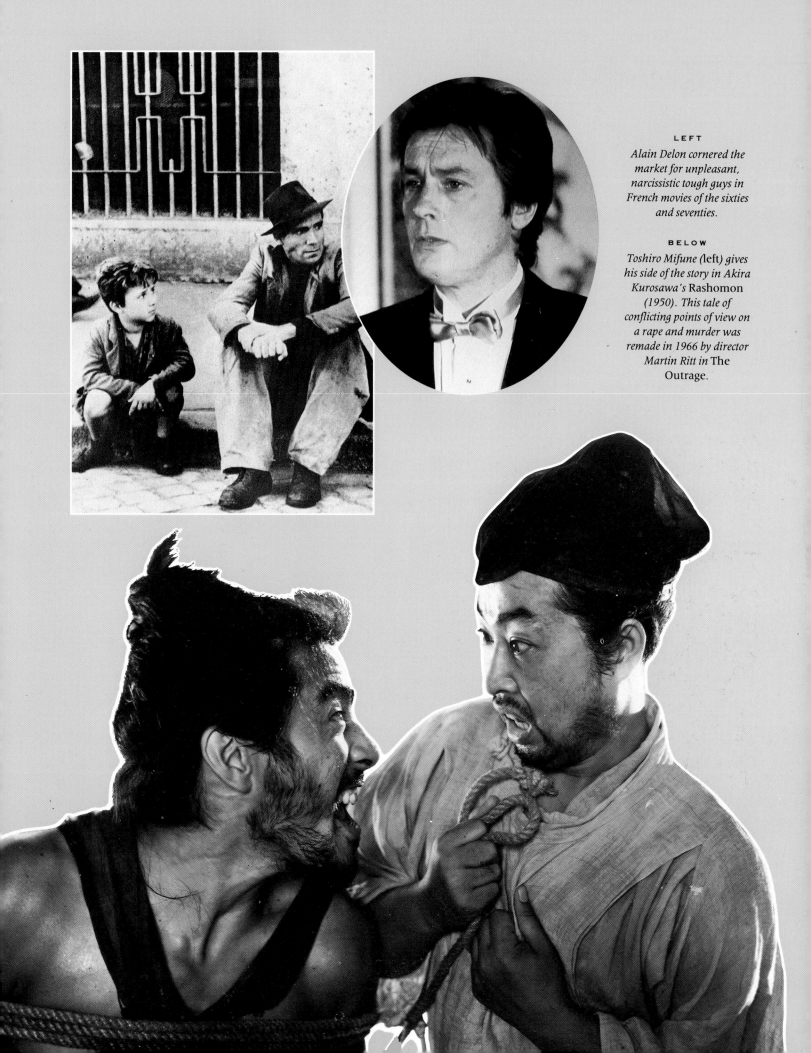

LEFT

Alain Delon cornered the market for unpleasant, narcissistic tough guys in French movies of the sixties and seventies.

BELOW

Toshiro Mifune (left) gives his side of the story in Akira Kurosawa's Rashomon *(1950). This tale of conflicting points of view on a rape and murder was remade in 1966 by director Martin Ritt in* The Outrage.

THE RISE OF THE AGENT AND THE PACKAGE DEAL

The butt of many a comedian's jokes, the agent, suddenly came to the fore in the power struggle in Hollywood. When the old studio system broke up, more and more films were made by independent producers who, however, had to make deals with the studios over distribution and, frequently, finance. The agents were ready to fill the vacuum that the demise of the studios had left. Top agents, such as MCA and William Morris, could approach a studio with a package deal that would consist of a screenplay by a well-known writer, a major star or two, an executive producer and a director – all of them under contract to the agency. The agents became the power brokers of Hollywood. And although much was written about the end of the star system, a few major stars had more power than ever before. In the sixties and seventies Barbra Streisand, Robert Redford, Jane Fonda, Marlon Brando, Dustin Hoffman, Steve McQueen, Paul Newman and others wielded immense power: their participation in a package could ensure a project would actually get off the ground.

The sixties, however, were not good years for Hollywood, until, at least, very late in the decade with 'youth' films such as *Easy Rider* and *The Graduate*. Gone were the days of family pictures and the Louis B. Mayer ethos of 'beautiful people in beautiful stories'. Hollywood was now willing to make money from anything; and if youthful

LEFT
A certain former American President started life as a sports commentator, then graduated to 'B' pictures and even some good guy roles in 'A' flicks. Along the way, he helped sell cigarettes for one of America's largest tobacco companies.

RIGHT
Dustin Hoffman as Bernstein of Woodward and Bernstein in All the President's Men *(1976). Directed by Alan Pakula, one of Hollywood's most successful directors in the seventies, the film documents how the* Washington Post *reporters tracked down the source of the Watergate break-in and cover-up.*

PARIS, TEXAS

NASTASSJA KINSKI

HARRY DEAN STANTON

"It brings magic back to the cinema..."

Derek Malcolm, The Guardian

A film by Wim Wenders Written by Sam Shepard
DEAN STOCKWELL-AURORE CLEMENT- and, for the first time, HUNTER CARSON
Music RY COODER Director of Photography ROBBY MULLER   Executive Producer CHRIS SIEVERNICH Art Director KATE ALTMAN
Editing PETER PRZYGODDA Assistant Director CLAIRE DENIS   An ARGOS FILMS, Paris – ROAD MOVIES, Berlin co-production.
Screenplay SAM SHEPARD Adaptation L.M. KIT CARSON Director WIM WENDERS with the participation of WDR, Cologne – PRO-JECT FILM, Munich, FILM FOUR INTERNATIONAL, London A PALACE PICTURES PRESENTATION

Grand Prize Winn Cannes F.l.

rebellion, after the heady days of 1968, was the fashion, then the new moguls were only too anxious to put youthful rebellion on screen. In the seventies, a further generation of American directors emerged, themselves steeped in Hollywood myths, and very often looking back to 'old Hollywood' for their inspiration: Steven Spielberg, Martin Scorsese, Francis Coppola, Brian De Palma and George Lucas. Spielberg, for example, has 'raided' Disney films for *Close Encounters of the Third Kind* and *ET*, whilst Scorsese reinvented the MGM musical with *New York, New York* and made a remake of Ford's *The Searchers* in *Taxi Driver*. These 'movie brats' were not only brilliant filmmakers, they knew how to make movies that became all-time box-office winners: *Jaws*, *Star Wars* and *Raiders of the Lost Ark*. Audience figures would never return to their 1946 peak, but mega-hits in the cinema could make more money than ever before for their makers, including directors and stars who were usually on a percentage of the box-office revenues.

One feature of the seventies was the emergence of national cinemas. Films that were both

ABOVE

Wim Wenders directed Harry Dean Stanton and Nastassja Kinski in 1984's Paris, Texas. *A bleak and perhaps rather pretentious view of eighties America by an outsider, the movie was a surprise commercial hit and elevated Stanton from supporting player to star.*

watchable and important started to emerge from countries as diverse as the Sudan and Argentina. One of the strongest was the Australian cinema, led by *Picnic at Hanging Rock*, *Mad Max* and *My Brilliant Career*. Australian directors Peter Weir, Bruce Beresford and Fred Schepisi went on to direct movies in America. The German cinema experienced something of a reawakening with directors such as Rainer Werner Fassbinder, Hans Werner Herzog and Wim Wenders. However, the British cinema as such was experiencing difficulty in maintaining a separate identity from the American industry, a situation that the French have never faced because they believe in an indigenous cinema and prove that by producing, on average, six times as many home-grown movies as the British do. Cinema had become truly international by the seventies and eighties with directors such as Italy's Bernardo Bertolucci, France's Louis Malle or Germany's Wim Wenders making films in their native countries, Hollywood and elsewhere. The art film circuit was established, and if a film failed to find a wide release in the cinema, it could always get showings on some of the many television channels that were sprouting up in every country. Video, and the fact that VCRs became part of almost every household, was the next challenge to cinema, but this time the businessmen behind the movie industry harnessed the new technology and turned it to their profit. For every one customer who sees a movie in the cinema, twelve now see it on video. In addition, the spread of cable and satellite television has added a new market for new and not-so-new films. New productions are very often financed by cable companies such as HBO in America, or by television channels such as Channel 4 in Britain. But Hollywood in the eighties generally played it safe with winning formulas repeated *ad nauseam*, spawning endless sequels, and even 'prequels'.

RIGHT
First Blood *(1982) has the stigma of being the first film to feature the 'character' of Rambo as played by Sylvester Stallone. Its huge success gave the green light to Stallone to play Rambo in seemingly endless sequels. Nightmare scenario for 2010:* Rambo 26?

FAR RIGHT
Harrison Ford as Indiana Jones in Raiders of the Lost Ark *(1981).*

RIGHT
Robert De Niro as Travis Bickle in Taxi Driver *(1976).*

No one can say with any certainty what the future holds for cinema. The accepted wisdom now in Hollywood is that 'no one knows anything', meaning it is all a gamble because nobody can gauge public taste or how the industry will develop. New technology is waiting in the wings with, for example, the means to summon up a film from a menu of films on your giant screen in your own front room, or 'virtual reality', which consists of involving the spectator directly in a created world, which he or she can, to a certain extent, control. In other words, Aldous Huxley's 'feelies' from *Brave New World* are just around the technological corner. In that context and with the inevitable continuing spread of cable and satellite television, it is impossible to state categorically that cinema as we have known it will survive. For example, the ownership of the Hollywood studios changes hands so rapidly nowadays, it is difficult to keep up with the latest deals. One thing that is certain is that the Japanese are now major players in the film industry game: their huge electronics firms need the 'software' of movies to back up their hardware. When Sony bought Columbia, Harry Cohn must have been whizzing around in his grave. 'Old Hollywood' has vanished forever.

What will survive without doubt are movies themselves, however we choose to view them. But it is the fervent hope of this writer, and many others, I suspect, that people will continue to come together in movie houses to share the anticipation as the opening credits and the musical score jointly tell us that we are about to participate in that unique entertainment experience: the cinema.

LEFT

Videos have not only extended the audience for movies, but have made films of the past more accessible.

*Eddie Murphy was one of
the major African–
American stars to emerge as
a box-office attraction in the
eighties.*

THE
MOVIE
MAKERS

INSET

*The camera operator poised
for action during shooting of
the Tom Cruise 1989 hit
Top Gun.*

LEFT

*One of the great directors of
the silent era, D.W. Griffith
at work during the shooting
of one of his early films.*

> ❖❖*I want to make beautiful pictures about beautiful people.*❖❖
>
> **LOUIS B. MAYER**

OUR KNOWLEDGE OF how movies are made has grown immensely since the early days of cinema. The Hollywood film industry, for example, has been studied in historical, industrial and sociological terms by many professional writers, cultural historians and sociologists. In addition to their work, there have been the personal testimonies of countless people who have been involved in the Hollywood filmmaking machine. The film industries of many other nations have also been 'written up' in this way, so we now presume to know how films came to be made, how they were put together as films, and in what social, political and historical circumstances they were produced.

However, despite all this 'knowledge', for a proportion of the cinema-going public any demystification of the mystique of the movies is unwelcome because, for them, movies belong to a separate world and are not part of day-to-day reality. Thus, there seems to be a never-ending consuming interest in the private lives of stars such as Madonna, Warren Beatty, Julia Roberts or Elizabeth Taylor. These stars are more than just actors on the screen; they act out our fantasies in their 'private' lives as well, and the public are allowed to peep into those lives voyeuristically through newspaper, magazine and television reports. There is often a confusion between their screen personas and their 'real selves'. They are 'creations' in both their professional and private lives and the watching public play their part in that creation.

Most movie makers have co-operated with this production of 'aura', of glamour, mystique and 'specialness'. As loyal employees of the studios, they were expected to support the concept of movies bringing harmless entertainment into the otherwise drab lives of the cinema-going public. The most damaging description that could be applied to a director in Hollywood, for example, was that he was an artist, an intellectual or a propagandist. That is partly why those Hollywood directors, such as Ford and Hitchcock, who were 'discovered' by intellectual cri-

tics in the forties and fifties continually denied that they had something to say in their movies. That was anathema to their employers, who claimed movies were only about entertainment, and not about art, philosophy or a social critique.

A minority of directors and actors have been unwilling to play according to the rules of the game and have distanced themselves from the production of 'glamour' and 'special aura'. Swedish director Ingmar Bergman, for example, has always resisted the blandishments of Hollywood and created an intimate world of filmmaking in which he works repeatedly with trusted colleagues and actors who are equally uninterested in glamour. Numerous stars have been weighed down by the demands of stardom and have fought, some successfully and others in more self-destructive ways, against the straitjacket imposed on them by the publicity machine. Whatever you may feel about his career in the movies, Marlon Brando, for example, has clearly tried to be his own person, as have Jane Fonda, Jessica Lange and other contemporary female stars. However, everyone involved in filmmaking in key roles in production or performing has, to some extent, to participate in the surrounding ballyhoo that seems to be inextricably linked with the film world. Stars like Brando or De Niro who seldom give interviews

are vastly outnumbered by other film personalities who pay money to press agents to get their names mentioned in the media, whatever the reason for this attention may be.

At the centre of this general ballyhoo and glamour were, and are, the Hollywood studios. In the heyday of the studio system, the major studios not only employed vast armies of technicians, artists, directors and actors, they also set up elaborate publicity machines to fabricate material for the other media – print, radio and television – to feed off, so that the information and publicity apparatuses were interdependent.

The famous Hollywood gossip writers, Louella Parsons and Hedda Hopper, needed the studios, and the studios definitely needed people like Parsons and Hopper to generate interest in movie personalities and, of course, the products they had to sell, the movies.

This section of the book looks at the studios in the great days of Hollywood, and at some of the most famous of the people at the centre of the movie-making process – the directors – who have made films in the leading cinema nations of the world.

BELOW

The Big Four who established United Artists – Douglas Fairbanks, Mary Pickford, Charles Chaplin and D.W. Griffith. United Artists represented an attempt to wrest control of movies away from the enterpreneurs and back to the artists.

THE STUDIOS

FROM THE MID-TWENTIES on, Hollywood film production functioned within the studio system. The system established a factory production style, in essence no different from a Ford assembly line except that what rolled off the production line were not automobiles but movies. To the moguls who ran the studios, and the money men who controlled the finances in New York, movies were first and foremost a business.

In fact, the 'Big Five' (MGM, Paramount, Fox, Warners and RKO) had more money invested in real estate than in film production. This real estate was in the form of first-run cinemas in the best positions in the principal cities of America. The studios had to make enough major features to service these cinemas and also the affiliated chains with which they had special agreements. As we have seen, each of the five majors was involved in the three aspects of the movie business: production, distribution and exhibition.

None of the majors made enough top-notch features in a year to service their own cinemas, which normally required weekly changes of programme, so the cinemas they owned showed the products of other studios as well. For example, if MGM had a huge hit on its hands, the other companies would benefit from that success by the box-office returns from the cinemas they owned that showed the MGM movie. The major studios were nominally in competition with one another, but in fact they formed an oligopoly that dominated the American film industry and successfully blocked entry to lesser fry. It would be the late forties before the American government would act decisively to force the majors to divest themselves of their exhibition function and thereby end the monopoly that had lasted over twenty years.

ABOVE
The logos of Hollywood's 'Big Five' studios: MGM, Paramount, Twentieth Century-Fox, Warner Brothers and RKO.

The other large studios, Columbia, Universal and United Artists (the company formed by Pickford, Fairbanks, Chaplin and Griffith), were known as the 'Little Three'. They were prevented from competing with the five majors because they did not have the control over the exhibition side of the business that the majors wielded. However, they were still big studios capable of producing major films.

In addition, there were the 'Poverty Row' outfits such as Republic and Monogram, and independent producers who would hope to sell their product to one of the majors.

By 1919, the American film industry had established a dominant position in the world film markets. It is a position that has never seriously been challenged. American cinema is dominant and that dominance had its foundations in the studio system. Even though that system began to break up in the fifties, the studios, or most of them, survive in some form to this day, despite the many changes in ownership and function.

MGM

MGM is probably the most famous of all the Hollywood studios. Its proud boast that it had more stars than there were in heaven typifies the studio's general approach: give the public glamour, gloss and glitz. MGM filmmakers had a motto they were meant to subscribe to: 'Make it good, make it big, give it class.' 'Ars Gratia Artis' was the legend that appeared below Leo the Lion, MGM's trademark, which is loosely trans-

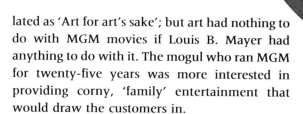

lated as 'Art for art's sake'; but art had nothing to do with MGM movies if Louis B. Mayer had anything to do with it. The mogul who ran MGM for twenty-five years was more interested in providing corny, 'family' entertainment that would draw the customers in.

The beginnings

MGM came into being in 1924 with the merger of Metro Pictures, Goldwyn Pictures (minus Sam Goldwyn) and Louis B. Mayer's company. It was the studio production arm of Loew's Inc., headed by Marcus Loew in New York, which is where all the financial decisions were made.

Louis B. Mayer and the 'boy wonder' Irving Thalberg were in charge of production at Culver City, the home of MGM. From the start they put their faith in stars and in top technicians. Curiously, MGM was never a particularly happy hunting-ground for directors: the studio's producers and the heads of the various technical departments were more powerful. Their main task was to create showcases for the glamorous stars MGM took enormous trouble to groom and market. Thalberg would work very closely with his producers and with the writers to produce vehicles for these stars, and only when they had the 'product' right did they assign a director to a picture.

1925–1940

Two silent hits for MGM were the 1925 version of *Ben Hur* with Ramon Navarro and King Vidor's *The Big Parade*, a war movie of the same year. The 1929 musical *The Broadway Melody* was the first talking picture to make big bucks for the studio. Garbo was an MGM star and she starred in her first sound film *Anna Christie* in 1930, and

LEFT
Irving Thalberg, the production chief of MGM during its golden years in the thirties.

BELOW
Greta Garbo in MGM's Grand Hotel *(1932). Perhaps this is not one of her better roles. She plays a ballerina holed up in a large hotel and expiring of love. Nine years later, Garbo retired from the screen for reasons that have never been clarified.*

BELOW RIGHT
Clark Gable as Rhett Butler, the part that Americans demanded he play in Gone with the Wind, *according to screen publicists anyway, sweeps Vivien Leigh as Scarlett O'Hara off her feet while in the background Atlanta burns.*

in 1932 *Grand Hotel* featured a roster of MGM luminaries: Lionel Barrymore, Joan Crawford, John Barrymore and Wallace Beery. The latter, along with child star Jackie Cooper, also made audiences weep in the aisles in *The Champ* (1931).

The 'look' of MGM films was glossy – 'stars shot through cellophane wrapping' – but two of their most popular stars in the thirties went against the house style: Wallace Beery and Marie Dressler. Garbo was the ultimate ethereal star and MGM exploited her in *Queen Christina* (1933), and in *Camille* (1936) with Robert Taylor as Armand. Two other major stars emerged in the thirties: Clark Gable and Joan Crawford. These two were teamed together in eight movies, almost all of them entirely forgettable. Gable made a lot of money for the studio in *Mutiny on the Bounty* (1935, with Charles Laughton as Captain Bligh going well over the top) and in *San Francisco* (1936). The decade ended with the première of *Gone with the Wind* (1939), which David Selznick produced for MGM.

The most magnificent picture ever!

DAVID O. SELZNICK'S PRODUCTION OF MARGARET MITCHELL'S

"GONE WITH THE WIND"

CLARK GABLE
VIVIEN LEIGH
LESLIE HOWARD OLIVIA de HAVILLAND

A SELZNICK INTERNATIONAL PICTURE · DIRECTED BY VICTOR FLEMING · SCREEN PLAY BY SIDNEY HOWARD · METRO-GOLDWYN-MAYER INC · Music by MAX STEINER

G GENERAL AUDIENCES   METROCOLOR ®

MGM had found a gold mine in the series of Andy Hardy pictures they had started in the late thirties, featuring Mickey Rooney. The family entertainment these movies offered (and their endorsement of American small-town values) warmed Louis B. Mayer's heart and filled Loew's coffers. The Freed Unit at MGM under producer Arthur Freed produced a series of 'teenage musicals' with Rooney and Judy Garland, and then graduated to elaborate technicolor musicals that created new standards for the genre: *Meet Me in St Louis* (1944), *On the Town* (1949), *An American in Paris* (1951), *Singin' in the Rain* (1952) and *The Band Wagon* (1953). MGM's musical stars were the best in the business: Gene Kelly, Fred Astaire, Judy Garland and Cyd Charisse. They also employed the most talented directors of musicals: Vincente Minnelli, Gene Kelly, Stanley Donen and Charles Walters.

However, musicals were expensive to produce and did not bring great returns on investment during a period when MGM badly needed an upturn in its profits. In 1951 Mayer was replaced as head of production by Dore Schary, but the more radical and adventurous former RKO man did not manage to halt MGM's downward slide, although *Quo Vadis* (1952), *Cat on a Hot Tin Roof* (1958) with Elizabeth Taylor, *Gigi* (1958) and *Ben Hur* (1959) with Charlton Heston as Ben all did well for the studio.

1960 onwards
. . . .

In the mid-sixties MGM had a few good years based on the box-office returns of some major hits: *How the West Was Won* (1962), *Doctor Zhivago* (1965), *The Dirty Dozen* (1967) and *2001* (1968). The early seventies saw new owners selling off backlots and studio props and cutting back to four or five movies a year, but the studio had recovered sufficiently by the early eighties to be able to purchase United Artists. MGM is still in the movie-making business but the great days of Gable, Garbo, Kelly, Astaire, Tracy and Hepburn are gone forever. The doyen of the studio system at its zenith, MGM produced the most wish-fulfilling of all the fantasies of the dream factory.

BELOW
Singin' in the Rain (1952) expressed an optimism about life and the movie business itself that found its ultimate expression in Gene Kelly's title number.

BOTTOM
The 1954 Seven Brides for Seven Brothers *was one of the most successful MGM musicals not to feature Gene Kelly.*

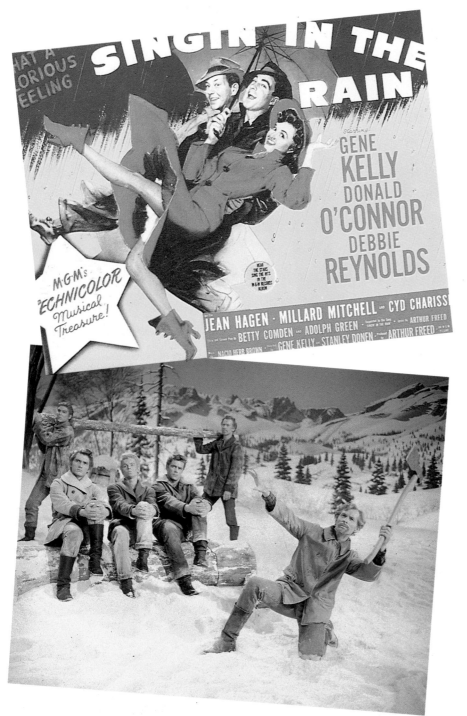

PARAMOUNT

Paramount was born in 1916, from the merging of Adolph Zukor's Famous Players Film Company with Jesse Lasky's company and the Paramount distribution company. Zukor would become one of Hollywood's most hard-nosed moguls, building the empire that would eventually make Paramount Hollywood's biggest studio. As a businessman he realised that you could only play in the ballpark if you were heavily involved in the three major aspects of the film business: production, distribution and exhibition. Thus Paramount, like the other four majors, became a vertically integrated business wielding enormous influence in the film market.

1916–1929

Zukor set great store by star names as is evidenced by the name of his first company: Famous Players. Among the stars he had in the early years were Douglas Fairbanks, Mary Pickford, Wallace Reid, Billie Burke and William S. Hart. In the twenties Valentino made huge profits for the studio in *The Sheik* and *Blood and Sand*. Cecil B. De Mille directed his first version of *The Ten Commandments* in 1923, whilst Ronald Colman made an early version of *Beau Geste* in 1926. *The Covered Wagon* in 1923 was the first epic western. *Wings* (1927) was a spectacular 'flying' movie set in World War I.

The thirties

Paramount in the thirties was the studio where the Marx Bros., Mae West and W.C. Fields exploited their particular forms of comic mayhem. The western was also one of Paramount's favourite genres: the laconic Gary Cooper starred in *The Plainsman* (1936) whilst Joel McCrea strapped on the gun holsters for *Wells Fargo* in 1937. De Mille donned his religious hat to direct *The Sign of the Cross* (1932) and *The Crusades* (1935), and in between these efforts he miscast Claudette Colbert as *Cleopatra* in 1934. Prestige productions came in the form of Preston

LEFT
Mary Pickford.

BELOW
Wallace Reid was one of the leading men of the early silent years.

ABOVE
Billie Burke made dithery matrons her speciality.

RIGHT
Rudolph Valentino as The Sheik *(1921).*

Sturges's comedies, Frank Borzage's *A Farewell to Arms* (1932) starring Gary Cooper and Helen Hayes, and the exotic fantasies dreamed up by Josef von Sternberg for Marlene Dietrich: *Morocco* (1930), *Shanghai Express* (1932) and *The Scarlet Empress* (1935). But it was in the musical field that Paramount really competed. Jeanette MacDonald starred with Maurice Chevalier in three musicals, including the delightful *Love Me Tonight* directed by Rouben Mamoulian. Bing Crosby was a major Paramount star as were Bob Hope, Betty Grable, George Raft and Dorothy Lamour.

1 9 4 0 – 1 9 6 0

Hope and Crosby with their series of *Road* pictures boosted Paramount profits enormously in the forties and fifties. Other major Paramount stars were Alan Ladd with *This Gun for Hire*, *The Glass Key* and *The Blue Dahlia*. Victor Mature and Hedy Lamarr wooed the audiences away from

their television sets in 1949 with *Samson and Delilah*, whilst Bing Crosby and Barry Fitzgerald did a good P.R. job for the Catholic church in *Going My Way*. Hope without Crosby made big bucks with *The Paleface* and *Son of Paleface*. An all-star cast including James Stewart and Betty Hutton made De Mille's *The Greatest Show on Earth* (1951) a huge success. Alan Ladd had the greatest role of his career in the 1953 *Shane*, whilst De Mille could not avoid preaching again in the extremely vulgar *The Ten Commandments* of 1956 with Charlton Heston as Moses parting the Red Sea. Critical plaudits as well as box-office success came with Hitchcock's *Rear Window* (1954), starring Stewart with Grace Kelly, and *Psycho* in 1960. Among famous directors who worked at Paramount during this period were Billy Wilder (*The Lost Weekend* and *Sunset Boulevard*), Preston Sturges (*The Miracle of Morgan's Creek*, *Hail the Conquering Hero*) and William Wyler (*The Heiress*).

ABOVE
Yul Brynner as the Pharoah and Charlton Heston as Moses in the 1956 version of The Ten Commandments, *directed by (who else?) Cecil B. De Mille.*

RIGHT
A poster for the French release of Billy Wilder's Sunset Boulevard *(1950), in which Gloria Swanson plays a silent movie star who is convinced that De Mille wants her for a very late comeback.*

The sixties onwards

· · · · · · · · · ·

The Carpetbaggers (1964) gave Paramount a hit movie and the studio also did very well with the 1968 *Rosemary's Baby*, directed by Roman Polanski, and the glutinous *Love Story* in 1970. However, it really hit the jackpot in 1972 with *The Godfather*, directed by Francis Coppola. *Godfather II* also did well in 1974, but not on the scale of *Saturday Night Fever* (1977) and *Grease* (1978), both starring John Travolta. These box-office receipts were eclipsed in the eighties by the Indiana Jones movies *Raiders of the Lost Ark* and *Indiana Jones and the Temple of Doom*. Eddie Murphy arrived as a major star in *Beverly Hills Cop* and Paul Hogan surprised the studio by making it a lot of money with *Crocodile Dundee*. Other hits included *Top Gun*, *Terms of Endearment*, *Trading Places*, the *Star Trek* movies and *An Officer and a Gentleman*.

BELOW

John Cazale as the weak son, Fredo, weeping over the shooting of his father, Don Corleone (Marlon Brando) in the 1972, Francis Coppola-directed The Godfather. *The movie made megabucks at the box-office, prompting the making of* Godfather II *in 1974 and* Godfather III *in 1990.*

> ♦♦*An executive cannot expect love – ever!*♦♦
>
> **DARRYL ZANUCK**

Paramount now

· · · · · · · · · ·

In 1966 Gulf & Western took over Paramount. The days of Adolph Zukor and the great movie entrepreneurs were long gone. Paramount was now part of a much larger company that had had no previous experience in the film industry. Despite that, the studio has continued to have its successes and seems set to remain a major presence in the industry for as long as movies survive as a mass entertainment.

AXEL FOLEY
IS BACK.

BACK WHERE
HE DOESN'T
BELONG.

EDDIE MURPHY
BEVERLY HILLS
Cop II

THE HEAT'S BACK ON!

ABOVE

*Beverly Hills Cop was a
big mid-eighties hit for
Paramount, making a star
of Eddie Murphy and
spawning the inevitable
sequel.*

RIGHT

Shirley Temple was a top box-office attraction in the thirties, which is the main reason Louis B. Mayer wanted to steal her for MGM, especially to play the part of Dorothy in The Wizard of Oz *(1939). Relax, the little moppet never got to sing 'Over the Rainbow' on screen.*

20th CENTURY-FOX

William Fox began in nickelodeons, then built picture palaces, moved into film distribution and finally production. He was one of the entrepreneurs who challenged the monopoly of the Motion Picture Patents Company. Fox's first film was made in 1914 (*Life's Shop Window*), but it was the emergence of Theda Bara as a major star that helped establish the Fox Film Company. In the mid-twenties Fox managed to acquire cinemas in prime sites and strengthened the company's position in relation to its main rivals. However, hard times followed when the stock market crash of 1929 hit the company; Fox was forced to sell his shares. Five years later Fox merged with 20th Century Pictures under Darryl Zanuck and Joseph Schenck: 20th Century-Fox was created.

The pre-1940 Fox movies

What Price Glory?, *Sunrise*, and *Seventh Heaven* were three of the more memorable Fox silents. Janet Gaynor was the studio's top silent star, and she was joined in the thirties by Spencer Tracy (until he went to MGM), Warner Baxter, Will Rogers, Alice Faye, Sonja Henie, Don Ameche, Tyrone Power and the biggest box-office attraction of them all, Shirley Temple. *Little Miss Marker* (1934), *The Littlest Rebel* (1935), *Dimples* (1936), *Wee Willie Winkie* (1937), *Rebecca of Sunnybrook Farm* (1938), *The Little Princess* (1939), and several others starring the diminutive but resistible moppet, made Fox big money: she was the envy of other moguls, including Louis B. Mayer at MGM, who, according to Judy Garland, was obsessed with Temple.

Alice Faye, Don Ameche and Sonja Henie were the musical stars and Tyrone Power was the

Tyrone Power was one of the most admired of romantic heroes in the Hollywood of the thirties and forties.

BELOW
You can imagine what the low scribes of Hollywood made of the teaming of Monroe and Jane Russell in Gentlemen Prefer Blondes *(1953). However, both women performed creditably in the Howard Hawks-directed tale of ocean voyages and millionaires. The humour of the piece depended on one of Hawks's staple themes: the reversal of male and female roles.*

ABOVE
Betty Grable starred in a series of harmless, mindless but cheerful musicals in the forties and fifties. She was a manufactured star who happened to meet the requirements her employer, Fox, demanded of her; she was blonde, had good legs and could sing and dance a little.

A L I E N

In space no one can hear you scream.

RIGHT

One of the most impressive of the sci-fi/horror movies of the last twenty years, Alien *(1979) was a huge success on its initial release. It contains a famous scene where the phallic-type creature bursts out of John Hurt's chest in a horrible parody of the birth process. Battling against the Freudian implications of the whole thing was the redoubtable heroine Ripley, played by Sigourney Weaver.*

romantic leading man in *In Old Chicago, Alexander's Ragtime Band, Rose of Washington Square, The Rains Came* and *Jesse James*. John Ford directed Henry Fonda in *Drums along the Mohawk* in 1939.

1940 onwards

The forties started auspiciously for Fox with John Ford's adaptation of Steinbeck's *The Grapes of Wrath*, and *The Oxbow Incident*, directed by William Wellmann. Betty Grable and Carmen Miranda starred in a series of brash musicals whilst Jennifer Jones attempted to raise the tone somewhat in *The Song of Bernadette* (1943). Clifton Webb was a huge hit in *Cheaper by the Dozen* and Olivia de Havilland suffered in *The Snake Pit* (1948). Cary Grant and Ann Sheridan sparred in *I Was a Male War Bride*. In the fifties, with a decrease in audiences hitting Hollywood, Fox led the industry in introducing CinemaScope with *The Robe* (1953). They had Marilyn Monroe as a

star now and she helped make *How to Marry a Millionaire, Gentlemen Prefer Blondes* (both 1953) and *The Seven Year Itch* (1955) successful. Film versions of stage musicals such as *South Pacific* and *The King and I* featured in the fifties. In the early sixties Fox had a major disaster with the $38 million *Cleopatra* with Elizabeth Taylor. Fox finances were helped hugely, however, by the stupendous success of *The Sound of Music* (1965). *Butch Cassidy and the Sundance Kid* (1969), *M*A*S*H* (1970) and *Patton* (1970) with George C. Scott were also hits.

The *Star Wars* series brought Fox enormous box-office returns in the late seventies and early eighties, as did the Damien trilogy, starting with *The Omen* (1976). *Alien* and *Aliens* with new star Sigourney Weaver did well but were surpassed at the box-office by the truly awful *Porky's* series. However, times were rocky for the studio by this time and, as if to prove it, Rupert Murdoch was able to purchase it in 1985.

WARNER BROS.

There were four Warner brothers, Albert, Harry, Sam and Jack. The whole family helped run a nickelodeon, then the brothers branched out into distribution. Soon they were into production and Warner Bros. came into being in 1923. Among their first successes were the Rin Tin Tin movies starring a lovable dog, while Ernst Lubitsch, a director of sharp comedies, gave the studio's productions some tone during the silent years. It was Warners' *The Jazz Singer* and its huge success that revolutionised Hollywood. Warner Bros. had truly arrived.

Warner Bros. and the depression

Warners attempted to build on the success of the Al Jolson movie with a number of musicals, but the public soon tired of this fare. Warners then turned to gangsters and social realism, and if there is one studio associated with the Depression and the New Deal, it is surely this one. Whereas MGM and Mayer were associated with a devout Republicanism, the Warner brothers were more sympathetic to Roosevelt. Criticism of a society indifferent to poverty and hardship was implicit in the movies that starred Edward G. Robinson, James Cagney and Paul Muni. Movies such as *Little Caesar*, *I am a Fugitive from a Chain Gang* and *The Public Enemy* reflected the underside of the American Dream and made criminals anti-heroes. Then the studio's products changed course, partly due to condemnation from official sources and pressure groups. In 1933 Busby Berkeley made three musicals for the Depression, *42nd Street* (directed by Lloyd Bacon), *Gold Diggers of 1933* and *Footlight Parade*. They offered audiences eroticism and spectacle whilst acknowledging in passing the reality of poverty in contemporary America.

Errol Flynn was a major Warners star in the thirties and forties with movies such as *Captain Blood* (1935), *The Adventures of Robin Hood* (1938) and *The Sea Hawk* (1940). Paul

If you want to send messages, use Western Union.

HARRY COHN

Muni scored in *The Story of Louis Pasteur* (1936), *The Good Earth* (1937), *The Life of Emil Zola* (1937) and *Juarez* (1939). Bette Davis became a major star in *Of Human Bondage* (1935), *Jezebel* (1938), *Dark Victory* (1939), *The Old Maid* (1939), *Elizabeth and Essex* (1940, with Errol Flynn), *The Letter* (1940), *The Great Lie* (1941), *The Little Foxes* (1942), *Now Voyager* (1942) and *Old Acquaintance* (1943). She was the undisputed queen of the melodramas.

Warners returned to its 'social conscience' style with the 1939 *Confessions of a Nazi Spy* with Edward G. Robinson, which was clearly anti American isolationism in intent.

From Pearl Harbor on

With America's entry into the war, Warners rallied to the flag with stirring, patriotic movies such as *Sergeant York*, *Yankee Doodle Dandy*, *Across the Pacific* and *Casablanca*. The latter became one of the most famous cult pictures ever shot and made Humphrey Bogart a major star, while doing no harm to the career of Ingrid Bergman. Bogart went on to star in *The Maltese Falcon* (1941), *To Have and Have Not* (with his future wife, Lauren Bacall; 1945), *The Big Sleep* (1946) and *The Treasure of the Sierra Madre* (1948). Meanwhile, Joan Crawford had moved over to Warners from MGM, leaving her glamour girl persona behind her and settling for maternal roles. She shone in *Mildred Pierce* (1945), *Humoresque* (1946), and *Possessed* (1947), suffering dramatically at the hands of husbands, lovers and children.

Alfred Hitchcock made three movies for the studio, *Rope* (1948), *Under Capricorn* (1949) and *Dial M for Murder* (1953). Judy Garland made her 'comeback' film for Warners, *A Star is Born*

RIGHT

Bette Davis as Charlotte Vale in New Voyager *(1942), one of the classic 'women's pictures' of the forties.*

BELOW

Christopher Reeve was superhero in the first of the Superman *series (1978). As with the later* Batman *(1990) and* Dick Tracy *(1991), Hollywood believed it could only resurrect comic book heroes if they indulged in affectionate send-up. Reeve's performance as the quick-changing defender of the American Way of Life is in line with the series's tongue-in-cheek quality.*

(1954), whilst director Elia Kazan made James Dean a star in *East of Eden*. Nicholas Ray used Dean again in *Rebel without a Cause* (1955) and George Stevens directed the new star in Dean's last picture, *Giant*, before he was killed in a car crash. In the sixties the studio scored with *Bonnie and Clyde*, *Bullitt* and *Who's Afraid of Virginia Woolf*. Its production of *My Fair Lady*, however, failed to make the impact expected of it.

A demonic thriller, *The Exorcist*, and the first *Superman* movie made big profits in the seventies as did the disaster movie, *The Towering Inferno*. Clint Eastwood did well with *Every Which Way But Loose* and *Any Which Way You Can*, and Barbra Streisand and Kris Kristofferson helped make the third version of *A Star is Born* a major hit. The story of the uncovering of the Watergate scandals gave Alan Pakula, the director, and Dustin Hoffman and Robert Redford, the stars, opportunities to shine, whilst Streisand again and Ryan O'Neal helped make *What's Up, Doc?* a success. In the eighties, Steven Spielberg's influence on *Gremlins* and *The Goonies* helped create hits. The follow-up *Superman* movies did well at the box-office, as did the dire series of *Police Academy* movies.

Warner Bros. today

Warner Bros. is now part of the giant Warner Communications conglomerate, a multinational involved in all aspects of the mass media. The brothers have all vanished from the scene, but the studio's great movies with Bogart, Davis, Crawford, Flynn and Cagney are still favourites with all true cinema lovers.

FATEFUL FASCINATION!   ELECTRIC TENSION!   The screen's top romantic stars in a melodramatic masterpiece!

CARY GRANT · INGRID BERGMAN

Adventurous Man!   *Notorious Woman!*

in ALFRED HITCHCOCK'S

NOTORIOUS!

with CLAUDE RAINS
LOUIS CALHERN

Directed by ALFRED HITCHCOCK   Written by BEN HECHT
An SRO Release

RKO

RKO is an abbreviation for the Radio-Keith-Orpheum Corporation, which was the result of various mergers between a small movie production and distributing company and the Radio Corporation of America.

David Selznick was an early production chief at the studio and he set himself the difficult task of giving RKO movies some quality whilst keeping the budgets very tight. In the thirties producer Pandro S. Berman made the series of Astaire-Rogers musicals including *Top Hat* (1935), *Swing Time* (1936), *Shall We Dance?* (1937) and *Carefree* (1938). Another famous producer, Merian C. Cooper, produced the classic *King Kong* (1933) which teamed an outsize ape with Fay Wray. Other quality pictures included *Alice Adams* with Katharine Hepburn and *The Informer* with Victor McLaglen, directed by John Ford. *The Hunchback of Notre Dame* (1939), directed by William Dieterle, and starring Charles Laughton as Quasimodo, also brought critical and commercial success.

RKO was notable for the number of independent productions it financed. Orson Welles's *Citizen Kane* and *The Magnificent Ambersons* were both independent productions which the studio lost money on, but these two movies alone ensured that the RKO name would live on. During the war RKO did its bit with John Wayne in *Back to Bataan* and Gregory Peck as a brave Russian resistance fighter in *Days of Glory*. After the war RKO was one of the leading producers of what came to be known as film noir: *Out of the Past* and *Crossfire*, both released in 1947 and both starring Robert Mitchum, have become noted films of this genre. The movie that brought in most revenue for the studio, however, was the sickly sweet *The Bells of St Mary's* with Bing Crosby. Cary Grant and Ingrid Bergman starred in Hitchcock's *Notorious*, but James Stewart in *It's a Wonderful Life*, directed by Frank Capra, failed to attract the expected customers.

Howard Hughes arrives
. . . .

In 1948 Howard Hughes bought up the ailing studio and proceeded to indulge his obsessions to the detriment of the studio's product and finances, though Fritz Lang managed to direct *While the City Sleeps* and *Rancho Notorious* at the studio during Hughes's reign. RKO stars in the fifties included Jane Russell, with whom Hughes was infatuated, Robert Ryan, Jane Greer and Dana Andrews. But too many RKO movies were substandard action and war flicks, and finally Hughes sold out to General Teleradio who were no better at making successful movies. Finally, in 1958 the studio was sold to Desilu, owned by Lucille Ball and Desi Arnaz, who used it to churn out episodes of *I Love Lucy*. It was a sad ending to the film studio that had made the Astaire-Rogers series, the Orson Welles classics and some of the best of film noir.

LEFT
Eccentric and reclusive movie mogul Howard Hughes, with Jane Greer in Out of the Past *and a scene from* Clash by Night, *starring Robert Ryan.*

BELOW
Marlene Dietrich gave one of the best performances of her later career for Fritz Lang and RKO in Rancho Notorious *(1952).*

COLUMBIA

Founded by brothers Jack and Harry Cohn in 1924, Columbia was for twenty years a comparatively minor studio, partly because it owned no cinemas itself and was therefore squeezed by the majors' monopolistic practices. The 1948 divorcement decree that forced the majors to sell their cinemas helped Columbia establish itself on an equal par with the giants of the industry. Not that the studio under Harry Cohn had not had its successes up to that point: its first great hit was the 1934 *It Happened One Night* with Gable and Colbert. Comedy scored again in *Twentieth Century* with John Barrymore and Carole Lombard. But Columbia was also the studio for cheaply

ABOVE
Columbia's Harry Cohn was known to be a monster even by Hollywood standards, and that's saying something! Rod Steiger played a Cohn-type character in The Big Knife *(1955) in which he drove Jack Palance (playing one of his studio's actors) to castrate himself. Harry Cohn asked for similar sacrifices in real life …*

produced series such as the *Blondie* films, for serials such as *Batman* and for The Three Stooges comedy shorts. On a more prestigious level, Jean Arthur and Gary Cooper starred in Frank Capra's *Mr Deeds Goes to Town* (1936). The screwball comedy *His Girl Friday* with Cary Grant and Rosalind Russell was a hit in 1940.

Rita Hayworth was the studio's only big star in the forties and she made *Cover Girl* with Gene Kelly in 1945 and *Gilda*, the steamy film noir, with Glenn Ford in 1946. The studio made big bucks with *The Jolson Story* and *Jolson Sings Again*. In the late forties and early fifties the studio produced a string of quality pictures: *All the*

> ◆◆*It's not a business,
> it's a racket.*◆◆
>
> **HARRY COHN**
> **(HEAD OF COLUMBIA)**

King's Men, Born Yesterday, On the Waterfront and *From Here to Eternity. The Bridge on the River Kwai, Guess Who's Coming to Dinner, Funny Girl, Easy Rider* and *A Man for all Seasons* were all winners for the studio in the sixties and seventies, whilst post-1970, Spielberg's *Close Encounters of the Third Kind, Kramer vs. Kramer, Tootsie, Ghostbusters* and *The Karate Kid* series ensured that Columbia stayed in the major league. Columbia was bought by the Sony Corporation in the eighties. The studio founded by the detestable mogul, Harry Cohn, had come a long way from its Poverty Row beginnings.

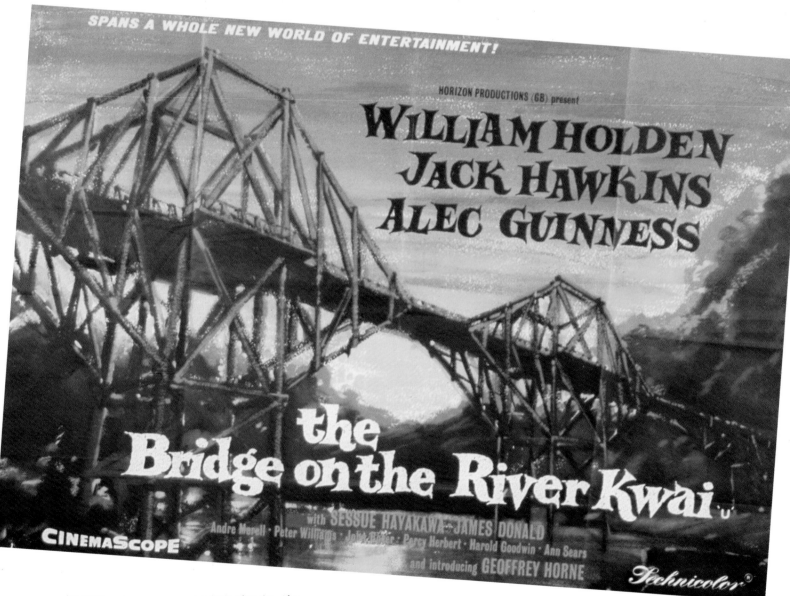

ABOVE
David Lean's The Bridge on the River Kwai *(1957) was the first of his blockbusters. William Holden played out the unconvincing heroics, Alec Guinness was a mad British colonel and Jack Hawkins was Jack Hawkins, in a confused anti-war statement.*

UNIVERSAL

In 1915 Carl Laemmle, the founder of Universal, bought a large piece of land in the Hollywood Hills and named it Universal City. It became a factory for churning out films, very few of which were at all memorable. Erich Von Stroheim, however, made *Foolish Wives* there before Laemmle's general manager, Irving Thalberg, sacked him from his next movie. Once the studio adapted to sound, they produced *All Quiet on the Western Front* in 1930. This was a rare prestige production in a steady stream of routine dross.

However, the studio was best known for its horror movies and its horror stars, Boris Karloff and Bela Lugosi. *Dracula* (1931), *Frankenstein* (1931), *The Bride of Frankenstein* (1935), *The Mummy* (1932) and several sequels, and *The Invisible Man* series all made profits. In the forties the studio's only big money-maker was Claudette Colbert in *The Egg and I*. But in the fifties

BELOW
Universal horror stars Basis Rathbone, Boris Karloff and Bela Lugosi in Son of Frankenstein *(1939). Why were horror movie stars often British or European rather than American? Does this tell us something about American notions of foreignness?*

Universal had big hits with a series of melodramas produced by Ross Hunter and directed by Douglas Sirk: *Written on the Wind*, *Magnificent Obsession*, *The Tarnished Angels* and *Imitation of Life*. *The Glenn Miller Story* and *Winchester 73*, both starring James Stewart, also earned money. Gradually Universal-International, as it was now known, was climbing into the big league. Giant hits such as the 1970 *Airport*, the 1973 *The Sting* and *Jaws* (1975) ensured this. Even these box-office successes were eclipsed in the eighties by Spielberg's *ET* and *Back to the Future*. *Out of Africa* was another major hit in 1985.

Universal is now a massive presence in film and television production. For a long time excluded from the top table in Hollywood, Universal now hands out the invitations and has seen former mighty rivals struggle and even disappear from the scene.

ABOVE

Paul Newman and Robert Redford co-starred in The Sting *(1973). This movie hit followed on the earlier Newman–Redford hit* Butch Cassidy and the Sundance Kid *(1969); both were directed by George Roy Hill.*

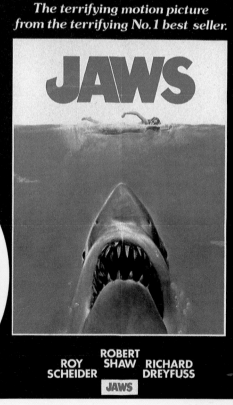

The terrifying motion picture from the terrifying No. 1 best seller.

JAWS

ROY SCHEIDER   ROBERT SHAW   RICHARD DREYFUSS

JAWS

LEFT AND ABOVE

Steven Spielberg had a lot of trouble with his mechanical shark during the filming of Jaws *(1975), but no problem with the box office returns when it was released.* Jaws *is basically a remake of the 1954* The Creature from the Black Lagoon *with some social significance via Ibsen's* Enemy of the People *thrown into the mix.*

UNITED ARTISTS

United Artists was formed by Mary Pickford, Douglas Fairbanks, Charlie Chaplin and D.W. Griffith in 1919 to protect their financial and artistic interests. Griffith left the company in 1924, and his place as a partner was taken by Joseph Schenck who added some much-needed business acumen. By 1928 the balance sheet was in the black, with Chaplin's *The Circus*, Fairbanks' *The Gaucho* and *The Iron Mask*, and Keaton's *Steamboat Bill Jr* adding to the profits.

BELOW
Douglas Fairbanks in one of the adventure roles that made him famous. The Gaucho was made in 1927, when sound was just around the corner. Fairbanks's brand of athleticism and manly charm did not ensure that his career would last into the sound era.

In the thirties the studio produced *The Front Page* (1931), *Les Misérables* and *The Call of the Wild* (both 1935), *Dodsworth* (1936) and *Dead End* (1937). Other memorable pictures included *Stella Dallas* and *The Prisoner of Zenda* with Ronald Colman. Laurence Olivier starred in both *Wuthering Heights* and *Rebecca*. Alexander Korda, the British producer, was associated with United Artists, making *Things to Come* (1936) and *The Man Who Could Work Miracles* (1937). Westerns

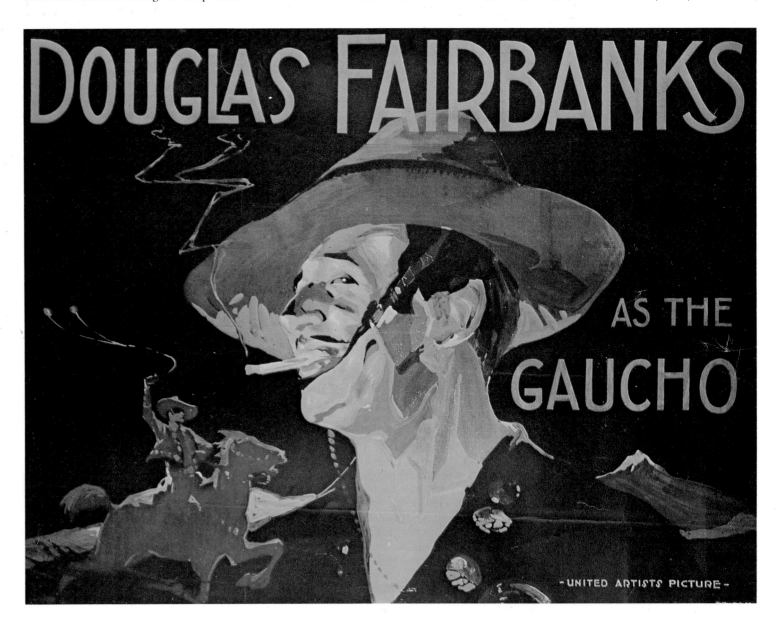

JAMES BOND 007
BACK IN ACTION!
ALBERT R. BROCCOLI &
HARRY SALTZMAN PRESENT
SEAN CONNERY
IN IAN FLEMING'S
GOLDFINGER
HONOR BLACKMAN
AS PUSSY GALORE
GERT FROBE
AS GOLDFINGER
TECHNICOLOR® UNITED ARTISTS
SCREEN PLAY BY RICHARD MAIBAUM & PAUL DEHN
PRODUCED BY HARRY SALTZMAN & ALBERT R. BROCCOLI
DIRECTED BY GUY HAMILTON EON PRODUCTIONS LTD

ABOVE
Sean Connery's third outing as James Bond was in the 1964 Goldfinger. Honor Blackman starred in the role of the less-than-subtly-named Pussy Galore and Gert Frobe was a worthy adversary for the superhuman Bond, a character who was only bearable for many people when Connery played him.

included John Ford's classic *Stagecoach* (1939) and the lamentably bad but notorious *The Outlaw*, the Howard Hughes–Jane Russell fiasco, which was made in 1941 but not released till much later.

Chaplin continued to make films for his company: *The Great Dictator* (1940) and *Monsieur Verdoux* (1947). Selznick produced two hit films for UA in the forties: the wartime family drama *Since You Went Away* and Hitchcock's *Spellbound*. Hard times followed until the early fifties produced such hits as *The African Queen* and *High Noon*. Another mega-hit was Mike Todd's *Around the World in Eighty Days*. By the mid-fifties, both Chaplin and Pickford had sold their shares in the company.

The Bond movies, *West Side Story*, *Tom Jones* and *Midnight Cowboy* helped make the sixties a profitable decade for UA, who were taken over in 1967 by the Transamerica Corporation, an insurance conglomerate. Heavy losses were incurred in the early seventies until hits such as *One Flew over the Cuckoo's Nest*, the *Rocky* series, the *Pink Panther* series and *10* turned the tide. In the eighties UA have continued to finance the Bond series and continued to profit from *Rocky* and the Stallone persona. Woody Allen is one director-star who makes his movies for the 'new' UA. MGM took over UA in 1981; thus, the company set up to protect artists from the tentacles of the majors at last succumbed to one of the giants of the industry.

THE DIRECTORS

W̶HO IS THE author of a movie? The screenwriter? The actors? The producer? The director? The studio? Can we ever claim that there is one overall author of a finished commercial film?

The French critics in the fifties were in no doubt. They looked at the commercial products of the Hollywood studios and they made a ranking list of directors who qualified for *auteur* status. An 'auteur' was a director who could claim to be the author of 'his' films by creating a personal vision of the world. According to the auteur theory, these directors used the conventional elements of Hollywood filmmaking – the

generic forms of the western or melodrama, the star system, the general mode of production – to project an individual view of the world, whether it be a covert criticism of American society or some personal obsession.

Directors such as Alfred Hitchcock and Howard Hawks were cited as two of the 'genius' directors who used conventional formats (Hitchcock with his thrillers, Hawks across a whole range of genres – westerns, screwball comedy, actioners, science fiction, musicals) to pursue their particular themes and obsessions. Suddenly, relatively unknown Hollywood directors were elevated to auteur status. Little did 'B' picture directors such as Joseph H. Lewis and Budd Boetticher realise when they were making cheaply produced gangster pictures and westerns

D.W. Griffith (left) poses beside the camera with two Hollywood functionaries around 1920.

respectively that they would one day be fêted by European critics as artists with a coherent philosophy of life embedded in their movies.

Younger British critics in the early sixties took up the auteur theory, mainly in the pages of *Movie* magazine, and discovered their own heroes. Indeed, the first edition of *Movie* had definitive lists of 'great', 'excellent', 'talented' and merely 'competent' directors. To qualify for the top rankings, a director had to have a coherent vision that informed most of the movies he made. Thus, not only Hitchcock and Hawks qualified, but also Fritz Lang, Otto Preminger, Orson Welles, John Ford, Vincente Minnelli, Nicholas Ray and numerous others. Most of these directors were very surprised when such critics pointed out to them that a coherent vision of the world shone through their films.

Filmmaking is a collaborative process. Undoubtedly directors are key figures in that process. However, it is a mistake to imagine that most films 'belong' to a director, especially when the assembly-line mode of production that operated in Hollywood is considered. In old Hollywood, more often than not, a director would have little or no control over script, casting, technical aspects, the editing of the final negative or marketing. Very often the producer and/or the studio would be the final arbiter of how a movie would turn out. For example, producers such as David Selznick had a powerful influence over the movies they supervised (Selznick used at least three directors on his most famous film, *Gone with the Wind*). Directors were employees of the studios and producers were there to make sure they did what the studio required.

> ◆◆ *John Ford isn't exactly a bum, is he? Yet he never gave me any manure about art. He just made movies and that's what I do.* ◆◆
>
> **JOHN WAYNE**

There were some free spirits who used the system, some more successfully than others, to make the films they wanted to make. Orson Welles is the outstanding example of a talented director who, after having made two outstanding movies, was sidelined by Hollywood because he was too much of an individualist. Hitchcock, on the other hand, won for himself a great deal of freedom by becoming the producer of his own movies and working out a deal over distribution with various major studios. A director had much more control over how he made 'his' film when he had some economic involvement in the production, otherwise the studios who were putting up the money could largely dictate to him. In this situation, for a director who wanted to 'say something' in movies, it was a matter of imposing some personal angle or trait where he could. However, there were some directors who had the confidence of the studios and producers and were given their head to a certain extent because they delivered the product in a form that was not only artistically satisfying but also made big bucks for the studio at the box-office.

Since the break-up of the Hollywood studio system, numerous filmmakers have won themselves much greater freedom over how they make their films. The packaging of a movie project (a script, a bevy of stars, a director, producer and an independent company) is done by agents who then deal with the studios who may act merely as distributors or bankers. Directors such as Steven Spielberg or Woody Allen have far greater artistic control over their movies than those who worked under the old Hollywood studio system.

In one sense, the wheel has turned full circle because, in the very early days of Hollywood, directors such as Griffith and Von Stroheim had almost total control over how their movies turned out. For a privileged few in the Hollywood of today, that is once again true. Elsewhere, directors who have won themselves a reputation, such as David Lean, Bernardo Bertolucci or Claude Chabrol, have considerable freedom. However, that kind of freedom is not always productive because a director can be self-indulgent and tedious just as writers can. The studio system may have been stifling to many talents, but the fact is that it also trained directors to work within certain disciplines; work of a surprisingly high quality was often produced in a business dedicated to making money.

LEFT
Anthony Perkins as Norman Bates, mother's boy par excellence, *in Hitchcock's* Psycho *(1960).*

BELOW
James Stewart as an ex-cop with problems in high places, in Hitchcock's 1958 Vertigo. *For Hitchcock, a story was only important to him as a director in as far as it gave him opportunities to manipulate the audience and to explore his obsessions: guilt, sexuality and punishment.*

'OLD
HOLLYWOOD'
GREATS

Alfred Hitchcock

Of all the Hollywood directors the French critics 'rediscovered' in the fifties Hitchcock was the one who received the most attention and praise. His forte was the suspense thriller and he rarely changed the formula, but he used the genre, consciously and often unconsciously, to work through his own fears and obsessions. However, his first responsibility, as he saw it, was to make the audience squirm. He was a master of audience manipulation, presenting its fears, lusts, nightmares and weaknesses in the movies he directed; but in the process he revealed more about himself than he thought he was doing.

Born in Leytonstone, London, in 1899, Hitchcock had a lonely and repressed childhood, which left him with emotional scars he spent the rest of his life exposing on screen. He had a Catholic upbringing and this left him with a fear of authority, a sense of guilt, especially about sex, and the expectation of punishment. All these obsessions regularly surface in his movies. His obesity also gave him a complex about his unattractiveness to women. He usually cast very

BELOW

Alfred Hitchcock (the fat gent) explains there's meant to be a corpse in the trunk to (from left to right) Farley Granger, James Stewart and John Dall in Rope *(1948). Granger and Dall bump off a friend for the kicks of planning the perfect murder. They stuff the body in the trunk and then invite their ex-professor round to their apartment. Hitchcock experimented by shooting the film in a series of ten-minute takes.*

personable actors in the leading roles in his movies (Cary Grant, James Stewart, Gregory Peck) and cast cool blondes opposite them; these women would be subject to abuse, humiliation and murder. Joan Fontaine was the subject of Cary Grant's murderous intentions in *Suspicion* (the studio insisted that Grant be cleared of suspicion at the end of the movie because it might have damaged his image), Grant was beastly to Ingrid Bergman in *Notorious*, Ray Milland tried to murder Grace Kelly in *Dial M for Murder*, Kim Novak was thrown off a high tower (twice) in *Vertigo*, Janet Leigh was slaughtered in a shower in *Psycho*, Tippi Hedren was attacked by birds in *The Birds* and variously humiliated by Sean Connery in *Marnie*, and various women were raped and murdered in the repellent *Frenzy*.

Hitchcock's own favourite movie was *Shadow of a Doubt*, starring Joseph Cotten as a charming uncle-figure who happened to have the distressing habit of bumping off widows for their money. No two fans would agree on Hitchcock's six best films, but here is my choice: *Shadow of a Doubt, Notorious, Rear Window, Vertigo, North by Northwest* and *Psycho*.

Whether consciously or not, Hitchcock challenged the audience to consider themselves as voyeurs. He knew we are fascinated by the process of watching and the cinema makes voyeurs of us all. He played on our fantasies and made us feel guilty about what they reveal about ourselves. He could manipulate us to feel anxiety for the 'wrong people': for example, after Norman Bates has murdered Marion Crane (Janet Leigh) in the shower scene in *Psycho*, albeit dressed as his mother, we watch anxiously as he cleans up the blood, remembers the newspaper containing the money in the bedroom at the last moment, stuffs the dead body into the boot of Leigh's car and drives to the swamp. When the car stops halfway down in the swamp, we want it to continue to submerge even though it contains the murdered body. Hitchcock has successfully transferred our sympathy from the victim to the murderer, manipulating our emotions in a manner that leaves us feeling distinctly uncomfortable. He was a master cinematic storyteller, but there are depths to his films that go well beyond the conventional suspense thriller.

John Ford

John Ford consistently denied any serious artistic purpose in his work and hooted with laughter at the idea of any consistent philosophy permeating the movies he directed. But critics have marked him down as one of the great originals of the Hollywood scene; some see him as a poet of the cinematic image, and certainly some of his films could be accused of looking good while having some distasteful elements to them (racism, extreme conservative values, mindless violence). He is best known for his westerns: *Stagecoach*, *Drums Along the Mohawk*, *My Darling Clementine*, *Fort Apache*, *She Wore a Yellow Ribbon*, *Rio Grande*, *Wagonmaster*, *The Searchers* and *The Man Who Shot Liberty Valance* are among his best known. His politics were a kind of maverick right-wing extremism, which may explain why he used stars with similar political beliefs, such as John Wayne and Ward Bond, so often in his movies.

Don't ever forget what I'm going to tell you. Actors are crap.

JOHN FORD

Howard Hawks.

LEFT

One of John Ford's best films, The Searchers *has been 'remade' in different forms by Martin Scorsese (*Taxi Driver; *1976) and Paul Schrader (*Hardcore; *1979). It provided John Wayne with a complex character to play for once, a racist.*

LEFT

John Ford before his eye-patch days. Ford's reputation ebbs and flows: some see him as a seminal director in the American cinema, others as a sentimental and reactionary filmmaker with pretensions to cinematic poetry.

Ford's films generally deal with groups of men in situations where they have to show their courage and loyalty to one another. He could be extremely sentimental at times, especially in his 'Oirish' movies such as *The Quiet Man* and *The Last Hurrah*. American Indians are portrayed as savages in almost all of the westerns till *The Searchers* (1956), but there is a belated attempt to redress the balance in the 1964 *Cheyenne Autumn*. At its best, Ford's work has a warmth and humanity about it (*The Grapes of Wrath, The Long Voyage Home*); at its worst it celebrates a kind of mindless, brutal machismo (*They Were Expendable, Donovan's Reef*). Running through the body of his films is a lament for an America that has vanished forever, a lawless frontier culture that was obliterated by the march of civilisation and the law book.

Howard Hawks

Hawks is a test case for the theory that certain directors have a consistent vision that shines through all the films they direct, because he was the archetypal journeyman director elevated to auteur status. He directed movies across a wide range of genres: actioners (*Barbary Coast, Only Angels Have Wings, To Have and Have Not, The Big Sky*), westerns (*Red River, Rio Bravo, El Dorado*), screwball comedies (*Twentieth Century, Bringing Up Baby, His Girl Friday*), gangsters (*Scarface*), private eye thrillers (*The Big Sleep*), science fiction

(*The Thing*), musicals (*Gentlemen Prefer Blondes*) and epics (*Land of the Pharaohs*).

One theme that does emerge from a number of the movies Hawks directed is gender roles and what happens when those are reversed: *Bringing Up Baby* has an assertive Katharine Hepburn leading a bemused Cary Grant through a series of misadventures. *His Girl Friday* has a tough Rosalind Russell being pursued professionally by Cary Grant; the latter dons women's clothes to pass as a wartime bride in *I Was a Male War Bride*, and Jane Russell cavorts in a swimming pool with the American Olympic team acting as chorus boys in *Gentlemen Prefer Blondes*. But in Hawks's movies women have to prove themselves in a man's world and are approved of if they turn out to be tough and no-nonsense types. He is quoted as saying 'For me the best drama is one that deals with a man in danger,' and that holds true for most of his movies. How much overall control he had over the content of his movies remains in doubt, however, and how much he deserves auteur status remains a matter of judgement.

When you find out a thing goes pretty well, you might as well do it again.

HOWARD HAWKS

THE
TALENTED
JOURNEYMEN

Frank Capra

Many would claim that Capra belongs in the first rank of American directors for the body of 'populist' films he made in the thirties and forties in which he celebrated the essential decency of the common man and the virtues of American democracy. Capra's populism consisted of his taking the side of the little guy against the battalions of big business and organized politics. A simplistic philosophy and wish-fulfilling happy endings are found in *Mr Deeds Goes to Town* (Gary Cooper inheriting wealth and going to New York to help poor farmers), *You Can't Take It with You*, *Mr Smith Goes to Washington* (James Stewart sorting out the political machine), *Meet John Doe* and *It's a Wonderful Life* in which Stewart again saves small-town America from perdition. In between these movies, Capra directed Harlow in *Platinum Blonde*, Gable and Colbert in *It Happened One Night*, Ronald Colman in *Lost Horizon* and Tracy and Hepburn in *State of the Union*. His later films were entirely forgettable: *Riding High* and *Here Comes the Groom* with Crosby, and *A Hole in the Head* with Sinatra.

BELOW

James Stewart as George Bailey and Donna Reed as his wife Mary in It's a Wonderful Life *(1947). Directed by Frank Capra, the movie is a hymn of praise to the virtues of small-town America.*

Michael Curtiz

Curtiz was Hungarian in origin and had a substantial career in European films before he came to Hollywood to direct some of the most famous films of the thirties and forties. He directed Errol Flynn in *Captain Blood*, *The Charge of the Light Brigade*, *The Perfect Specimen*, *The Adventures of Robin Hood*, *Elizabeth and Essex*, *Dodge City*, *Virginia City*, *The Sea Hawk* and *Sante Fe Trail*. He showed he had a feeling for romance and film noir in the classic *Casablanca* and *Mildred Pierce*. Associated with Warner Brothers primarily, Curtiz was the quintessential journeyman director, turning his directorial hand to most genres; however, very few critics, even the most obsessive of French auteurists, have made a case for Curtiz's 'vision'.

George Cukor

Cukor came to be known as a woman's director because of the sensitivity with which he handled top female stars and 'women's pictures'. He was also known for directing respectable screen adaptations of famous literary works such as *Little Women*, *David Copperfield*, *Romeo and Juliet* and *The Women*. Musicals included *A Star is Born*, *Les Girls* and *My Fair Lady*. Comedies were his forte: *The Philadelphia Story*, *Adam's Rib*, *Born Yesterday*, *The Marrying Kind* and *Pat and Mike*. He directed Garbo in *Camille*, Joan Crawford in *A Woman's Face*, Bette Davis in *The Actress* and Monroe in *Let's Make Love*. Cukor's main talent may have consisted of his ability to adapt literary and theatrical influences to the cinema and to serve up middlebrow entertainment in various forms over a period of forty years.

William Wyler

Wyler was known as a very hard taskmaster for actors; stars or not, he took no nonsense from them and would go for take after take if he felt it

[Hu]mphrey Bogart as Rick in *Michael Curtiz's [C]asablanca (1942). The [film] has achieved major cult [st]atus, and Woody Allen's [Pl]ay It Again, Sam (1972) pays due tribute to it.*

A Star is Born. *Surely one of the best films George Cukor directed, this 1954 musical has Judy Garland giving one of her very best performances as Vicky Lestor, a singer who makes it to the top with the help of alcoholic, self-destructive movie star on the skids, Norman Maine.*

ABOVE

Charlton Heston as Ben in MGM's 1959 version of Ben Hur, *directed by William Wyler. There is a heavy religiosity to the film which makes it hard to sit through, but the action scenes are spectacular.*

was warranted. Laurence Olivier always paid tribute to his influence on him as a director and actor after Wyler had directed him in *Wuthering Heights*. He also directed Bette Davis, a strong-minded individual, in *Jezebel*, *The Letter* and *The Little Foxes*. One of his important movies was *The Best Years of Our Lives* which examined the problems facing ex-GIs coming to terms with post-war America and which offered some liberal but simplistic solutions. Wyler was also entrusted with action pictures, notably *The Desperate Hours*, *The Big Country* and *Ben Hur*. Melodramas included *The Heiress*, *Carrie* and *The Children's Hour*, and he also had the task of directing Streisand in *Funny Girl*.

Vincente Minnelli

Minnelli was one of MGM's longest-serving directors, indeed, in a career spanning thirty-five years, he made only three films out of thirty-six for studios other than MGM. This makes him an interesting test case as a director: as a studio director how much control did he have over the movies he made?

Minnelli is best known for his musicals but he has also acquired a reputation for the melodramas he directed in the fifties. These include *The Cobweb*, *The Bad and the Beautiful*, *Some Came Running* and *Home from the Hill*. His best-known musicals are *Meet Me in St Louis*, *The Pirate*, *An American in Paris*, *The Band Wagon*, *Gigi* and *On a Clear Day You Can See Forever*. He is, in fact,

*The Band Wagon (1953)
was one of the best of the
MGM musicals directed by
Vincente Minnelli. With a
plot that is not much
different from the previous
year's* Singin' in the Rain,
Band Wagon *has Astaire
'Dancing in the Dark' with
Cyd Charisse, performing an
elegant soft-shoe shuffle
with Jack Buchanan, and
singing solo on 'By Myself'.*

known as the father of the modern movie musical and has other paternity claims as the father of Liza Minnelli, the product of his brief marriage to Judy Garland. His favourite film of the ones he directed himself was *Lust for Life* in which Kirk Douglas played Van Gogh. Minnelli was revered by critics as a stylist and for his feeling for colour and design within the screen space.

Billy Wilder

Another European expatriate, Wilder specialised in rather sour comedy and noirish melodramas. He co-wrote, with Charles Brackett and then I.A.L. Diamond, many of the films he directed. As a writer he collaborated on Garbo's *Ninotchka* and the Stanwyck-Cooper *Ball of Fire*. As a writer-director his finest efforts have been *Double Indemnity* (on which he collaborated with Raymond Chandler) and *Sunset Boulevard*. Other notable films include *Ace in the Hole*, *The Seven Year Itch*, *Some Like It Hot* and *The Apartment*. His later films became increasingly raucous and vulgar: *Irma La Douce*, *Kiss Me Stupid* and *Avanti!*. Wilder is quoted as saying that the best director is the one you don't see; certainly, he is no stylist and his main talent may be as a writer and in his instinct for what works on screen.

George Stevens

Stevens's best film as a director is probably *Shane*, the classic western, and yet he was not a western specialist. He made a name in the thirties directing Hepburn in *Alice Adams* and again in *Woman of the Year*. His films tended towards the sentimental and the romantic, for example, *I Remember Mama* and *A Place in the Sun*. He directed Dean, Taylor and Hudson in the Texas epic *Giant* and was also responsible for *The Greatest Story Ever Told*.

COLOR BY TECHNICOLOR MUSICAL!

GET ABOARD THE BAND WAGON

HEAR THE MUSIC IN THE M-G-M RECORD ALBUM

Starring
FRED ASTAIRE · CYD CHARISSE
OSCAR LEVANT
NANETTE FABRAY · JACK BUCHANAN
with JAMES MITCHELL · Story and Screen Play by BETTY COMDEN and ADOLPH GREEN
Songs by HOWARD DIETZ and ARTHUR SCHWARTZ · Directed by VINCENTE MINNELLI · Produced by ARTHUR FREED
AN M-G-M PICTURE

John Huston

· · · · · · · · · ·

A talented director or a lucky son of a famous father who happened to get involved with some decent movies? Opinions divide over Huston, largely because there is little discernible pattern to his work as a whole. He directed some of the best of Hollywood movies: *The Maltese Falcon, The Treasure of the Sierra Madre, The Asphalt Jungle, The Misfits* and *Wise Blood.* However, he also directed some of the worst: *Moulin Rouge, Moby Dick, The Barbarian and the Geisha, The Bible* and *Victory.* The jury is still out on *Prizzi's Honour* and *The Dead.* However, there is no doubting his staying power or his icon status among old Hollywood directors.

> ♦♦*We can make bad pictures too . . . Costs more but we can make 'em.*♦♦
>
> **JOHN HUSTON**

BELOW

John Huston also acted in films from time to time, as here in Breakout.

RIGHT

One of the first American films to explore in detail the planning and execution of a robbery, The Asphalt Jungle *(1950) inspired a sub-genre of its own, the 'heist' movie.*

Huston's 'anti-western' The
Misfits (1960) was to be the
last film for both Clark
Gable and Marilyn Monroe,
with the death of its third
star, Montgomery Clift,
following shortly
afterwards.

LEFT

An early success for director
John Huston was The
Maltese Falcon (1941).
Bogart confronts Mary Astor
with Peter Lorre caught in
the middle.

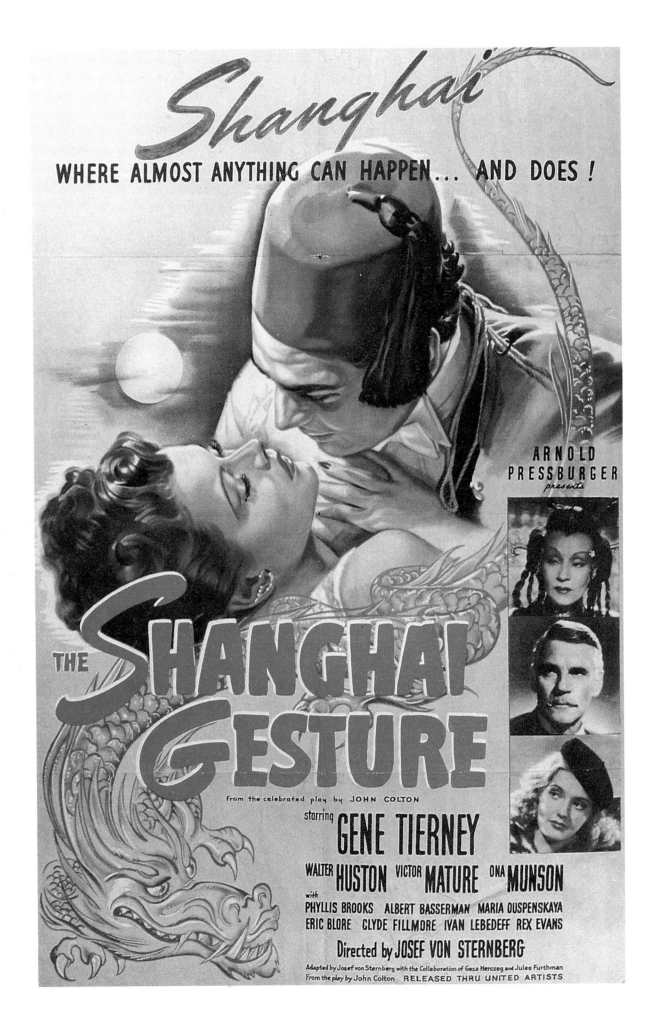

This section focuses on 'maverick' directors who, for one reason or another, did not quite fit in with the Hollywood system, or who carved out for themselves a unique position within that system.

Josef Von Sternberg

Another Hungarian expatriate director, Von Sternberg's career was closely associated with the films he directed Marlene Dietrich in. Neither of their careers ever really recovered from their professional split, though Von Sternberg suffered more than the star he 'created'.

Von Sternberg was known as a stylist, indeed he is quoted as saying that he cared little for the stories of his films, only about how they were photographed and presented. That is just as well because movies such as *Shanghai Express, Blonde Venus, The Scarlet Empress* and *The Devil is a Woman* teeter on the edge of being 'high camp' rubbish and only the 'look' of them saves them. Von Sternberg liked shooting through shutters and lattices, gauze and mists; he also decorated his sets elaborately to create a Hollywood concept of decadence.

After his films with Dietrich, his career went into a downward spiral; he directed the unfinished *I Claudius* for Korda and then made very few films until his death in 1969. He once said, 'The only way to succeed is to make people hate you. That way they remember you.' It seems that people remembered Von Sternberg's autocratic ways only too well, because very few of them offered him a directing job in his declining years.

LEFT

The Shanghai Gesture *(1941) was directed by a Joseph Von Sternberg well past his peak by this time.*

♦♦*Everyone denies I am a genius but no one ever called me that in the first place.*♦♦

ORSON WELLES

Orson Welles

The *enfant terrible* of Hollywood in the forties, Welles first came to fame when he terrorised America with his documentary-style radio version of *War of the Worlds*, convincing thousands of naïve Americans that their country really was being invaded by aliens. *Citizen Kane* (1941) then

BELOW

Orson Welles at the radio microphone, the instrument he used to terrify America with his radio version of H.G. Wells's War of the Worlds. *The notoriety Welles gained from this sensational radio event helped launch his career in Hollywood and led to his directing* Citizen Kane.

established his reputation as a director of movies; his story of a press baron, based on the life of William Randolph Hearst, was seen as innovatory in its use of deep-focus photography, overlapping sound, expressionistic sets and creative montage sequences. How much of the credit for these innovations should go to cameraman Gregg Toland and co-writer Herman J. Mankiewicz is still a matter of controversy. Welles's second film for RKO, *The Magnificent Ambersons*, was badly mauled by the studio, which added a spurious happy ending. Thereafter, Welles's relationship with the studio declined, and he was more often seen as an actor in films made by others, such as *Jane Eyre*, *Prince of Foxes*, *The Third Man*, *The Black Rose*, *Moby Dick*, *The Long Hot Summer* and *Roots of Heaven*. Some of the later films he directed have authentic Welles touches to them, notably *The Stranger*, *Macbeth*, *Othello*, *The Lady from Shanghai*, *Touch of Evil*, *The Trial*, *Chimes at Midnight* and *The Immortal Story*. The usual adjective used about his later work is 'flawed', but many of those flaws were caused by low and disappearing budgets. Welles said of himself, 'I started at the top and worked down,' and there is more than a grain of truth in that statement, including the implication that he may have brought many of his troubles upon his own head.

Nicholas Ray

Ray became an icon for many European critics and filmmakers, the symbol of the genius director partly destroyed by the studio system. His artistic background was with the left-wing Group Theatre, where he was a protégé of Elia Kazan. His first Hollywood film *They Live by Night* is probably his best; the story of the isolated and alienated young lovers on the run is given added impact by Ray's imaginative use of the screen space and his creative *mise-en-scène*. Ray clearly identified with the outsider and the young in American society and this was again reflected in his direction of James Dean in *Rebel without a*

Cause. The institution of the family gets a rough ride in several of his films, notably in *They Live by Night* and *Rebel* and also in *Bigger Than Life*, where James Mason takes some drugs and is transformed into an oppressive patriarch – his real self, the movie implies. Ray also made *In a Lonely Place*, a study of paranoia and violence starring Humphrey Bogart as a Hollywood writer; this movie was perceived as being a comment on the paranoia engendered by the McCarthyite investigations into Hollywood in the late forties and early fifties.

French critics in particular saw merits in later Ray films such as *Bitter Victory* and *Party Girl* that few other people could perceive, and they even found things to admire in two epics he directed in the early sixties, *King of Kings* and *55 Days at Peking*. Wim Wenders, the German director, paid one last tribute when he made a film about Ray when he was dying of cancer in 1979, *Lightning over Water*. It was a last defiant romantic gesture from a romantic director.

Elia Kazan

Kazan, of Greek descent, worked as an actor with the Group Theatre but later spectacularly renounced his radical past when he was a friendly witness in front of the Congressional committee investigating so-called communist infiltration into Hollywood. Kazan went so far as to 'name names' of past communist associates. His testimony did his career no harm at all.

His early films are far from personal: *A Tree Grows in Brooklyn*, *Gentleman's Agreement*, *Sea of Grass* and *Pinky*. He described MGM for whom he made *Sea of Grass* as an industrial compound run by businessmen. His first personal project was *A Streetcar Named Desire* with Marlon Brando and Vivien Leigh and, after his testimony to the Congressional committee, he concentrated on making movies which, to varying degrees, seemed to justify the stand he had taken. *On the Waterfront* justified 'snitching' on your friends when it showed Terry Malloy (Brando) turning stool-pigeon on his erstwhile gangster pals; the movie was also a huge success and gave Kazan carte blanche to tackle any film project he wanted to and have final cut rights over the movies he made. He went on to make *East of Eden*, *Baby Doll*, *A Face in the Crowd*, *Wild River*, *Splendor in the Grass* and *The Last Tycoon*. In between he made two films which he adapted

Marlon Brando (Stanley) menaces Vivien Leigh (Blanche Dubois) in A Streetcar Named Desire *(1951), directed by Elia Kazan and adapted from Tennessee Williams's stage play. 'I have always depended on the kindness of strangers', Blanche says, but Stanley shows her no kindness when he rapes her, and thereby catapults her into madness.*

from his own novels, *America America* and *The Arrangement*. In these films he represents his family's coming to America and finding the joys and tribulations of American capitalism. Kazan's main talents were his undoubted ability to direct actors and the emotional intensity he brought to his movies.

Douglas Sirk

Of Danish origin, Sirk worked in the German Expressionist theatre of the twenties before directing various European films and coming to Hollywood. His first major film was *Summer Storm* (1944), adapted

from a Chekhov short story, then he made a series of comedies for Universal including *Has Anybody Seen My Gal?*, *Meet Me at the Fair* and *Take Me to Town*. However, Sirk's reputation as an auteur rests squarely on the melodramas he directed in the fifties: *All I Desire*, *Magnificent Obsession*, *There's Always Tomorrow*, *All That Heaven Allows*, *Written on the Wind*, *The Tarnished Angels* and *Imitation of Life*. Supporters of Sirk's claims to seriousness say that he used the excesses of the melodramatic genre to criticise Eisenhower's America in all its materialism and conformity. Detractors of these claims say that

you can read anything you like into these excessively sentimental pieces of schlock if you really want to find an excuse for liking them. However, there is little doubt that Sirk used ironic and distancing devices in his direction to draw attention to the social points he wanted to make. His left-wing credentials endeared him to many film critics in Europe, but some feminist critics, although admitting his films were more than just examples of kitsch, pointed out they did tend to reinforce patriarchal structures while appearing to attack them.

Stanley Kubrick
· · · · · · · · ·

After two minor, low-budget films, Kubrick, who had been a photographer with *Life* magazine, made *The Killing* (1956), a semi-documentary crime thriller which brought him much attention. *Paths of Glory*, an anti-war movie set in First World War trenches with Kirk Douglas as a French officer defending three men wrongfully accused of cowardice, established his reputation as a major director. The epic *Spartacus* continued his association with Kirk Douglas and is usually seen as one of the few 'intelligent' epics.

Kubrick's desire to film challenging material led him to direct *Lolita* in 1962, and he used the movie to paint a picture of an America that was aimless and materialistic. His black comedy *Dr Strangelove* remains a very funny comment on the nightmare of the dangers of nuclear warfare and *2001* in 1969 took the space film into new dimensions. *A Clockwork Orange* was controversially violent and aroused a storm of protest (Kubrick later withdrew it), but *Barry Lyndon* was largely damned with the faint praise of being beautiful to look at but not much else. It is, however, one of the greatly underrated movies of the seventies. *The Shining* again aroused protests because of its violence, particularly towards women. *Full Metal Jacket* was Kubrick's Vietnam movie and it is certainly among the best of the crop of movies about that American nightmare.

Kubrick has insisted on independence as a producer-director and his films are always notable, though he has been criticised for being too interested in the sets and staging of events in his movies at the expense of the human characters. Certainly, since *Paths of Glory*, there has been a distancing of emotional involvement, but he remains a distinctive talent.

ABOVE

Posters for Douglas Sirk's All That Heaven Allows *and* Written on the Wind, *and Kubrick's* A Clockwork Orange.

THE DIRECTORS OF NEW HOLLYWOOD

John Cassavetes
. . . .

Cassavetes was never a hugely successful director, but he made the movies he wanted to in his own personal style. He was a successful Hollywood actor before he turned to directing (*Edge of the City* and *Virgin Island*), but it was his experimental *Shadows* (1961) that established his reputation for risk-taking: actors' improvisation, hand-held cameras, disjointed narrative and a refusal to portray human relationships sentimentally. He is quoted as saying, 'When I started making pictures, I wanted to make Frank Capra pictures. But I've never been able to make anything but these crazy tough pictures. You are what you are.' 'These crazy tough pictures' include *Faces* (1968), *A Woman Under the Influence* (1974), *Opening Night* (1978), *The Killing of a Chinese Bookie* (1978), *Gloria* (1980) and *Love Streams* (1983). Only *Gloria* achieved any substantial commercial success. His wife, Gena Rowlands, starred in most of his films and he also acted in some of them. Other favourite male actors he used were Peter Falk and Ben Gazzara, who were his personal friends. Almost all of the films Cassavetes directed have real flaws in them, but there is a rawness and honesty to them that delineates them sharply from the standard Hollywood product. Tragically, he died in 1989 at the age of sixty.

> ♦♦*I never know what my movies are about until I finish them.*♦♦
>
> **JOHN CASSAVETES**

Steven Spielberg
. . . .

Spielberg is the world's most famous and successful living film director. He makes movies for the mass market and is phenomenally successful at it. *Jaws, Close Encounters of the Third Kind, ET, Raiders of the Lost Ark, Indiana Jones and the Temple*

RIGHT
Stephen Spielberg on the set of The Colour Purple.

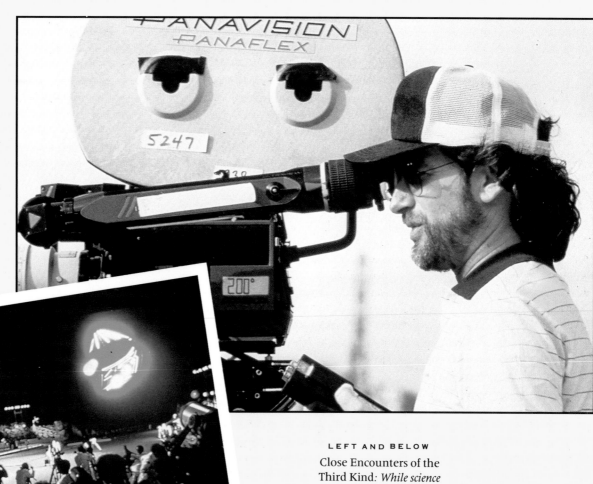

LEFT AND BELOW
Close Encounters of the Third Kind: *While science fiction movies of the fifties depicted aliens as a threat to the status quo and the American way of life, Spielberg's extra-terrestrials are intelligent, benevolent creatures.*

LEFT
John Cassavetes (left) as the bad guy in Brian de Palma's 1978 psychic thriller The Fury. *Cassavetes will undoubtedly be remembered more for his few directing achievements than for his many performances in other people's films.*

of *Doom* and *Indiana Jones and the Last Crusade* have made him a multi-millionaire and carved for himself a very powerful position within the American film industry. He is the most consistently successful of the 'movie brats', that group of movie-obsessed young men who conquered Hollywood in the seventies: George Lucas, Francis Coppola, Martin Scorsese, Brian De Palma, Peter Bogdanovich and Spielberg himself. He has garnered critical praise as well as commercial success.

Spielberg openly confesses his debt to Disney and the Saturday-morning serials, but his films

Robert De Niro in Martin Scorsese's Raging Bull *(1980). Based on the life story of champion boxer Jake La Motta, the film explores notions of masculinity and how society conditions the male psyche towards brutality and self-destruction.*

are also in the tradition of Frank Capra populism – they are for the individual against bureaucracy, the decent instincts of the ordinary people against the government that appears to act in their name. Witness the Richard Dreyfuss character in *Close Encounters* or the neighbourhood youngsters saving ET. Spielberg's directional touch has been less certain in his 'adult' movies: *The Colour Purple* and *Always*. His one really successful adult movie has been *Empire of the Sun* and that again had a boy as the main protagonist. It is a child's vision of the world that Spielberg brings to his films.

He has also been a very influential and successful producer of other directors' films: *Poltergeist*, *Gremlins 1* and *2* and *The Goonies*. Spielberg is a phenomenon, not only in terms of his success, but because he is a product of a movie culture which he now enriches.

Martin Scorsese

Scorsese directed *Taxi Driver*, one of the seminal movies of the modern American cinema. Like the rest of the 'movie brats' Scorsese is in love with cinema *per se* and his films persistently show his debt to old Hollywood. *Taxi Driver* is a very late film noir, *New York, New York* is in part a tribute to the MGM musical, *Raging Bull* owes something to *On the Waterfront* in its portrayal of the Jake La Motta protagonist, and *The Color of Money* is a late sequel to *The Hustler*. However, Scorsese brings his own personal obsessions to these movies: his ambivalence towards macho values, group and family loyalties, the concept of success and the price it demands. Several of his films have been criticised for their depiction of extreme violence, in particular *Mean Streets* (his first real success), *Taxi Driver* and *Raging Bull*; *The Last Temptation of Christ* aroused great controversy because of its perceived blasphemy.

Scorsese has consistently used his own experiences of growing up in the Little Italy section of New York as material in his films, and violence and Catholic guilt were intrinsic parts of that experience for him. He has a romantic trait and this comes out in *Alice Doesn't Live Here Any More* and *The Color of Money*. *King of Comedy* was a box-office failure but showed his talent for exposing through comedy the tawdry nature of the search for fame and success in modern America. Of all the movie brats, Scorsese may turn out to be the most important as a maker of films that reflect their times.

LEFT
Robert De Niro reaches his 'major chord' in New York, New York *(1977).*

ABOVE
New York, New York *was in part intended as a tribute to the MGM musicals of the forties and fifties.*

BELOW
Robert De Niro chats up Liza Minnelli in New York, New York *(1977).*

RIGHT
Liza Minnelli in New York, New York *(1977). Liza plays a forties singer very much in the mould of her mother, Judy Garland.*

Francis Coppola explains what he wants on the set of The Godfather *(1972), while Al Pacino, playing Michael Corleone, listens attentively. Coppola has taken enormous risks during his career with his own money and talent, as the documentary* Hearts of Darkness *(1992) about the making of* Apocalypse Now *(1979) makes very clear.*

Francis Coppola

Coppola first made it in movies as a writer; his writing credits include *This Property is Condemned* and *Patton*. His first success as a director was *The Godfather*, which he also co-wrote, and that was followed by *The Conversation*, a movie about paranoia, betrayal and Nixon's America. *The Godfather Part II* was even more effective than the first part. His most ambitious movie has been *Apocalypse Now*, an LSD picture of the Vietnam war. He sank a lot of the money he made out of the *Godfather* movies into this very expensive venture. He has, in fact, always been willing to risk his own capital, as shown when he founded his own studio, Zoetrope, in San Francisco and employed old Hollywood stalwart Gene Kelly and British director Michael Powell as associates, but this attempt to make films in a traditional studio-based set-up was doomed to failure. Movies such as *One from the Heart* and *Hammett* were more or less disasters at the box-office, leaving Coppola relatively impoverished. He then made two teenage melodramas from Susie Hinton novels, *The Outsiders* and *Rumble Fish*, which revived his fortunes, but failed to save the Zoetrope studios. *Peggy Sue Got Married* was a popular success but showed Coppola coasting, whilst *Tucker* was distinctly disappointing. Coppola's achievements with the *Godfather* movies, *The Conversation* and *Apocalypse Now* means he has already won himself an important niche in Hollywood history, but it is to be hoped he soon manages to produce pictures of that quality again.

Oliver Stone

As a writer Stone wrote *Midnight Express*, *Scarface* and *The Year of the Dragon*. He co-wrote and directed *Salvador*, a tough indictment of fascism in Latin America and America's covert support of it. Another film he wrote and directed, the Vietnam movie *Platoon*, won him an Oscar as a director; he had used his own experiences of the war as an ordinary 'grunt' for his screenplay. *Wall Street* was another huge success for him as a director and writer; this time his target was greed and corruption among junk bond dealers, but the radicalism of the movie was watered down by pinning the blame on a few rotten apples rather than the system itself. This lack of political edge may be why Hollywood has taken Stone to its flinty bosom and showered further awards on his second Vietnam movie, *Born in the USA*, which showed a paraplegic Vietnam vet winning through to become a public spokesman for his comrades. However, *JFK* (1991), a long rambling, somewhat confusing but brilliant analysis of one of the many conspiracy theories surrounding the Kennedy assassination, strengthened Stone's reputation for radicalism in an industry that spawns too many time-servers. Stone communicates a visceral intensity in his movies.

LEFT

Val Kilmer as Jim Morrison in Oliver Stone's 1991 movie The Doors. *The movie records Morrison's almost inevitable crawl towards self-destruction and a squalid death in a Parisian apartment.*

Quentin Tarantino

. . . .

His many admirers have been known to compare Tarantino with Orson Welles but those who are not his fans claim that this would send the great Falstaffian genius revolving in his grave. One could go as far as saying that placing Tarantino on a similar pedestal to Welles is like comparing cheap sparkling wine to Champagne or a hamburger with *filet mignon*. Stripped of their surface gloss, Tarantino's movies (*Reservoir Dogs*, *Pulp Fiction* and the script of *True Romance*) are basically splatter movies that appeal to the thinking and non-thinking viewer. These films are most likely destined to be double-bill fare on late night shows for years to come.

Tarantino's movies sell designer violence to the masses, portraying macho mayhem that Hollywood types like Tarantino would in fact give a wide berth to in real life. Only time will tell whether Tarantino manages to live up to the flattering hype that critics on both sides of the Atlantic have bestowed on him.

Michael Cimino

. . . .

Cimino's relatively short career has reached heights of success and real depths of failure. *The Deer Hunter* (1978) brought him enormous praise and commercial success, which he dissipated in the legendary flop, *Heaven's Gate*, an epic western that cost an enormous amount of money but was greeted with absolute derision, especially by American critics, and which subsequently bombed at the box-office.

Cimino's movies are a puzzling mixture: *Deer Hunter* was criticised by the left-wing for being very partial in its representation of Vietnam atrocities and for not examining America's real role in the war, and *Heaven's Gate* was accused of

BELOW

Pulp Fiction (1994) won Quentin Tarantino an Oscar for Best Screenwriter and showed the acting skills of John Travolta (left) in a new light.

being the first Marxist western. As Cimino co-wrote both films, it argues a certain confusion in his mind. Other movies he has made link him with macho, right-wing politics: he co-wrote, for example, *Magnum Force* and directed *The Year of the Dragon*, which was accused of racist attitudes. It may be that Cimino was a talent that flared briefly only to splutter out, but *Deer Hunter* and parts of *Heaven's Gate* show that he had talent as a director.

Names to watch
. . . .

Hollywood has discovered that there is a potentially huge black audience out there, predominantly young and conscious of their cultural heritage. African-American directors such as Spike Lee (*She's Gotta Have It*, *Do the Right Thing* and *Jungle Fever*) and John Singleton (*Boyz N the Hood*) are likely to be kept busy over the next decade. Women, too, at long last are breaking the male preserve in Hollywood. Directors such as Kathryn Bigelow (*Point Break*) and Penny Marshall (*Parenthood*) are now making big-budget films with major stars. Other interesting young filmmakers are the Coen brothers (*Blood Simple*, *Miller's Crossing*), Jonathan Demme (*Melvin and Howard* and *The Silence of the Lambs*), Steven Soderbergh (*Sex, Lies and Videotape*), and James Cameron (*The Terminator*, *The Abyss*).

LEFT

Spike Lee has come to prominence with movies such as Do the Right Thing *(1989),* Mo' Better Blues *(1990) and* Jungle Fever *(1991). In* Do the Right Thing *he represents the racial tensions between Italian–Americans and African–Americans, centred around a pizza parlour owned by Danny Aiello.*

ABOVE

Sex Lies and Videotape *was a surprise hit in 1989. Director Steven Soderbergh focused on the relationships of 'thirtysomething' types and offered a brew of voyeurism and pseudo-intellectualism.*

THE BRITISH

Carol Reed

Carol Reed brought a liberal outlook to a conservative British film industry and made some of the most enduring of British films. His first major film was *The Stars Look Down* (1939) about coal miners, then *Odd Man Out*, perhaps his best film, which sympathetically portrayed an IRA gunman played by James Mason. *The Fallen Idol*, from a Graham Greene screenplay, was expertly directed by Reed in 1948 and then he made his most famous film, *The Third Man*, with Orson Welles as the charming but criminal Harry Lime. *Outcast of the Islands*, adapted from the Conrad novel, was another distinguished film, but his later movies failed to match these successes, although *Oliver!* brought him a major international hit. Reed was one of the few British directors respected by the movie brats of Holly-wood.

Michael Powell

Working in collaboration with Emeric Pressburger, Powell directed some of the most colourful and interesting wartime and postwar British movies, including *The Thief of Bagdad*, *The Life and Death of Colonel Blimp*, *A Matter of Life and Death*, *Black Narcissus* and *The Red Shoes*. His films are distinguished by their elaborate design concepts, extravagant use of bright colour and some extreme silliness in the tradition of the upper-class Englishman. A horror film made in 1961, *Peeping Tom*, was met by total disapproval, although his reputation has been re-established and enhanced since then. Undoubtedly over-rated as a director, Powell nevertheless was one of the most creative directors around in British cinema.

David Lean

Lean's first big success as a director was *Brief Encounter* (1946), that quintessential British tale of unconsummated illicit love set mainly in a railway station. There followed two adaptations

ABOVE

James Mason peers over Carol Reed's shoulder during the making of Odd Man Out *(1946), undoubtedly one of the best British films ever made. It provided Mason with one of his best screen roles and established Reed's reputation as a premier British director.*

ABOVE

Michael Powell's The Thief of Bagdad *was typical of his concern with the technical side of* filmmaking, picking up Oscars for Colour Cinematography, Special Effects and Colour Art direction.

Peter O'Toole strikes up a suitably heroic attitude in the epic of sand and self-belief, Lawrence of Arabia, *directed by David Lean (shown right).*

of Dickens' novels, which many think are Lean's best films, *Great Expectations* and *Oliver Twist*. He took a leap into the multi-million-dollar budget product with *The Bridge on the River Kwai* and from then on it seemed that Lean could not make a 'small' picture. *Lawrence of Arabia* and *Dr Zhivago* were two major successes for him, but his penchant for epic scale and overblown scenes served him badly in *Ryan's Daughter*, a simple Irish love story that he attempted to inflate to epic dimensions. Critical raspberries for that film encouraged him to give up directing until he made *A Passage to India* in 1984.

Lean is a director with a banal visual imagination, but he has a talent for story-telling, which probably comes from his experience as a film editor. However, many people rate his films as serious movies. My advice is to wallow in them for what they are: overblown, enjoyable epics!

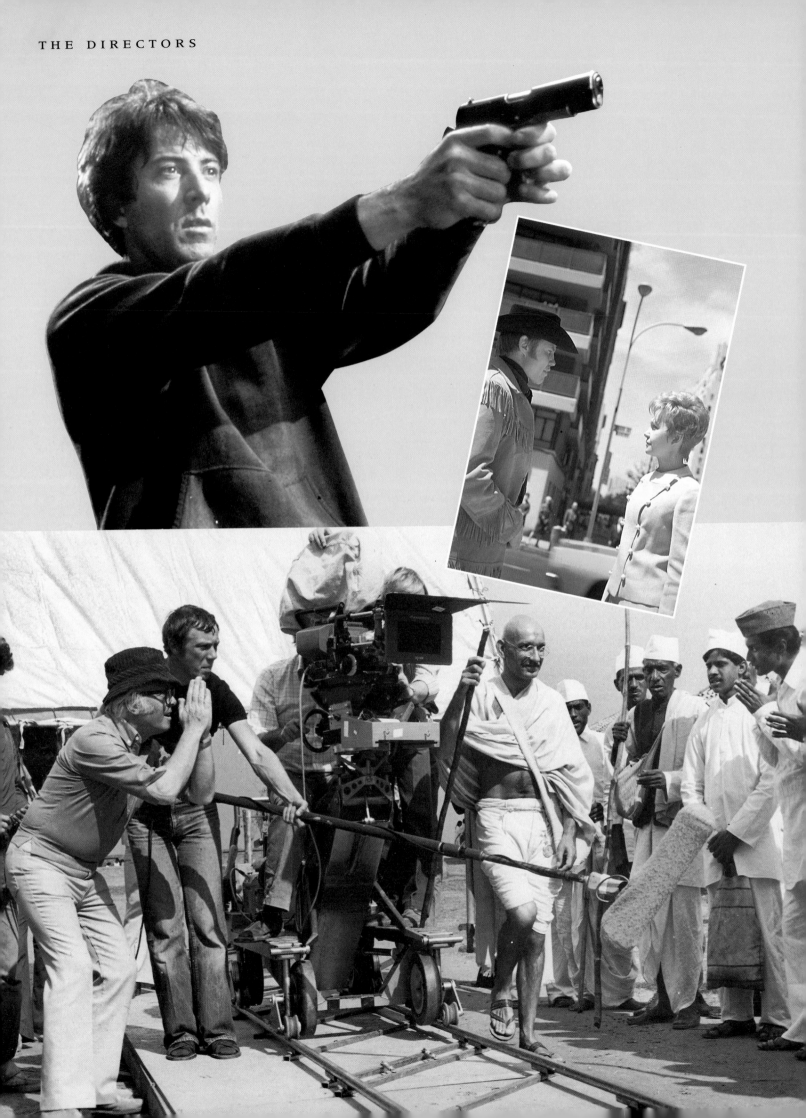

Lindsay Anderson

Anderson was first a critic, and then was involved in the 'Free Cinema' British documentary, making three shorts in the fifties, *O Dreamland, Thursday's Children* and *Every Day Except Christmas.* His first feature was *This Sporting Life* in 1964, a film about the northern working class and rugby league. This was followed by *If* in 1968, which was a huge success. Later movies have shown a tendency to high-minded sententiousness and to making 'state-of-the-nation' simplifications. These include *O Lucky Man* and *Britannia Hospital.* Anderson's former radicalism seems to have been transformed into a kind of nihilistic conservatism and he has since mainly worked in the theatre.

Richard Attenborough

'Dickie' had a long career as an actor in British films before turning to directing. He seems to be David Lean's natural successor in the overblown stakes. His first directorial effort, *Oh What a Lovely War*, managed to de-politicise the message of the original stage version, then he directed *Young Winston*, a film about the youthful adventures of Churchill. *A Bridge Too Far* and *Magic* did not add much to his directorial reputation, but *Gandhi* (1982) did and he won an Oscar for it. *A Chorus Line* (1985) was an unusual project for him, but he was back on more familiar territory with *Cry Freedom*, which dealt with the story of black South African campaigner, Steve Biko.

Alan Parker

It was the success of the 1977 *Bugsy Malone* that established Parker as a director, and this led to his directing *Midnight Express*, which was a huge hit. He even survived directing *Fame* and went on to make a very personal film about a marriage break-up, *Shoot the Moon*, which starred Albert Finney and Diane Keaton. *Birdy* and *Angel Heart* did not make many waves and it took the controversial *Mississippi Burning* to put him back on the cinematic map. Parker is an expert manipulator of audience emotions, but his films are frequently exploitative and simple-minded.

Roland Joffe

Joffe had a huge success with his first film, *The Killing Fields*, about the slaughter of the Cambodian people by the Khmer Rouge. However, *The Mission*, with Robert De Niro and Jeremy Irons, fared less well, whilst *The Shadow Makers* practically disappeared at the box-office. Roland Joffe has a radical point of view and it is to be hoped that he will be given worthwhile projects to direct in the future.

Other notables

Thorold Dickinson, director of *Queen of Spades* (1948) and *Secret People* (1952); Anthony Asquith, who made *The Way to the Stars* (1945), *The Winslow Boy* (1948), *The Browning Version* (1950), *The Importance of Being Earnest* (1951) and *Orders to Kill* (1958); Tony Richardson, director of the 'new' British school of the sixties, made *The Entertainer* (1960), *A Taste of Honey* (1961), *The Loneliness of the Long-Distance Runner* (1963), *Tom Jones* (1963), *The Loved One* (1965), *The Charge of the Light Brigade* (1968) and *The Border* (1982); John Schlesinger, who came to prominence with his documentary about Waterloo Station, *Terminus* (1960), and then went on to direct *A Kind of Loving* (1962), *Billy Liar* (1963), *Darling* (1965), *Far from the Madding Crowd* (1967), *Midnight Cowboy* (1969), *Sunday Bloody Sunday* (1972), *The Day of the Locust* (1975), *Marathon Man* (1976), *Yanks* (1977), *Honky Tonk Freeway* (1981) and *An Englishman Abroad* (1983); Ridley Scott, director of *The Duellists* (1978), *Alien* (1979), *Blade Runner* (1981), *Black Rain* (1989) and *Thelma and Louise* (1991).

Jean Renoir.

THE FRENCH

Marcel Carné
. . . .

Carné was the most important French director of the immediate pre-war and Occupation years, directing a number of poetic and atmospheric melodramas that somehow made statements about France and its situation. *Drôle de Drame* (1937), *Quai des Brumes* (1938) and *Le Jour Se Lève* (1939) are three classics of the French cinema. Who can forget Jean Gabin as the decent working-class man holding out against the massed forces of law and order in *Le Jour Se Lève*? *Les Enfants du Paradis* is a parable about the Occupation made right under German noses in 1944; it has Jean-Louis Barrault as a milksop mime artist, Pierre Brasseur as an exhibitionistic actor and sundry 19th-century nasties (who stood in for the Nazis), all quarrelling over Arletty, who represented France. Carné's post-war movies were not of the same standard, almost certainly because, apart from *Les Portes de la Nuit* (1946), he was no longer collaborating with screenwriter Jacques Prévert, who had written the screenplays for his most memorable movies.

Jean Renoir
. . . .

Jean was the son of the painter, Auguste Renoir; he had a long and distinguished career in the French cinema right from the silent years through to the late sixties. His best-known films include *La Chienne*, *Boudu Sauvé des Eaux*, *Le Crime de Monsieur Lange*, *Les Bas Fonds*, *Une Partie de Compagne* and two classics, *La Grande Illusion* and *La Règle du Jeu*. During the war and the post-war years, he made films in Hollywood which included *The Southerner*, *Diary of a Chambermaid* and *The Woman on the Beach*. Later movies were *The River*, *The Golden Coach* and *Lunch on the Grass*. Like Carné, Renoir's career peaked round the late thirties and he will be remembered for *La Grande Illusion* and *La Règle du Jeu*.

ABOVE
Carne's Le Jour Se Lève.

LEFT
La Règle du Jeu *is thought by many to be Renoir's masterpiece.*

ABOVE

La Grande Illusion *(1939),
directed by Jean Renoir, is
one of the greatest anti-war
films ever made. It starred
Jean Gabin, that archetypal
Frenchman, as a First
World War POW, with
Erich Von Stroheim as the
German commandant of the
camp.*

Marcel Pagnol
· · · · · · · · ·

Pagnol was a writer and director, best remembered for his Marseilles trilogy *Marius* and *Fanny* (script only) and *César* (directed and scripted). Other notable films include *La Femme du Boulanger*. *Jean de Florette* and its sequel, *Manon des Sources*, both directed by Claude Berri, were adaptations of Pagnol novels.

Jean-Luc Godard
· · · · · · · · ·

When Godard made *A Bout de Souffle* (*Breathless*) in 1960, he became the doyen of the 'New Wave' of French directors. His innovative techniques – jump cuts, hand-held cameras, semi-documentary approach and a disregard for 'normal' narrative – helped him to 'genius director' status. Subsequent films also gained a great deal of attention: *Une Femme Est Une Femme*, *Vivre Sa Vie*, *Le Petit Soldat*, *Les Carabiniers*, *Bande à Part*, *Une Femme Mariée* and *Alphaville*. Like most of the New Wave directors, Godard was besotted with the American cinema, especially film noir and 'B' movies. However, around the mid-sixties he went down with a bad case of Mao-itis and his films have never really recovered. In his attempts to interrupt classical story-telling in the cinema and hammer home political points, he has become a bore. He is quoted as saying, 'My aesthetic is that of the sniper on the roof'; the trouble is that he is shooting himself in the foot.

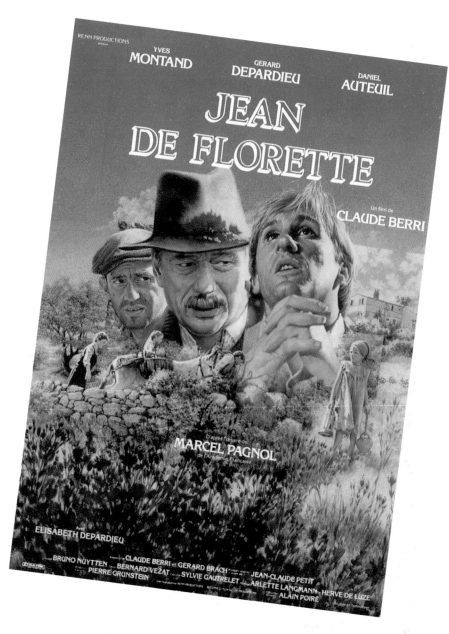

LEFT

Jean Seberg tells Jean-Paul Belmondo how many lovers she has had – a scene from Jean-Luc Godard's A Bout de Souffle *('Breathless', 1959). This movie encapsulated many of the features of the French New Wave: fragmented narrative, jump cuts, hand-held cameras, a homage to Hollywood, and a pervasive nihilism.*

ABOVE

Claude Berri's 1985 Jean de Florette *and its sequel,* Manon des Sources *(1986), brought Pagnol's works to public attention again.*

♦♦*Film is truth 24 times a second.*♦♦

JEAN-LUC GODARD

Claude Chabrol's Les
Biches *(1968): Themes and
variations on love, obsession
and madness on the French
Riviera.*

François Truffaut

· · · · · · · · ·

If Godard was the Marxist conscience of the French New Wave, Truffaut was its soft centre. Charm oozed from his films and this sometimes edges over into preciousness and sentimentality. However, his best films had an edge to them that belied his innately gentle nature: *Les Quatre Cent Coups, Shoot the Pianist, Jules et Jim, Fahrenheit 451, L'Enfant Sauvage, Anne and Muriel, La Nuit Americaine, Le Dernier Métro* and *Vivement Dimanche*. Truffaut also made a memorable appearance in Spielberg's *Close Encounters of the Third Kind* as the only scientist who was sympathetic to the ordinary people who tried to make direct contact with the aliens.

Louis Malle

· · · · · · · · ·

One of the French New Wave in the fifties, Malle has survived as a major director into the nineties. His first film, *Lift to the Scaffold*, was a Hitchcockian thriller with an improvised jazz score by Miles Davis. *The Lovers* caused a furore in the late fifties, because it showed a wealthy bourgeois French wife and mother (Jeanne Moreau) abandoning husband and children for a lover who has introduced her to sensual pleasures. Most of his other films also explored controversial territory. *Le Feu Follet* was a brooding, pessimistic study of the last day in the life of a self-destructive writer, while *Viva Maria* was, by contrast, a rather mindless romp starring Moreau and Bardot. *Souffle au Coeur* explored the theme of incestuous feelings between mother and son, while *Pretty Baby*, his first American film, dealt with child prostitution. Both his best films have dealt with aspects of the French Occupation: *Lacombe Lucien* and *Au Revoir Les Enfants*. *Atlantic City*, with Burt Lancaster, was another American film, an interesting treatment on the theme of regeneration. *My Dinner with André* was about two men talking in a restaurant about life and regeneration (again).

Claude Chabrol

· · · · · · · · ·

Most of the New Wave directors revered Hitchcock as 'the master' and none more so than Chabrol, many of whose films are very Hitchcockian and full of Catholic obsessions about transference of guilt and punishment. After his early successes with *Le Beau Serge* and *Les Cousins*, Chabrol directed *Les Biches*, *La Femme Infidèle, Le Boucher, Voilette Nozière, Les Menteurs, Blood Relatives, Cop au Vin* and *Inspector Lavardin*. The quality of his films varies enormously, but his forte is murder within a French bourgeois setting, with or without adulterous connotations but with scenes of families sitting down together for tense meals.

Bernard Tavernier

· · · · · · · · ·

A director in the tradition of classic French filmmaking, Tavernier's films have frequently had Philippe Noiret as their star: *The Watchmaker of St Paul's, Coup de Torchon, Sunday in the Country, Round Midnight, Life and Nothing But* and *These Foolish Things*.

THE ITALIANS

Vittorio De Sica

De Sica was best known to the general public as a comedy actor, but he was actually one of the leading directors of the post-war Italian Neo-realist school who influenced directors in the rest of Europe and in Hollywood. His most famous film is *Bicycle Thieves* (1948); set amidst the poverty of post-war Italy it concerns the theft of a bicycle from a working-class man who needs it desperately to carry out his treasured job as a bill-poster. Sentimental as it may be in parts, it would take a heart of stone not to be touched by the scene where his young son defends the beleaguered father when an angry crowd turns on him after he is forced to steal another man's bicycle to make up for the loss of his own. *Shoeshine* (1946) and *Umberto D* (1952) were two other Neo-realist classics, but of the later films he directed only *Two Women* (1962) with Sophia Loren and the 1972 *The Garden of the Finzi-Continis* made much of an impact.

Roberto Rossellini

Rossellini was the other Neo-realist leading director, but he became famous for other reasons – his affair with, and marriage to, Ingrid Bergman. A documentary style, the use of a mixture of amateur and professional actors, a refusal to glamorise, a radical social viewpoint – these are the characteristics of Rossellini's films such as *Open City, Paisa, Stromboli, Europa* and *Louis XIV Seizes Power*. The fashion for Neo-realism passed relatively quickly and Rossellini never found a niche in the commercial cinema.

Federico Fellini

Fellini's early films were clearly influenced by Neo-realism: *I Vitelloni, La Strada* and *Il Bidone*. However, he discarded Neo-realism to make highly personal and exhibitionistic movies, including films such as *La Dolce Vita, Boccaccio 70, 8½*

ABOVE
Bicycle Thieves (1948), an authentic picture of poverty directed by Vittorio De Sica, was the most successful of the postwar Italian Neo-realist movies.

RIGHT
Roberto Rossellini was the leading Neo-realist director along with De Sica. He starred his wife, Ingrid Bergman, in the 1949 Stromboli.

INGRID
BERGMAN
dans

STROMBOLI

Un film de **ROBERTO ROSSELLINI**

R K O
RADIO
FILMS

> ❖❖ *I've got your happy ending. We'll let the Germans win the war.* ❖❖
>
> LEWIS MILESTONE

(which was about his doubts about himself as a director), *Juliet of the Spirits* (which people either hate or love), *Satyricon*, *Fellini Roma*, *Amarcord* and *Ginger and Fred*. Fellini's world is a world of dreams and fantasies; he is consumed with memories of his childhood and his relationship with Catholicism. At his best he is skilful at depicting the uncertainties of human relationships, at his worst he is showily indulgent and modish. Feminists, on the whole, dislike his movies because he treats women as objects while pretending to worship them.

ABOVE

Jack Nicholson in a rare moment of exhilaration in the Michelangelo Antonioni film The Passenger *(1974). The movie is a bleak exploration of the meaning of identity and was the last Antonioni film to make any kind of impression.*

RIGHT

The infant Emperor from Bertolucci's The Last Emperor *(1988). The movie had a world-wide success, although many people consider it inferior to Bertolucci's best works.*

LEFT

Fellini's Satyricon *(1969). Fellini's later films became more exotic and indulgent, dividing critics and cinemagoers alike. He is a director who seemed to run out of things to say in his films, a state which he represented in his autobiographical 8½ (1963).*

Michelangelo Antonioni
· · · · · · · · ·

Antonioni came to international prominence with *L'Avventura* (1959), then he went on to make *La Notte* and *L'Eclisse*. The 1967 *Blow-Up* was a commercial success for him and this led MGM to give him the money to make *Zabriskie Point*, which failed at the box-office. He made *The Passenger* with Jack Nicholson in 1972, his last important movie. Antonioni is an intellectual whose films dissect bourgeois aridity and questions of identity. The pace of the films is slow and dialogue is sparse. He creates images that encapsulate the thematic content of the film.

Bernardo Bertolucci
· · · · · · · · ·

Bertolucci has left-wing views which inform most of his films. One of his best is *The Conformist* with Jean-Louis Trintignant as a fascist, and a study of fascism also makes both parts of *1900* interesting social documents. He made the controversial *Last Tango in Paris* with Marlon Brando and Maria Schneider in 1972, and *La Luna* with Jill Clayburgh in 1979. He had a surprising success with *The Last Emperor* which is not, however, one of his best films. Apart from politics, a Freudian view of sex is a strong feature of Bertolucci's work.

*Shadowed by angels. Wim
Wender's* Wings of Desire
*sends two spirits to
contemporary Berlin,
sympathically
eavesdropping into the
private thoughts of mortals.*

ABOVE
*Dean Stockwell has brother
troubles in* Paris, Texas
*(1984) and tries to break the
news gently to his wife.
Harry Dean Stanton plays
his long-lost brother,
striding purposefully
through the Texas desert,
going nowhere and
remembering very little.*

THE MODERN GERMANS

Rainer Werner Fassbinder
. . . .

Fassbinder, who died in 1982 at the age of 36, was a fashionable director of the seventies, but it remains to be seen whether the films he made stand the test of time. Personally, I could not bear to sit through *The Bitter Tears of Petra Von Kant* again, but Fassbinder undoubtedly has his supporters. His best-known films are *Effi Briest*, *Fear Eats the Soul*, *Despair*, *The Marriage of Maria Braun* and *Berlin, Alexanderplatz*. The last two are the most accessible of his work.

Werner Herzog
. . . .

Herzog appears to be an obsessive filmmaker and he often makes films that are about obsessives, such as the Klaus Kinski protagonist in *Fitzcarraldo*, who is determined to bring grand opera to the jungles of South America. His first major success was *Aguirre, Wrath of God*, but before that he had made *Even Dwarfs Started Small* and *Fata Morgana*. *The Enigma of Kasper Hauser* attracted a good deal of attention, as did his version of the legend of Dracula, *Nosferatu*, which reflected Murnau's silent original. Apart from *Fitzcarraldo*, the eighties did not bring him much success. He is quoted as saying that he is not out to win prizes, which he considers to be suitable only for dogs and horses.

Wim Wenders
. . . .

Wenders makes odd, often slow-paced movies that frequently pay some kind of oblique homage to Hollywood, but are described as pretentious by his detractors. *Kings of the Road* and *The American Friend*, for example, are recognisably reworkings of the road movie and thriller genres. In the latter, he gives a part to the cult American director, Nicholas Ray; then, in *Lightning Over Water*, the subject is Ray himself during the last few months of his life. Francis Coppola employed Wenders to direct *Hammett*, at Coppola's Zoe-

BELOW
Rainer Fassbinder's Fear
Eats the Soul *(1974)*
concerns the alienation felt
by Turkish migrant workers
in Germany.

trope studio, a convoluted treatment of film noir themes that involved a representation of Dashiel Hammett himself, but there were great difficulties during the making of the film and it is not clear how much of the final movie was directed by Wenders. *The Goalkeeper's Fear of the Penalty*, one of Wenders's first films, at least has a novel title. *Alice in the Cities* attracted attention, while *Paris, Texas* achieved minor box-office success made a star of Harry Dean Stanton.

AN
AUSTRALIAN
DIRECTOR

Peter Weir
· · · · · · · · ·

If one Australian director has to be chosen to represent the reborn Australian cinema, then it has to be Peter Weir. Other contenders would be Gillian Armstrong, Bruce Beresford and Fred Schepisi, but Weir has had more successes than any of them, both with the films he made in Australia and those he has made in America.

His first big success was *Picnic at Hanging Rock*, one of the first Australian films of the seventies to signal the revival in Australian cinema. It is an evocative, 'arty' and resonant film that raises more issues than it can adequately deal with, but it is still a real achievement. Weir followed this up with *The Last Wave*, which again had mystical and religious elements and tried to explore Australian guilt about the Aborigines. *Gallipoli* to a certain extent dealt with the theme of what it is

BELOW
Robin Williams as the charismatic teacher, John Keating, in Peter Weir's Dead Poets Society *(1989). Keating inspires his pupils to 'seize the day' and to live life to the fullest. Some of them take him at his word with disastrous results. He emerges as a kind of male Miss Jean Brodie.*

to be an Australian. Weir's first big-budget movie was one of the key films of the eighties, *The Year of Living Dangerously* with Mel Gibson, Sigourney Weaver and Linda Grant memorably cast as a male dwarf. It is about the conflict between the drive to succeed and the need to commit yourself to loving another person. After that success he directed Harrison Ford in *Witness* and *Mosquito Coast*. Both these films, and others he has directed, deal in part with culture clash and have a charismatic figure representing some kind of life force at the centre of the narrative. This is certainly true of the Robin Williams character in *Dead Poets Society*, which was another big success. However, his 1991 film, *Green Card*, with that other life force, Gérard Depardieu, may be thought of as somewhat disappointing from a director who has made other such unusual movies to date.

FIVE INTER-
NATIONAL
DIRECTORS

Ingmar Bergman

Bergman is a Swedish writer-director who first came to international prominence with his medieval allegory, *The Seventh Seal*. This success led to the release outside Sweden of earlier films such as *Summer with Monika, Sawdust and Tinsel* and *Smiles of a Summer Night. Wild Strawberries* was another major film in 1957. Bergman's films tend to the austere and gloomy, notably in *The Virgin Spring, Through a Glass Darkly* and *The Silence*. Women are very often the central protagonists in his movies, for example in *Persona, Cries and Whispers* and *Autumn Sonata*. The impossibility of man-woman relationships and bourgeois marriage is a recurring theme. However,

BELOW

A group of travellers await the chilly hand of death in Ingmar Bergman's The Seventh Seal *(1957), a sombre meditation on mortality. The Knight, played by Max Von Sydow, plays chess with Death, until all his escape routes run out. The movie presents a picture of the Middle Ages as cruel and primitive. Its visual power and poetic insights make it one of Bergman's major achievements.*

Fanny and Alexander revealed a warmer, more humanistic side to his artistic personality when he used his affectionate memories of his Stockholm childhood to paint an evocative picture of extended family life. Bergman is the 'art house' director *par excellence*, but his movies are both 'entertaining' and involving with an emotional intensity that is disturbing at times. Bergman must rank as one of the most talented directors ever to have worked in the medium. He is also an extremely creative stage director.

Bergman usually creates his own screenplays, then imposes his personal vision on the material. As he has created considerable independence for himself, he of all directors can surely be seen as an auteur.

Fanny and Alexander,
*Bergman's evocative family
saga set in turn-of-the-
century Stockholm explores
how memory and
autobiography serve art.*

ABOVE

*Alf Sjöberg, himself a
director, plays a selfish and
irascible professor on his
way to Stockholm to accept
an honorary degree in
Bergman's* Wild
Strawberries *(1957).
Unknown to him, this is the
last day of his life, and he
recalls memories from his
childhood and young
adulthood. Modern
marriage comes under the
steely eye of the director and
scarcely survives the
examination.*

Akira Kurosawa
. . . .

The Japanese director built up an international following with *Rashomon* (1950) and *The Seven Samurai* (1954), the latter being remade in Hollywood as *The Magnificent Seven*. Later films such as *Throne of Blood* and *The Hidden Fortress* reinforced his reputation for action movies within the samurai tradition; he was often likened to John Ford. His most recent films have been praised, but seem too leisurely and indulgent for some tastes, as if he has been too conscious of his artistic status, as in, for example, *The Shadow Warrior* and *Ran*. Apart from his samurai epics, he has directed modern-day pictures, including the impressive *Living* and *The Lower Depths*.

Andrei Tarkovsky
. . . .

Some people would rather watch paint dry than sit through one of the late Russian director's films again; others see Tarkovsky as a genius of the modern cinema. He died in 1986 at the age of 54, having directed a handful of long, slow paced arty movies that elevated him to major auteur status in many people's minds. In constant bother with the pre-glasnost Soviet authorities, Tarkovsky first came to prominence with *Andrei Rublev* (1966); his obscure movie about space, *Solaris* (1972), then captured audiences in the West. *Mirror* and *Nostalgia* were more overtly personal and political statements. It is tragic that Tarkovsky died before the present thaw in the Soviet Union happened; it would have been interesting to see what kind of movies he would have made in his homeland in the new circumstances.

Roman Polanski
. . . .

Polanski first came to international prominence when he directed *Knife in the Water*. Thereafter, he made all of his films outside his native country, Poland. His films are full of violence, sexual quirks and the occult. *Repulsion* and *Cul de Sac* are odd, claustrophobic studies of repression. He then had a major Hollywood success with *Rosemary's Baby* which dealt with devil-worship. Tragically, Polanski's own life became inextricably linked with the macabre and the occult when his wife Sharon Tate was one of the victims of ritual murder at the hands of the Charles Manson 'family'.

ABOVE

Toshiro Mifune plays the clown for the amusement of the peasants in Kurosawa's 1954 samurai epic The Seven Samurai. *Mifune is an eccentric young samurai who is desperate to be accepted by the older professionals. The samurai defeat the forces of the local bandits and save the peasants, who quickly turn their backs on them and get on with their lives. Perhaps there is some kind of militaristic message behind all this, but most people just like the action scenes and the comic antics of Mifune.*

Polanski's version of *Macbeth* emphasised the witchery and the violence, while *Chinatown*, probably his best film, was a brilliant reworking of film noir themes. Polanski has also had his out-and-out commercial flops, including *What?* and *Pirates*. *Tess* was a surprisingly subdued version of the Thomas Hardy novel. *The Tenant* explored themes of gender and identity; *Frantic* was only a partially successful thriller starring Harrison Ford. Along the way Polanski picked up a charge of statutory rape in America for allegedly sleeping with a minor, which means he has to work abroad unless he is prepared to return to the States to stand trial.

Satyajit Ray
. . . .

Ray's *Apu* trilogy in the fifties put Indian cinema firmly on the international film map. *Pather Panchali*, *Aparajito* and *The World of Apu* are brilliant representations of Indian life. What makes Ray so accessible to western audiences is his command over film technique and his control of the narrative and acting in his films. Other distinguished films he has made include *The Music Room*, *Company Limited*, *Distant Thunder*, *The Middle Man*, *The Chess Players* and *Days and Nights in the Forest*. Ray could be described as rather a 'literary' director in that his films are often adaptations of novels, strong on plot and character, but he has a genuine instinct for what can hold an audience in the cinema.

THE STARS

> **You make a star, you make a monster.**
>
> **SAM SPIEGEL (PRODUCER)**

A ravishing studio portrait of Marilyn Monroe. Monroe donned the mantle of 'glamour' to attract the attention she craved, and then found she could not escape from the persona she had created and which the world devoured.

MOVIE STARS ARE said to be America's version of royalty and it is true that the most famous screen actors do achieve an almost legendary status. They become the 'Greta Garbo' or 'Clark Gable' of myth rather than of reality. If cinema is about our dreams, then these larger-than-life figures are given the onerous task of enacting those dreams.

Some observers of the mass media see something sinister in how stars are used in movies. Herbert Marcuse, the German-American philosopher, wrote this about how star images were used in Hollywood: 'They are no longer images of another way of life but rather freaks or types of the same life, serving as an affirmation rather than a negation of the established order.' In other words, stars have an ideological function; they make life more palatable for us by ironing out the contradictions and worries that inevitably work their way into even the sunniest of movies. For example, if a 'good Joe' star such as James Stewart is shown to be poor but happy with his lot and the American Way of Life, then it is more likely we will be seduced into feeling the same way.

There is no doubt that stars *are* symbols. They signify something 'extra' in a movie, especially if they have created a star persona from numerous films. John Wayne signified a kind of macho integrity, promising straight-shooting and straight-talking. Henry Fonda carried an aura of incorruptibility with him into almost all of his movies; he was the personable, archetypal 'liberal' star. Monroe encapsulated for many an innocent joy in sex, for others a child-like vulnerability. All the major stars had their dominant persona, arousing audience expectations. Sometimes a star would be cast against 'type', so occasionally Gregory Peck or even Fonda would play a villain, but even that is an example of how star personas can be used, as casting 'against type' is still dependent on our expectations as an audience of what these stars signify to us.

During the heyday of the Hollywood studio system, there was an elaborate grooming process for potential stars. They generally had to be glamorous, above reproach, and recognisable American types. If the moguls considered they were wanting in some area, then the remodelling process could be severe. Rita Hayworth, for example, had to have her hairline raised by an inch through electrolysis, a very painful exercise, because Harry Cohn, Columbia's boss, thought she would look better that way. Names were the first thing to go if an actor's real moniker did not fit: Marion Michael Morrison became John Wayne; Doris von Kappelhoff became Doris Day; Britain's Diana Fluck became Diana Dors. The fan magazines and gossip writers would be handed publicity material to boost the public's awareness of up-and-coming stars, and, once they were established, their reputations would be protected and continually polished.

Under old Hollywood the stars were constrained by seven-year contracts with options every six months to be picked up or dropped by the employing studio. This contract tied the stars to their employers; the option clauses were used to make them toe the line and force them to make the movies the studios wanted them to make. Bette Davis and Olivia de Havilland took

on their studios in the courts in an attempt to break this feudal hold the moguls had over them. They helped break up the old studio system, and the stars were in time largely released from the tyranny of the long-term contract. Burt Lancaster and Kirk Douglas were two early examples of producer-stars who took a financial risk in their own films and formed companies to make independent productions which they then sold to the studios to market and distribute.

Soon the major stars became enterprises in themselves; millions of dollars for a movie budget could be raised on one star name. Their agents became enormously important because the really powerful ones could promise a package of several stars and probably a top director, a successful screenwriter and a commercial vehicle for them all to participate in. Contemporary stars such as Sylvester Stallone or Robert Redford are as much businessmen as actors.

Movie actors have moved on since the early days of the silents when the figures on the screen were anonymous, but, in a sense, the Biograph Girl was the predecessor of a star such as Barbra Streisand who now produces and directs her own films.

FAR RIGHT

The star system has produced few people with such large reputations from so few films as James Dean. Giant (1956), in which he portrayed the development from enthusiastic youth to embittered middle age of a self-made man, was his last part before his tragic death.

BELOW

Burt Lancaster's roles have run the gamut from tough guys and cowboys to pirates and prophets.

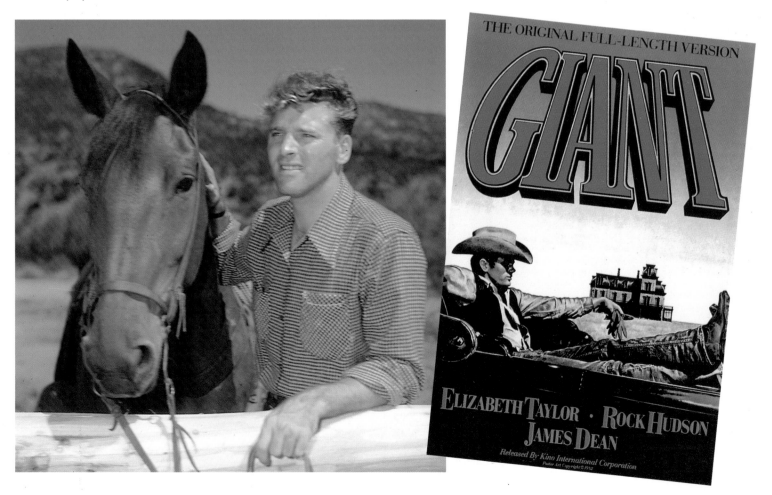

THE SCREEN GODDESSES

There have been many contenders for the status of screen goddess. To qualify, the star must have become immensely popular with millions of people, to signify something transcendental to her fans, to have conquered the medium of film through her beauty, charisma and talent, and to have acquired a cult status either before or after her death. Every movie fan would have a different short-list, so I offer these four stars very tentatively as contenders for the title.

Mary Pickford

Pickford was known as the 'world's sweetheart' during the heyday of silent movies. Her forte was a child-like demureness allied to an all-American steeliness, for beneath her girlish locks was the mind of an astute businesswoman who knew her own market worth in the industry that made her world-famous. Sam Goldwyn stated that it took longer to frame one of Pickford's contracts than it did to shoot her movies. With Douglas Fairbanks, to whom she was married, Charlie Chaplin and D.W. Griffith, she was one of the cofounders of United Artists in 1919.

Pickford earned mega-bucks even by today's standards, Paramount paying her $675,000 dollars a year at one time. A succession of 'child-woman' parts in movies such as *The Little Princess*, *Rebecca of Sunnybrook Farm*, *Pollyanna* and *Tess of the Storm Country* gave her immense clout with her bosses. Other movies she made included *Little Lord Fauntleroy*, *Dorothy Vernon of Haddon Hall*, *Little Annie Rooney* and *My Best Girl*. By the time sound arrived in Hollywood she was in her mid-thirties; she could no longer play *ingénues* and she was so identified with the silents that there was clearly no future for her. However, she stayed active in the business through United Artists and lived on till 1979. Pickford lived out the American Dream, reaching dizzying heights of popular and financial success. Unlike many other Hollywood luminaries, however, she was a survivor. 'Rebecca of Sunnybrook Farm' was no pushover.

ABOVE

Mary Pickford aka 'America's Sweetheart'. Pickford was actually a Canadian who played child-women all her screen life. She ended up as a studio mogul, however, through her part-ownership of United Artists.

Greta Garbo

Garbo was born Greta Gustafsson in Stockholm in 1905. Her early Swedish films show her as a rather plump young woman, more tomboyish than alluring. But her early silent movies in America, *The Torrent*, *The Temptress* and *The Flesh and the Devil*, established her as a woman men would die for, or at least commit adultery with.

With the talkies she went for a more realistic image in *Anna Christie* and *Susan Lennox*, then

Greta Garbo, whose name
has become synonymous
with movies. To many, a
screen goddess; to Hollywood
wag, Herbert Kretzmer, 'a
plain mortal girl with big

resorted to ethereal parts such as *Queen Christina* and *Camille*. She lost her heart to John Barrymore in *Grand Hotel* and to Fredric March in *Anna Karenina*, but no male co-star was really good enough for her, according to her admirers. Her fans adored her mixture of spirituality and sensuality. She also had an androgynous quality that meant she had a wider appeal than more overtly heterosexual stars. William Daniels was her favourite cameraman and he made sure, as she herself did, that the lighting and the poses she struck were always kind to her.

But could she act? The jury is still out on that one. Sometimes she is very bad indeed (witness her part as the ballerina in *Grand Hotel*) but to Garbo fanatics, questions about her acting skills are totally irrelevant. They worship her as a transcendent symbol of beauty, of the human spirit and as an embodiment of love.

The hard fact was that Garbo was always much more popular in Europe than in the States, so when America entered the Second World War and the European markets for American films were cut off, the studios were none too keen to make more films with her, especially as her last, *Two-faced Woman*, had been a flop. Her famous 'I want to be alone' retirement cue line may be misleading; her screen career was almost certainly in serious decline by then. However, that is doubtless sacrilege to the many millions of fans who, despite her recent death, will go on worshipping at her shrine.

Marlene Dietrich

Dietrich was another screen goddess with an androgynous appeal. Like Garbo, she was European-born – in Berlin in 1901. Her first big hit was in the German movie, *The Blue Angel*. Director Josef Von Sternberg also directed her first American film *Morocco* (1930) in which she starred with Gary Cooper. Von Sternberg was a key figure in Dietrich's Hollywood career, directing her in *Dishonoured*, *Shanghai Express*, *Blonde Venus*, *The Scarlet Empress* and *The Devil is a Woman*. In all these movies Dietrich played the vamp, the imperious mistress for whom men ruined themselves. Von Sternberg's wife certainly thought Dietrich played that part in real life because she served a writ on Dietrich accusing her of alienating her husband's affections.

After Von Sternberg's professional relationship with Dietrich ended, her career was never quite the same. Indeed, she was labelled 'box-office

ABOVE
Marlene Dietrich was one of the most manufactured of all the female screen goddesses. Director Joseph Von Sternberg fashioned her till she became the focus of many a camp fantasy.

poison' for a time, before movies such as *Destry Rides Again*, *Rancho Notorious* and *Witness for the Prosecution* partly revived her film career. Finally, in the fifties, and in her own fifties, she embarked on an international cabaret career which brought her new fans and fame.

For those who adored Dietrich, there was no one like her. For those who found her eminently resistible, it was puzzling why she won herself such cult status. Dietrich was never an acting talent; what she had was a certain bisexual appeal, an icy beauty, an exotic style and a ravenous ego that saw to it that she was shown on the silver screen in as flattering a light as possible.

Marilyn Monroe
· · · · · · · · ·

More words have been written about Monroe than any other movie star. A mixture of fantasy, fact, legend and downright fabrication make up the Monroe legend; indeed, 'Marilyn Monroe' is now an industry even thirty years after her death. Fans of 'Norma Jean' collect everything associated with her, writers never tire of writing about her, and her movies are still very popular. Along with James Dean, she is the Hollywood star who has provoked and continues to provoke, the most intense cult worship.

Born in Los Angeles in 1926, Norma Jean Mortenson had a paranoid schizophrenic mother, no father, various unbalanced relatives and several foster homes. These childhood experiences must have contributed hugely to her later instabilities and her search for that solid parent figure, particularly the male parent, that led her into disastrous relationships and marriages with older men. The hardships she endured undoubtedly also gave her the drive to

ABOVE

Monroe posed for thousands of glamour portraits in her time and was sold as the ultimate female sex object. The Monroe industry continues unabated to this day as collectors avidly acquire everything that is written and published about her.

succeed, to get herself out of this morass of abuse and poverty.

To do this, Monroe was forced to exploit her looks: her (dyed) blonde hair, her appealing face and her voluptuous body. Evidence has piled up that her early film career was greatly helped by various elderly gentlemen in the movie business. Monroe is quoted as saying she spent a lot of time on her knees in her early starlet days. Her first significant role was in *The Asphalt Jungle*, directed by John Huston, in which she played elderly Louis Calhern's mistress. She looked beautiful and she was also rather touching in this small part.

Undoubtedly Monroe had a quality when she was on screen. She could play dumb blonde parts with an instinctive grasp of comedy, as in *How to Marry a Millionaire, Gentlemen Prefer Blondes, The Seven Year Itch* and *Some Like It Hot*. Male viewers were attracted by her sexuality but felt unchallenged by her 'little girl' voice and general helplessness; men were allowed to lust after her and be a father as well. Because she played powerless young women, this angered the more feminist of cinemagoers, who dismissed her as a middle-aged man's fantasy object, but many women liked her because of her vulnerability.

Marriages to James Dougherty, baseball star Joe DiMaggio and playwright Arthur Miller all failed. Attracted to the mixture of power and sex that John Kennedy exuded, Monroe had an affair with the President, who seemingly asked brother Bobby to take care of her when she started to get 'troublesome'. Bobby himself had an affair with her and then the scenario becomes blurred. Whether Monroe's death through an overdose of barbiturates was an accident, suicide or murder has not yet been finally established. Certainly, what we do know about the end of her life exposes the seamier side of Hollywood's connections with power politics.

Monroe is often written about as a victim figure, and undoubtedly she was treated shabbily at times. But she was a determined woman, driven by her need to make up for childhood deprivations of material and emotional security. Finally, she never achieved that security because she was never allowed, in the years of her fame, to be herself. The men who became involved with her went to bed with Marilyn Monroe but made sure they never woke up with Norma Jean Mortenson. Perhaps what fans worship about Monroe is the Norma Jean they sense under the Marilyn exterior.

THE ROMANTIC HEROES

Romantic heroes, male heart-throbs, call them what you will, there have been numerous major stars who were famous for their combination of good looks, devil-may-care screen personas and their on-screen womanising. Here is a short list of four outstanding ones.

I am paid not to think.

CLARK GABLE

In 1961 twelve days after filming ended on *The Misfits* Gable died of a heart attack, probably brought on by the action scenes he had insisted on doing himself in the movie. Perhaps it was a case of Gable's screen image catching up with the man.

Rudolph Valentino

Valentino was the screen's first 'Great Lover', a title that caused him problems both with other men and his wives. He danced a tango in *The Four Horsemen of the Apocalypse* (1921) and set pulses racing. His preposterous role in *The Sheik*, a desert chieftain with propensities towards rape, found an ecstatic audience. Marital difficulties with actress Jean Acker and designer Natasha Rambova and problems with Paramount put a great deal of pressure on the superstar, as did press insinuations of bisexuality. He died of a ruptured appendix in 1926 at the age of thirty-one. The scenes of extravagant mourning at his funeral have passed into Hollywood legend. The Valentino phenomenon is evidence of the power of the screen image over a mass audience hungry for erotic fantasy.

Clark Gable

Gable was known as 'The King' of Hollywood. He was certainly the most popular male star of the late thirties and forties with his most famous role, Rhett Butler in *Gone with the Wind*. He was popular with men because he was an uncomplicated action hero and did not make a big deal about his success with the ladies. Women liked him for his sexuality, his ready charm and his easy-going persona. He won an Oscar for *It Happened One Night* but was never perceived as a great screen actor, although for his performance in his final film with Marilyn Monroe, *The Misfits*, he won critical praise. He was married to Carole Lombard for a few years before she died in an air crash in 1942.

LEFT
Rudolph Valentino, in The Sheik *(1921). In roles like this Valentino was the quintessence of high camp, but in his day he was worshipped by his female fans.*

BELOW
Clark Gable was marketed as the acme of happy-go-lucky masculinity, an uncomplicated, outdoor guy, beloved by women and admired by men. No other actor was even considered for the part of Rhett Butler in Gone with the Wind.

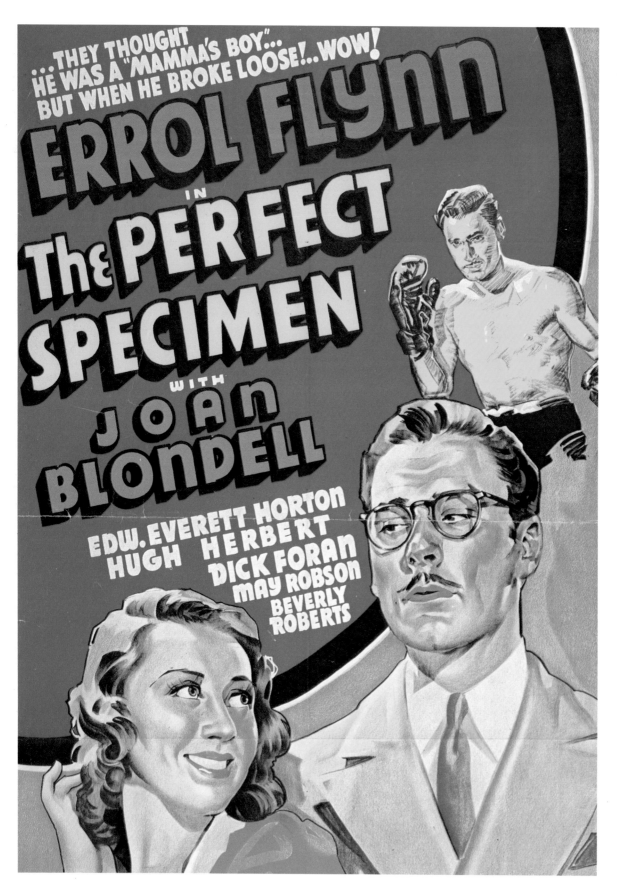

Errol Flynn in the 1937 The Perfect Specimen, *a comedy role for the swashbuckler and general all-round hero. The title of the movie is not accidental: Flynn was sold as the 'perfect' male specimen.*

Errol Flynn
. . . .

The greatest of the swashbuckling stars, Flynn was as famous for his off-screen antics as his celluloid heroics. Determinedly self-destructive, Flynn drank his health and wealth away and died in 1959 at the age of 59. At his peak in the thirties and early forties, he was very big at the box-office in movies such as *Captain Blood, The Charge of the Light Brigade, The Sea Hawk, They Died With Their Boots On* and *Elizabeth and Essex*. By the fifties his alcoholism had ruined his outstanding good looks and he was reduced to starring with Anna Neagle in film versions of *Lilacs in the Spring* and *King's Rhapsody*. He played a drunk in *The Sun Also Rises* and *Too Much Too Soon* (as John Barrymore), but the end was near. His body finally gave out in a Vancouver hotel when he died of a heart attack. Since his death bizarre rumours have linked him with Nazi espionage and the IRA. Flynn, even in death, is seldom far from a headline.

Robert Redford
. . . .

Redford is unlike Valentino, Gable and Flynn in that he is not predominantly an action hero. However, he has become a symbol of male beauty whether he likes it or not. His roles in *Butch Cassidy and the Sundance Kid, The Candidate, The Way We Were, The Sting, All the President's Men* and *The Natural* have made him a major star, albeit not in the tradition of Gable. Redford has no great range as an actor. He tends to play the honest guy trying to make his way in the world in as honourable a manner as he can. In the process, however, he always looks impossibly handsome in the tradition of Hollywood roman-tic heroes.

ABOVE

Redford has always suffered for being 'too good-looking'; male critics, in particular, underestimate his dramatic talents on the basis that anyone that handsome couldn't be any good as an actor.

♦♦ *They throw that word 'star' at you loosely and they take it away equally loosely. You take the responsibility for their lousy movie, that's what that means.* ♦♦

ROBERT REDFORD

THE
SENSITIVE
ANTI-HEROES

In the fifties there appeared a new kind of male star: the intuitive, almost feminised hero. Usually anti-authoritarian in stance, these stars grew out of the naturalistic, 'Method' school of acting and the commercial need to give Hollywood's dominant audience in the fifties – young people of between sixteen and twenty-five – stars they could identify with.

Montgomery Clift

Clift was the first of the sensitive, emotional actors to make it as a major star. His mumbling, hesitant style suited his roles in *A Place in the Sun*, *The Heiress*, *I Confess*, *From Here To Eternity*, *The Young Lions*, *Suddenly Last Summer* and *The Misfits*. His spectacular good looks did not harm his career either, but a serious car smash in 1957 altered his appearance and probably eventually shortened his life. Insecure in his private life, uncertain about his sexual identity, he resorted to drink and drugs and died prematurely at the age of 46. Clift influenced other young stars of the fifties and was undoubtedly, in his own way, a powerful screen presence.

James Dean

An enormous world-wide cult has grown around James Dean which, almost thirty years after his death at the age of twenty-four, shows no sign of dying out. Like Monroe, he is still big business. People who have never seen his films buy posters and other memorabilia of him because he represents something about youth, rebellion and charisma.

In real life, Dean rebelled against the strait-jacket that Hollywood tried to put him into; he would not conform to the image-makers' idea of what a Hollywood star should be, and in this he was just like his great hero, Marlon Brando. Dean's style is similar to Brando's except it is even more mannered, boyish and self-conscious. But he had tremendous screen presence, and an

ABOVE
James Dean as Cal Trask in the 1955 East of Eden. *With only three major films under his belt, Dean acquired mythical status after his death in 1956. With his death, the cult grew and grew.*

LEFT
Montgomery Clift in his costume for Raintree County *(1957). Clift's career and personal life never really recovered from the major car accident he was involved in during the making of this movie.*

ability to dominate the screen space and force the audience to look at him.

All actors are narcissistic but Dean seemed to have narcissism to excess. The need to display himself and his emotions on screen was overwhelming whatever he might have said about remaining a private person. But he did acknowledge that acting was about an actor's inner fantasies: 'My neuroticism manifests itself in the dramatic. Why do most actors act? To express the fantasies in which they have involved themselves.' Dean's talent lay in his power to involve mass audiences in those inner fantasies.

He had made only three major films by the time of his death: *East of Eden* and *Rebel without a Cause* (both 1955) and *Giant* (1956). In *East of Eden* he played Cal Trask, the moody, disaffected son of Adam Trask, played by Raymond Massey.

Elia Kazan directed the movie and has written about how Dean's improvisatory style irritated Massey, who was of the old school of actors believing in knowing your lines and your moves. In one famous scene in the movie, Dean throws his arms round Massey's neck imploring him to say he (his father) loves him. This had not been rehearsed and completely threw Massey, though the scene as it was shot remains in the film. Kazan admits that he used the antagonism between Dean and Massey to generate on-screen tension – in fact, he surreptitiously encouraged it between the two stars.

Rebel without a Cause had Dean as a disturbed high school teenager on the verge of becoming a fully-developed teenage delinquent largely because of the lack of love and stability in his home life. Although Natalie Wood and Sal Mineo form a kind of substitute family, Dean completely dominates. Nicholas Ray, the director, privileged him by allowing him to steal scenes and placing him in the dominating space on the screen. Dean in this persona, and in his playing of Cal Trask, seemed to encapsulate a rebellious attitude among America's youth that was to boil over into the mass protests of the sixties.

Giant was his last film (only *East of Eden* had been released by the time of his death). In it he co-starred with Rock Hudson and Elizabeth Taylor, playing another outsider part, Jet Rink, the penniless orphan who becomes an oil millionaire. His hesitant style suited the young Jet Rink, but when he had to age in the later parts of the movie, his lack of technique showed through and his acting is almost amateurish.

On 30 September 1955 Dean was killed while driving his Porsche along a Californian highway. He died a death that fed the legend of the rebel who lived for kicks, speed and fighting adult hypocrisy and conformity. The myths grew around him: was he homosexual or bisexual? Was his death an accident or was he murdered by proxy by Rock Hudson, a one-time lover? Truth never mixes well with legend so it is unlikely we will ever know the real James Dean. The only Dean that really counts is the one who appeared in those three films, but the cultists want much more than that from this icon of the cinema. The Dean legend represents something meaningful to millions of people and shows no sign of disappearing from our culture.

Paul Newman

At the beginning of his career Paul Newman was accused of copying Brando, but he went on to become a superstar in his own right. His first success was playing an inarticulate boxer in *Somebody up There Likes Me*. This was followed by Billy the Kid in Arthur Penn's *The Left-Handed Gun*, a western that aimed to demythologise cowboy legends. Newman's sensitive style suited his roles in *Cat on a Hot Tin Roof* and *The Hustler* but was less successful in comedies such as *Lady L* and *The Secret War of Harry Frigg*.

Of the new breed of actor, Newman was always more macho than the rest, notably in *Hud*, *Hombre* and *Cool Hand Luke*. He had great success in the seventies with *Butch Cassidy and the Sundance Kid* and *The Sting*. He also turned to directing, including directing his wife Joanne Woodward in *Rachel Rachel*.

His pursuits in real life include liberal politics and these liberal sentiments are reflected in some of his movies: *WUSA*, *Absence of Malice* and *The Verdict*. He is quoted as being sick of morons coming up to him and asking him to remove his dark glasses so they can see his steely blue eyes. Then he feels like a stupid male sex object, a stereotype he has always fought against.

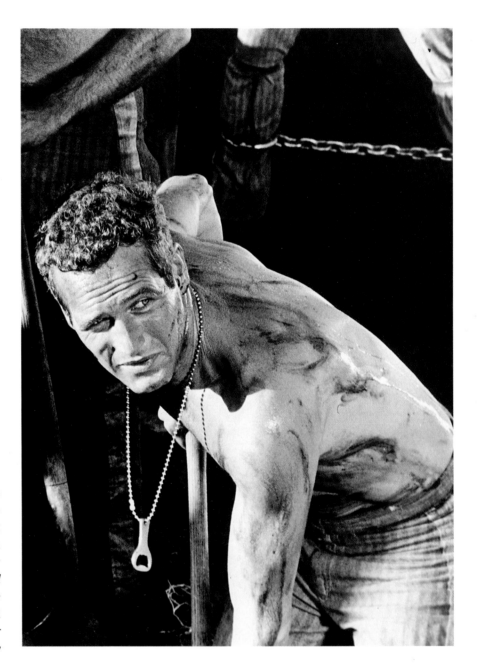

ABOVE

Paul Newman as the irrepressible hero of Cool Hand Luke *(1967). He plays a non-conformist imprisoned for sawing the heads off parking meters and forced to work on a chain gang. His numerous attempts at escape end in failure and finally in death. A classic Newman role, in line with his screen persona of the rebel who won't lie down.*

William Hurt

Of all the leading movie actors who emerged in the eighties, Hurt most symbolises 'the new man'. He won an Oscar for his performance as the transvestite in *Kiss of the Spider Woman* and has played 'loser' roles in *Body Heat*, *The Big Chill* and *The Accidental Tourist*. Some variety to his roles has been added by his appearances in *Altered States*, *Gorky Park*, *Children of a Lesser God* and *Broadcast News*. Hurt is likely to remain one of the most watchable of the most recent crop of Hollywood stars.

Mickey Rourke

Many would dispute that Rourke exudes sensitivity because he has taken on 'hard man' roles in *The Year of the Dragon* and *A Prayer before Dying*, but his charismatic screen presence in *Diner*, *Rumble Fish*, *Angel Heart* and *Johnny Handsome* have shown other aspects of his acting persona. The slightly high-pitched voice, the muted delivery, the narcissism, the cultivated scruffiness – all these characteristics mark Rourke down as a natural successor to the anti-heroes of the fifties.

Dustin Hoffman

Hoffman became a star with his role of the unsure young man eaten up by Mrs Robinson in *The Graduate*. Other notable anti-heroic parts have been in *Midnight Cowboy*, *Little Big Man*, *Kramer vs Kramer*, *Tootsie* and *Rain Man*. Hoffman obviously prides himself on the range of parts he has attempted; he has also appeared in overtly violent movies (*Straw Dogs*, *Papillon* and *Marathon Man*) but he basically always plays the decent individual with doubts and inadequacies struggling against a cruel and indifferent world.

ABOVE
The 1967 comedy The Graduate *was an international hit and established Dustin Hoffman as a major star.*

RIGHT
Mickey Rourke emerged as a star in Coppola's Rumble Fish *(1983). His forte is soft-spoken menace, encapsulating a kind of 'new man' machismo.*

Marie Dressler and W.C.
Fields as Tillie and Gus
(1933). They eye each other
like the old cynics they
pretend to be on screen.
However, there is a good
deal of evidence to show that
Fields' screen image was
very close to his real
personality.

THE COMEDY STARS

Charlie Chaplin

The little man with the baggy pants and bowler hat became one of the icons of the cinema. However, opinions divide over Chaplin and I find myself having to admit I find his movies unfunny. They are also spoiled by a gross sentimentality. But there is no denying Chaplin's fame and popularity. Early movies such as *The Tramp*, *The Pawnshop* and *Easy Street* established him as a major star and *The Kid*, *The Gold Rush*, *The Circus* and *City Lights* are perceived as masterpieces by Chaplin fans. In the thirties *Modern Times* and *The Great Dictator* showed Chaplin's brand of sentimental liberal politicising and it was this aspect of his work that gave ammunition to reactionaries in America who demanded that his passport be withdrawn until he could prove his 'moral worth'.

Monsieur Verdoux (1947), Chaplin's best film perhaps, was followed by *Limelight* (1952), *A King in New York* (1957) and *A Countess from Hong Kong* (1967). Finally, Hollywood 'forgave' Chaplin and awarded him a special Oscar in 1972. 'Charlie Chaplin' was a cinematic phenomenon; however opinions diverge about his worth as a performer and director, his fame illustrates how cinema is a world-wide form of communication that crosses barriers of language and culture.

W. C. Fields

Fields played misogynistic braggarts and cheats, who viewed the world cynically and through a whisky bottle. He communicated his dislike for women and children in his 'act', which almost certainly owed a great deal to the real-life Fields. His comic appearance with that bulbous, whisky-red nose meant he could never play for pathos, although, unlike Chaplin, he was temperamentally unwilling to milk tears anyway. His biggest successes were *The Old-Fashioned Way*, *It's a Gift*, *David Copperfield* (as Mr Micawber), *Poppy*, *You Can't Cheat an Honest Man*, *My Little Chickadee*, *The*

Bank Dick and *Never Give a Sucker an Even Break*. His alcoholism caught up with him on Christmas Day, 1946.

LEFT
Charlie Chaplin in his tramp guise. 'The son-of-a-bitch is a ballet dancer,' said W.C. Fields about his comedian rival and it is true that Chaplin's skill of movement and mime are intrinsic to his screen presence.

Groucho Marx

Groucho Marx and Margaret Dumont square up to each other in A Night at the Opera *(1935). Dumont was Groucho's favourite sparring partner, the target for his remorseless insults: 'Marry me and I'll never look at another horse!'*

The only one of the Marx Bros. really to count. It was Groucho who gave the brothers class and wit in movies such as *Animal Crackers, Monkey Business, Horse Feathers, Duck Soup, A Night at the Opera, A Day at the Races* and *Room Service*. His best partner in comedy was the mountainous matron, Margaret Dumont, whom Groucho systematically insulted. Irretrievably sexist, Groucho still managed to be funny and sharp. His trademarks were a painted-on moustache, heavy eyebrows, steel-rimmed spectacles, a cigar and a mad, crouching walk. He was a verbal and physical clown whose humour depended on elaborate wordplay and puns. Perhaps it was this aspect of his clowning that gained him intellectual fans, including T.S. Eliot, with whom he conducted a long correspondence. 'Marry me and I'll never look at another horse!'

Bob Hope
· · · · · · · ·

Hope at the peak of his career was among the biggest box-office stars, especially in the series of 'Road' movies he made with Bing Crosby. Paramount made a mint out of these (*Road to Singapore*, *Road to Zanzibar*, *Road to Morocco*, *Road to Utopia*). Other Hope hits were *The Cat and the Canary*, *The Ghost Breakers*, *My Favorite Blonde*, *Monsieur Beaucaire*, *The Paleface* and *The Lemon Drop Kid*. His screen persona was based on a cowardly and narcissistic nincompoop, always falling for Crosby's streetwise ruses and seldom getting the girl.

As his films deteriorated in the late fifties and sixties he turned more and more to television. He also became extremely reactionary in his politics and was associated with jingoistic tours of Vietnam. But Hope was also something of a national institution and the resident White House clown.

BELOW
Bob Hope with Jackie Gleason in How to Commit Marriage.

129

Woody Allen
. . . .

Allen could have appeared in the section on directors because he has directed and written most of his most important films. However, he is best known in the public mind as a performer in worldly, New York comedies such as *Play It Again, Sam, Annie Hall, Manhattan, Stardust Memories, Broadway Danny Rose, The Purple Rose of Cairo* and *Radio Days*. He leans heavily for his humour on his Jewish background and his show-business career. His obsessions are death, sex, potency, his looks and his Jewishness. Allen started in stand-up comedy and those origins are reflected in the one-liners that pepper his scripts. There is a knowing, self-conscious quality to the writing that flatters the audience who congratulate themselves on picking up the Freudian or cultural references. He has also directed 'serious' movies such as *Interiors* and *September*, which are very much influenced by his cinematic hero, Swedish director Ingmar Bergman.

Woody Allen divides people like few other performers: if you are an Allen fan, you tend to be a devotee who becomes boring after a while recounting favourite bits from the movies; if you're not, you can't see what all the fuss is about. His view of life? 'I don't believe in an after-life, but I'm bringing along a change of underwear.'

THE GLAMOUR QUEENS

In the heyday of Hollywood, female stars usually had to conform to a stereotyped image of female beauty as defined by men. Hopefully, the pressure on contemporary actresses to present a manufactured glamour image is now less intense, witness stars such as Kathleen Turner and Glenn Close. In the days of old Hollywood, however, there were many contenders for the role of glamour queen or sex object.

Jean Harlow
. . . .

Harlow is one of the prime candidates for the dubious honour of being the all-time Hollywood victim. She died at the age of twenty-six, after a short but highly successful career playing blondes-on-the-make. Harlow was one of Howard Hughes's 'starlets', in other words, one of his mistresses whose careers he boosted. She had little acting talent but came over on the screen as a brash, vulgar but determined young woman.

She co-starred with Cagney in *Public Enemy*, then she became *The Platinum Blonde*. MGM bought up her contract and with them she made *Dinner at Eight*, *Red Dust*, *Reckless* and *Saratoga*. Her marriage to Paul Bern, MGM executive, landed her in scandal as Bern, shortly after their marriage, either shot himself because he was impotent or was murdered by a former woman friend. Harlow's frenetic existence came to an end in 1937 when she died of uremic poisoning.

> ♦♦*I have decided that while I am a star, I will be every inch and every moment the star. Everyone from the studio gateman to the highest executive will know it.*♦♦
>
> **GLORIA SWANSON**

ABOVE

Jean Harlow in a characteristic studio glamour pose.

Mae West

Of all the manufactured female sex objects, Mae West was the most self-conscious and processed. Both a sex symbol and a parody of a sex object, West appealed to a wide spectrum of audience. Her forte was the unsubtle double entendre such as 'Is that a gun in your pocket or are you just glad to see me?' Lines like that made West notorious and helped give ammunition to the Legion of Decency and other vigilante censorship groups to clamp down on Hollywood licentiousness. She looked like a man in drag, presenting a grossly stereotypical image of what passed for female sexuality. But she knew what she was doing and was no dumb blonde, writing her own scripts and proving herself to be an expert self-publicist and business-woman. Her films include *She Done Him Wrong* (1933), *I'm No Angel* (1933), *Belle of the Nineties* (1934), *Klondike Annie* (1936) and *My Little Chickadee* (1939). She made a late and disastrous appearance in the dire *Myra Breckinridge* (1970), and died at the age of eighty-eight in 1980.

Rita Hayworth

Hayworth could be seen as another victim of the Hollywood system. When she said that the years that she was married to Orson Welles were the happiest of her life, Welles replied that, if that was her idea of happiness, what must the rest of her life have been like? But in the forties Hayworth became *the* glamour queen, enduring painful transformations of her appearance to reach the standard of Hollywood glamour that her studio bosses demanded.

Her best films were *Cover Girl*, *Gilda* and *The Lady from Shanghai*, the latter directed by husband Orson Welles who dyed her hair blonde and made her portray a duplicitous femme fatale. In the fifties her most notable films were *Miss Sadie Thompson*, *Salome*, *Pal Joey* and *Separate Tables*. In 1949 Hayworth had married Prince Aly Khan, a Muslim leader-cum-playboy, but they were divorced in 1953. Alzheimer's Disease came to her at the early age of sixty-two; for the last few years of her life she had to be cared for like a baby

Lana Turner

Turner was another totally manufactured Hollywood glamour object. Rarely was she ever anything other than wooden in her roles, but she did achieve some credibility as an actress in *The Bad and the Beautiful* and *Imitation of Life*. Earlier films included *Ziegfeld Girl*, *Dr Jekyll and Mr Hyde*, *The Postman Always Rings Twice* and *The Three Musketeers*. Even the legend of her so-called discovery at Schwab's Drugstore on Sunset Boulevard has been exposed as a manufactured myth.

Her early film career prospered with her label as the 'Sweater Girl' and she acquired husbands at a rate of knots: seven in all, including Artie Shaw the bandleader, and Lex Barker, one of many screen Tarzans. In 1958 she was involved in a steamy scandal when her fourteen-year-old daughter stabbed to death her lover, a Mafia hood. Her career survived and even thrived on the notoriety. But parts eventually ran out for an ageing glamour queen with few acting resources to fall back on in her old age.

Jane Russell

'Discovered' by Howard Hughes who was fascinated by her breasts, Russell survived the furore surrounding her debut in *The Outlaw* to show, in some movies, that she was more than a male fantasy object. Her best films were *Macao* and *Gentlemen Prefer Blondes*. Russell in later life found God, perhaps as a response to the crudeness with which Hollywood marketed her shape in movies such as *Double Dynamite*, *The French Line* and *Underwater*.

Ava Gardner

Carrying the burden of the tag of the 'world's most beautiful woman' could not have been easy, but Gardner appeared to be quite a tough cookie until her later years, when the ravages of alcohol and burning the candle at both ends finally took their toll on her with her premature death at the age of 67 in 1989. Along the way she survived marriages to Artie Shaw, Mickey Rooney and Frank Sinatra. Gardner was never a great actress, but she had a certain screen quality of warmth mixed with resilience that went beyond mere beauty. After serving her time in a succession of minor movies, she finally made the big time with the role as Kitty in *The Killers*

LEFT
Jane Russell surrounded by Olympic athletes as her chorus line in Howard Hawks's Gentlemen Prefer Blondes *(1953).*

playing opposite Burt Lancaster. In the fifties, major film followed major film: *Show Boat, Pandora and the Flying Dutchman, The Snows of Kilimanjaro, Mogambo, The Barefoot Contessa, Bhowani Junction, The Sun Also Rises* and *On the Beach*. Roles were harder to come by in the sixties and seventies, but she did continue to work right into the eighties. Gardner was undoubtedly the product of the Hollywood glamour machine and, as such, she was never allowed to show whether she was a more capable actress than her limited roles suggested.

RIGHT
Ava Gardner was undoubtedly one of the most beautiful of the old-time Hollywood glamour queens. Sometimes she could be surprisingly effective as an actress too. But alcoholism took its toll and she died in relative obscurity in 1989 at the age of sixty-seven.

LEFT
Lana Turner was marketed as the provocative 'sweater girl' in the forties, until she moved on to 'mature' roles in the fifties and sixties. Her best role was in The Bad and the Beautiful *(1952).*

Elizabeth Taylor

. . . .

At the height of her career Taylor was the highest-paid star of them all. Born in England of American parents, she joined MGM as a child star and appeared in *Lassie Come Home* and *National Velvet* during the war. Graduating to adult parts, she was dubbed the screen's most beautiful woman and starred in *A Place in the Sun* (1951), *Giant* (1956), *Cat on a Hot Tin Roof* (1958) and *Butterfield 8* (1960). The ponderous epic *Cleopatra* (1963) almost bankrupted 20th Century-Fox, partly because of the long delays caused by her ill-health. During the shooting of the movie, she began an affair with Richard Burton, whom she subsequently married (twice). Taylor and Burton became the most famous show-business couple since Fairbanks and Pickford, earning huge salaries for appearing in some worthless movies (with *Who's Afraid of Virginia Woolf?* and *The Taming of the Shrew* as exceptions), and indulging in conspicuous consumption that merely added to their rather tawdry public image.

After her relationship with Burton finally ended, Taylor's career nose-dived and recent years have seen her more in the news for her fight against alcoholism, her 'pigging out' and her repeated adventures in the operating theatre than for her acting career. But whatever estimation might be made about her abilities, it cannot be denied that she is nothing if not resilient.

LEFT
The young Elizabeth Taylor was supposed to be 'the most beautiful woman in the world'. Opinions divided sharply about her acting talents, but no one can deny her survival instincts. All those marriages, tragic deaths, critical illnesses, drugs, booze and 'pig-outs' have taken their toll, but she's still with us.

THE
GOOD JOES

The 'good Joe' stars are the 'Mr Reliables', the archetypal quietly-spoken heroes who don't make a lot of fuss but who are around to sort things out when things turn nasty.

Gary Cooper
. . . .

Cooper's screen persona consisted of the straight-down-the-line, on-the-level, slow-talking, slow-burning but handsome American good guy. *Mr Deeds Goes to Town* typified the Cooper archetype – the incorruptible, unworldly Mr Average who defeats the crooks in the end by sheer integrity. Cooper was also used in westerns and adventures, such as *The Plainsman*, *Beau Geste*, *The Westerner* and *Unconquered*. He was a natural choice for the World War I hero *Sergeant York* and won an Oscar for his most famous role as the isolated marshal in *High Noon*, interpreted by many as an anti-McCarthy movie. If it was, Cooper was unaware of it because he was one of the stars who publicly testified to the Congress investigating committee about alleged communist infiltration into Hollywood: 'From what I hear about communism, I don't like it because it isn't on the level.'

RIGHT

A studio portrait of Gary Cooper. Never one of Hollywood's intellectuals, Cooper represented a straight-talking, straight-shooting version of personable masculinity.

James Stewart

· · · · · · · · ·

Stewart is another slow-speaking, drawling star who played his share of 'honest Joe' parts, notably in Frank Capra's *Mr Smith Goes to Washington* and *It's a Wonderful Life*. Hitchcock and Anthony Mann were two other directors who played important roles in Stewart's career, Hitchcock using Stewart in *Rope, Rear Window, The Man Who Knew Too Much* and *Vertigo*. Mann made eight westerns with Stewart including *Winchester 73* and *The Man from Laramie*. John Ford also used Stewart when he needed an actor who could communicate integrity: *Two Rode Together* and *The Man Who Shot Liberty Valance*. Other major movies for Stewart were *The Philadelphia Story, Harvey, Anatomy of a Murder* and *Shenandoah*. He played real-life American heroes in *The Stratton Story, The Glenn Miller Story* and *The Spirit of St Louis* (about the aviator, Charles A. Lindbergh).

Henry Fonda

· · · · · · · · ·

Fonda seemed to be first choice for playing presidents, presidential candidates or senators:

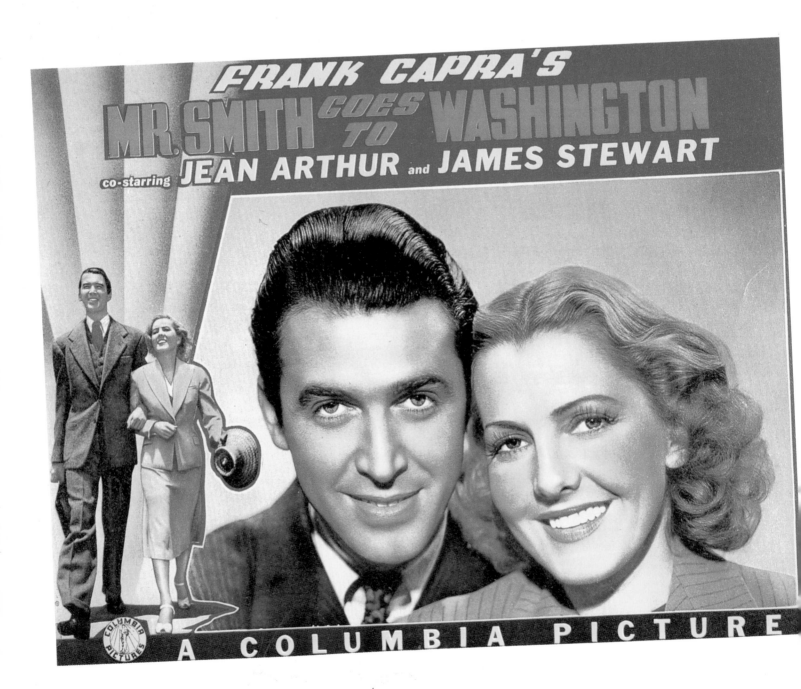

Young Mr Lincoln, Advise and Consent, The Best Man and *Fail Safe*. He often played the soft-spoken hero who represents American justice and free speech. In *The Grapes of Wrath, The Ox Bow Incident* and *Twelve Angry Men* he variously defended the downtrodden and through his presence signified that the American way of life was basically fair and just. He played American heroes such as Frank James, Alexander Graham Bell and Wyatt Earp. Only rarely did he not play the good guy, notably in *Once Upon a Time in the West*. He was rather irascible in his last movie, *On Golden Pond*, a role perhaps closer to his real-life persona. He gave up Hollywood between 1948 and 1955 and returned to the stage, until the good guy part in *Mister Roberts* drew him back to the screen. While shooting that film, he reputedly had a fist fight with director John Ford. As the actor himself once said, 'I'm not really Henry Fonda. Nobody could have that much integrity.'

Spencer Tracy

Solidity was Tracy's trademark – he could always be relied on and trusted. Tracy had a strong screen presence, although his range was limited and he sometimes allowed himself to edge over into sentimentality. For example, he played priests in *Boys' Town, San Francisco* and *Men of Boys' Town*. His limitations as an actor were exposed when he played *Dr Jekyll and Mr Hyde* but he scored in comedies with Katharine Hepburn: *Woman of the Year, State of the Union, Adam's Rib* and *Pat and Mike*. His power was used profitably in *Fury, Northwest Passage* and *The Last Hurrah*. His liberal politics were reflected in some of the movies he made: *Keeper of the Flame* (about American fascism), *Bad Day at Black Rock* (anti-racism), *Inherit the Wind* (anti-religious fundamentalism), *Judgement at Nuremberg* (as a judge of war crimes) and *Guess Who's Coming to Dinner* (as a father coming to terms with his daughter's marrying Sidney Poitier). Tracy was separated for a long time from his wife and family and had a long relationship with Katharine Hepburn. But the demon drink proved to be his enemy and contributed to his death in 1967.

Gregory Peck

Opinions vary about Peck's acting abilities, and in some parts such as Captain Ahab in *Moby Dick* and Scott Fitzgerald in *Beloved Infidel* he was clearly out of his depth. He is at his best in solid, caring roles: as Atticus, the southern lawyer in *To Kill A Mockingbird*, he won an Oscar, and he had other good guy roles in *The Keys of the Kingdom*, *The Yearling*, *Gentleman's Agreement*, *The Man in the Grey Flannel Suit*, *The Big Country* and *On the Beach*. He has tried to break the heroic pattern by playing villains in *Duel in the Sun* and *The Boys from Brazil*, and has also had his share of romantic lead parts, notably in *Spellbound*, *David and*

LEFT
Gregory Peck has been one of Hollywood's elder statesmen for years now. For a romantic hero, he has a curiously sexless quality which, perhaps, is one of the secrets of his appeal.

Bathsheba, *The Snows of Kilimanjaro*, *Roman Holiday* and *Arabesque*. Man-of-action roles have included *The Gunfighter*, *Captain Horatio Hornblower*, *Twelve O'Clock High*, *Pork Chop Hill* and *The Guns of Navarone*. Peck has become a pillar of the Hollywood establishment representing the more liberal side of filmland's politics.

Charlton Heston

Heston is mainly associated with roles in epics but basically he plays good guys whether he is Moses, Ben Hur or El Cid. However, Heston takes himself very seriously as an actor (witness his autobiography *An Actor's Life*). His career really took off when he played Moses in De Mille's *The Ten Commandments* and this was followed by *Ben Hur*, *El Cid* and *The Agony and the Ecstasy* (as Michelangelo). Other epic parts included *The War Lord*, *Khartoum* (as General Gordon) and *55 Days at Peking*. His westerns have included *The Big Country*, *Major Dundee* and *Will Penny*. Sci-fi roles in *Planet of the Apes*, *Soylent Green* and *The Omega Man* gave his career a boost,

but Shakespearian roles in *Julius Caesar* and *Antony and Cleopatra* failed to make the critics enthuse. He has returned to the stage and dabbled in directing and even appeared in the television series *The Colbys* for a season.

Kevin Costner

Costner is seen as resembling Stewart and Fonda in his quiet but authoritative style. His first big success was as Elliot Ness in *The Untouchables* and this was followed by his roles as the duplicitous spy in *No Way Out*. *Field of Dreams* was a Capra-esque exercise in nostalgia and downhome American values, but *Revenge* involved Costner in a macho tale of betrayal and bloodletting.

However, it was *Dances with Wolves* (1990) that put the seal of major stardom on Costner's career. Directing this 'liberal' reappraisal of the myth of the American frontier and the white man's interaction with native Americans brought Costner a Best Director Oscar. *Robin Hood, Prince of Thieves* was also a major box-office success for him and further insurance that he would be a major star for a long time to come.

BELOW

Charlton Heston, as usual, completely in charge whether delivering messages from God, winning chariot races or leading thousands of extras into battle.

THE HEAVIES, VILLAINS AND DOWNRIGHT CADS

Baddies come in all shapes and sizes, and the actors awarded honoured status in this section represent all three categories. Sometimes a heavy is not quite a villain; however, a villain is always a villain, whereas a cad may be a villain but he's charming with it.

Bela Lugosi

Of Hungarian origins, Lugosi was the screen's most famous Dracula in *Dracula* (1930), *Mark of the Vampire* (1935), *The Return of the Vampire* (1943) and *Frankenstein Meets the Wolf Man*. He was totally typecast in horror movies such as *Murders in the Rue Morgue*, *White Zombie*, *The Raven* and *The Ghost of Frankenstein*. In the latter part of his career all that was left for him to do was appear in spoof versions of the Frankenstein and Dracula legends: *Abbott and Costello Meet Frankenstein*, *Bela Lugosi Meets a Broadway Gorilla* and *Mother Riley Meets the Vampire*.

Boris Karloff

Karloff in real life was an Englishman of the old school, a pillar of the insufferable British colony in Hollywood who liked to show the natives how to dress for dinner and keep a straight bat. On screen he was the Creature in the 1931 *Franken-stein* and was involved in *The Old Dark House*, *The Mask of Fu Manchu*, *The Mummy*, *The Bride of Frankenstein* and *The Raven*. In the mid-forties he made three more notable movies: *The Body Snatcher*, *Isle of the Dead* and *Bedlam*. In the sixties he appeared in three Roger Corman spoofs of the horror genre: *The Raven*, *The Terror* and *Comedy of Terrors*. In 1968 he made his last film and one of his best, *Targets*, which was Peter Bogdanovich's first movie. Karloff was refreshingly modest about his achievements: 'You could heave a brick out of the window and hit ten actors who could play my parts. I just happened to be on the right corner at the right time.'

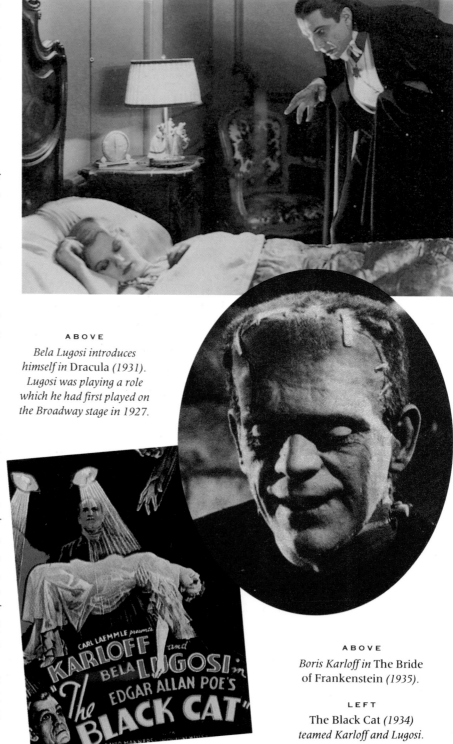

ABOVE

Bela Lugosi introduces himself in Dracula *(1931). Lugosi was playing a role which he had first played on the Broadway stage in 1927.*

ABOVE

Boris Karloff in The Bride of Frankenstein *(1935).*

LEFT

The Black Cat (1934) teamed Karloff and Lugosi.

George Sanders

Sanders was the archetypal British cad – smooth, urbane and as trustworthy as a car salesman in Mayfair. He was the cad in *Rebecca*, but then had a saintly spell in *The Saint* and *The Falcon* series. He was the Gauguin figure in *The Moon and Sixpence*, another cad in *Summer Storm*, *The Picture of Dorian Gray*, *Hangover Square*, *Forever Amber* and, memorably, in *All About Eve*. Sanders was never really committed to his profession and used to disparage his work. Perhaps it was not surprising that he took his own life in 1972, writing in his suicide note that he was bored and that he was glad to be leaving 'this sweet cesspool that was the world'. A cad to the last.

Sydney Greenstreet

One of the screen's great fat men, Greenstreet's film debut could hardly have been more auspicious: he played the villainous Kasper Guttman in *The Maltese Falcon* (1941). He came up against Bogart again in *Casablanca* and *Passage to Marseilles* and was another heavy in *The Mask of Dimitrios*. None of his later roles brought him similar success, and when he died aged seventy-five in 1954, he had packed all his film career into nine years.

ABOVE

Edward G. Robinson never gave an underplayed performance on screen, but he was mightily effective in tough, cynical roles. Here he looks uncharacteristically benevolent.

RIGHT

George Sanders as Addison de Witt in All About Eve *(1952). Sanders played cad after cad of the Mayfair car salesman variety usually. In this movie, he was the scabrous drama critic who 'helps' Anne Baxter's career.*

Edward G. Robinson

It is probably doing Robinson a disservice to include him in this section, but it is as a movie baddie he will largely be remembered. The 1930 *Little Caesar* made him a star and a succession of gangster roles in the thirties created Robinson's tough guy screen persona. He was a memorable insurance claims investigator in *Double Indemnity*, and, in the forties, was more often the good guy in movies such as *Woman in the Window*, *The Stranger* and *Scarlet Street*. He returned to playing villains in *Key Largo*, *Black Tuesday*, *The Ten Commandments* (he dared to take on Moses!), *Two Weeks in Another Town* and *Seven Thieves*. His small stature and menacing looks meant he would never be cast as a hero, but he brought real quality to many of his roles.

ABOVE

Charles Laughton as Henry VIII in The Private Life of Henry VIII *(1932). At his worst, Laughton was insufferably hammy and seemingly difficult to direct. Even the authoritarian Alfred Hitchcock said the best a director could hope to do on a Laughton picture was referee it.*

RIGHT

Even when sitting on a studio chair, Rod Steiger cannot help hamming it up.

Charles Laughton

Laughton certainly played a variety of roles but he was always at his most watchable when he played an over-the-top villain such as Nero in the 1932 *The Sign of the Cross*, the incestuous Mr Barrett in *The Barretts of Wimpole Street* (1934), Captain Bligh in the 1935 *Mutiny on the Bounty*, the unrelenting policeman in *Les Misérables* (1935) and the newspaper proprietor in *The Big Clock* (1948). He also played Quasimodo in *The Hunchback of Notre Dame*, a weak but finally courageous schoolteacher in *This Land is Mine* and a wily Roman senator in *Spartacus*. He is remembered as well for his direction of *Night of the Hunter*. Married to Elsa Lanchester for years, he was nonetheless seemingly tortured by his homosexuality.

Vincent Price

Price is another over-the-top actor who has made a career out of horror films. He was unpleasant in *Laura* and *The Three Musketeers* and then appeared in the 3-D *House of Wax*. *The Bat* and *The Fall of the House of Usher* further enhanced his horrible screen persona and these exercises in grand guignol were followed by *The Pit and the Pendulum*, *The Raven*, *The Tomb of Ligeia*, *The Abominable Dr Phibes*, *Theatre of Blood* and *Journey into Fear* as well as numerous others. He brings a quality of high camp to his roles.

Rod Steiger

'You shoulda looked after me, Charlie' complains Brando to Steiger in the famous taxi cab scene in *On the Waterfront*. Steiger's naturalistic acting style, and his tendency to ham, made him one of the best of the fifties villains in movies such as *Oklahoma*, *The Harder They Fall* and *Al Capone*. He clearly loved playing Mr Joyboy in *The Loved One* and outacted everyone else in *Dr Zhivago* as the repellent time-server. He won an Oscar for his bigoted policeman in *In the Heat of the Night* and was a psychopathic killer in *No Way to Treat a Lady*. He played Napoleon in *Waterloo* and Lucky Luciano in the 1973 movie of the same name. His career has had its troughs and he has certainly made far too many bad movies, but he has allowed his talent to shine through in a handful of worthwhile films.

The publicity material for the horror flick, House of Wax *(1953). Vincent Price took over the mantle of Lugosi and Karloff in the horror stakes and added his own contribution of high camp.*

Lee Marvin as Sheriff Big Track Bascomb in The Klansman, *in which he starred with Richard Burton (1965).*

Lee Marvin

· · · · · · · · · ·

Marvin made his reputation playing psycho-pathic villains and, even when he was nominally the hero, he always managed to bring an ambiguous quality to his roles. He threw hot coffee in Gloria Grahame's face in *The Big Heat* and was Brando's adversary in *The Wild One*. He was one of the villains in *Bad Day at Black Rock* and Liberty Valance in *The Man Who Shot Liberty Valance*. He won an Oscar for his role as the drunken gun-fighter in *Cat Ballou*. Around this time he began to play tough guys with some kind of integrity, as in *The Professionals*, *Point Blank*, *The Dirty Dozen*, *Prime Cut* and *Emperor of the North*. Off-screen he had a reputation for being a drinker and a wild man; latterly, seemingly, he settled down, but perhaps too late to reverse his declining health. He died at the age of 62 in 1987.

> ♦♦ *You know why I get so many dates? Because I have a 40-foot face.* ♦♦
>
> RICHARD DREYFUSS

THE QUEENS OF MELODRAMA

The characteristic of melodrama, and screen melodrama in particular, is excess. These five queens of melodrama were adept at unleashing extremes of emotion on the screen. In the heyday of old Hollywood the performances of these actresses gave the so-called 'woman's picture' a good name.

Bette Davis
. . . .

Davis was an actress of the large theatrical gesture and killing look. Sometimes she was very bad (*The Private Lives of Elizabeth and Essex* and

BELOW

Bette Davis was a tough woman on and off the screen. She fought Warners for better roles, and usually played determined women on screen. Here Charles Boyer helps her on with her cape in the 1940 All This and Heaven Too.

The Anniversary) but she was mostly very effective in 'wicked women' roles such as in *The Little Foxes*, *The Letter*, *Mr Skeffington*, *A Stolen Life* and *Whatever Happened to Baby Jane?*. She was noble in *Dark Victory*, *The Old Maid*, *The Corn is Green* and *Old Acquaintance*. She suffered for love in *Now Voyager* and *Deception*. Her later grand guignol roles included *Hush Hush Sweet Charlotte* and *The Nanny*.

At the height of her career in the late thirties and forties Davis was one of Hollywood's biggest box-office stars. She took on her studio, Warners, over the seven-year contract system and,

although she lost the court case, she ultimately helped to free movie actors from that form of bonded slavery. Always independent and forceful she acquired a reputation for being difficult, which may have contributed to the fact that her career in the fifties suddenly went into decline, so much so that she had to put an advertisement in *The Hollywood Reporter* announcing she needed work. Her most famous role may be Margo Channing in *All About Eve*, a movie in which she utters the immortal line, 'Fasten your seatbelts, it's going to be a bumpy night.' Most impersonators of stars can do a passable Bette Davis: tha New England throaty voice with its cutting edge those large eyes and the exaggerated inhaling o a cigarette.

> ◆◆*When I saw my first film test, I ran from the projection room screaming.*◆◆
>
> **BETTE DAVIS**

Joan Crawford graduated from flapper girl or secretary roles to suffering matron parts in the forties and fifties. Another actress who could never be accused of underplaying, she tenaciously clung to her screen career almost to the end of her life, refusing to give up on a stardom that she had chased ruthlessly.

Joan Crawford

Another great 'sufferer' was Crawford, but only in the latter part of her long film career. Christened Lucille Le Sueur, Crawford in her early film parts was cast as a 'flapper' and some misguided studio executives thought she could dance. In the thirties and early forties she made eight mostly forgettable films with Clark Gable. Her archetypal roles were as the ambitious stenographer in *Grand Hotel* and as Sadie Thompson in *Rain*. When MGM dropped her in the forties she signed a new contract with Warners and came into her own as the chief rival of Davis in the melodrama stakes. Movies such as *Mildred Pierce*, *Humoresque*, *Possessed*, *Daisy Kenyon*, *Sudden Fear*, *Torch Song* and *Autumn Leaves* had her suffering at the hands of her husbands, lovers, children and society in general. Her screen persona lent itself more to 'victim' roles than Davis's, but Crawford, with a limited range of acting ability, still managed to project a powerful screen image.

Off screen Crawford built up a reputation for her ruthless pursuit of success and cleanliness. As her screen career wilted, she married a Pepsi-Cola executive and the soft drink manufacturer had to defend itself from the attentions of the widow when her executive husband died. Her adopted daughter wrote a damning account of her as a mother in *Mommie Dearest*, which was later filmed with Faye Dunaway as Crawford. Crawford and Davis co-starred in *Whatever Happened to Baby Jane?* in one scene of which Davis pushes Crawford, crippled in a wheelchair, down a staircase. It was a case of Hollywood feeding off its own legends again.

> ◆◆*The public likes provocative feminine personalities but it also likes to know that, underneath it all, the actresses are ladies.*◆◆
>
> **JOAN CRAWFORD**

Ingrid Bergman

A Swedish actress, Bergman made her first Hollywood film in 1939, *Intermezzo* with Leslie Howard, and became Hollywood's top female star in

the forties. *Casablanca* opposite Bogart cast her again as a woman destined to end up suffering for love, as did *For Whom the Bell Tolls, Spellbound* and *Notorious*, the latter two directed by Alfred Hitchcock. She also suffered in *Dr Jekyll and Mr Hyde, Gaslight, Joan of Arc* and *Under Capricorn.* Then she had a real-life affair with Italian director Roberto Rossellini, who was married at the time, as was Bergman. She had Rossellini's child and scandalised hypocritical Hollywood. She made a series of films with Rossellini (*Stromboli, Europa '51, We the Women*) before returning to a contrite Hollywood who rewarded her with an Oscar for her role in *Anastasia.* She had further successes with *Indiscreet* and *The Inn of the Sixth Happiness* but her great days at the box-office were over. Late in her career she made *Autumn Sonata*, directed by Ingmar Bergman, and she revealed what she might have achieved if her Hollywood roles had been more consistently worthwhile. Bergman had a beauty that escaped Hollywood stereotyping and a quality of 'goodness' that illuminated her roles.

Barbara Stanwyck
. . . .

Stanwyck was more working class in origin and manner than Davis or Crawford. She also employed an iciness in her screen portrayals that the other two could not match. Her greatest role was as Phyllis Dietrichson in *Double Indemnity*, the femme fatale who snares insurance salesman Walter Neff, played by normally 'good guy' actor, Fred MacMurray, in her murderous plans. Stanwyck and MacMurray deserve to be as famous for those roles as Bogart and Bergman were for their parts in *Casablanca.*

Other archetypal Stanwyck roles were in *Stella Dallas* (as a sacrificial mother), *The Lady Eve, Ball of Fire, The Strange Love of Martha Ivers, The Two Mrs Carrolls* and *Sorry Wrong Number.* She lost Fred MacMurray to Joan Bennett in Douglas Sirk's *There's Always Tomorrow* and must have known her screen career was on the wane when she starred with Elvis Presley in *Roustabout.* However, her television series *The Big Valley* was a success in the sixties and she later co-starred with Richard Chamberlain in *The Thorn Birds.* A very underrated actress, Stanwyck had tremendous power on screen and this despite her quite ordinary looks. She was married to Robert Taylor, considered by some to be a glamour boy, for a number of years.

Faye Dunaway
. . . .

A contemporary star with something of the Davis-Crawford 'over-the-top' style. Indeed, Dunaway played Joan Crawford in an unintentionally hilarious 'biopic' of the old-time star in *Mommie Dearest.* She came to stardom in *Bonnie and Clyde* and followed this up by playing opposite Steve McQueen in the ultra-smooth *Thomas Crown Affair.* After that, her career seemed to mark time until she made *Chinatown, 3 Days of the Condor, Network* and *Mommie Dearest.* Dunaway has always played the star off-screen as well, which is in itself a throwback to the old days of Hollywood. She has found it hard to sustain her box-office appeal, however, and satisfactory roles have been few and far between in the last decade.

ABOVE

Barbara Stanwyck was undoubtedly one of the best Hollywood actresses of her generation. Tough, tender or comic in turns, she was a strong presence in a variety of roles: killer, cattle-rancher, gambler or even, occasionally, a woman-in-peril.

LEFT

A portrait of Ingrid Bergman that emphasizes her simple beauty and purity. The American public turned their backs on her for a while, however, when she went off with married man Roberto Rossellini.

THE GREAT MUSICAL STARS

Fred Astaire

Nominated by most people as the greatest dancer in movies, Astaire danced with Ginger Rogers in a series of highly successful musicals in the thirties: *The Gay Divorcee, Roberta, Top Hat, Follow the Fleet, Swing Time, Shall We Dance?, A Damsel in Distress, Carefree* and *The Story of Vernon and Irene Castle*. Astaire was the effortless top-hat-and-tails dancer who made love to his leading ladies through his dancing, but he had a curiously sexless quality. Some fans prefer the movies he made in the latter part of his career: *Easter Parade, The Band Wagon, Daddy Long Legs, Funny Face* and *Silk Stockings*. Astaire was a perfectionist and a great worrier about his dance routines, which he usually worked out for himself with the help of choreographer Hermes Pan. His singing voice was also very pleasant and he could interpret a standard by Gershwin or Berlin like few others. A modest man, he could never really understand why people made such a fuss over his movies. 'I just dance,' he once said. Most people are glad he did. After his first screen test, some conventional studio functionary reported: 'Can't act. Can't sing. Slightly bald. Can dance a little'.

Betty Grable

Grable is living proof of Hollywood's power to fragment the female body and make big bucks out of it: Grable's legs were supposedly insured for millions of dollars with Lloyds of London. A musical star of only average singing and dancing abilities, she was tailored to be the wartime pin-up of the American forces. Basically, she was a glamorised version of the American girl-next-door. Overt sexuality was absent in her movies; she was sold on the basis of peaches-and-cream, kid sister appeal. This star persona proved very successful at the box-office in a series of anodyne musicals such as *Million Dollar Legs, Down Argentine Way, Tin Pan Alley, Moon over Miami, Footlight*

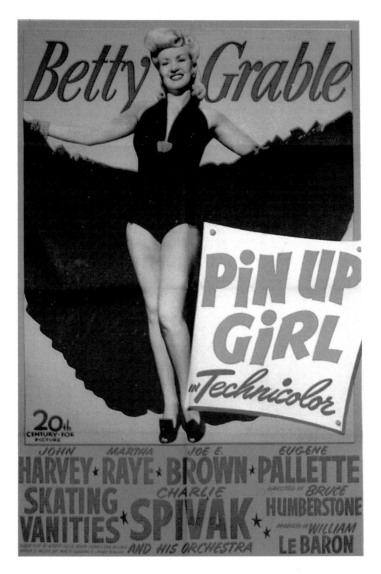

Betty Grable films were always harmless, cheerful family romances centred round show people.

Fred Astaire was not always paired with Ginger Rogers in his musicals. Here he dances with Marjorie Reynolds in Holiday Inn.

Serenade, Springtime in the Rockies, Coney Island, Sweet Rosie O'Grady and *Pin Up Girl*. Her career lasted well into the fifties with musicals such as *Mother Wore Tights, The Beautiful Blonde from Bashful Bend, My Blue Heaven* and the nonmusical *How to Marry a Millionaire*. When these movies are seen today, you ask yourself what all the fuss was about, but then, forty years from now, they'll be asking the same question about Madonna. The answer will be the same: publicity and money.

Gene Kelly
. . . .

Kelly has been dogged all his movie career by comparisons with Astaire. The fact is that he is very different: Kelly is overtly masculine, athletic and sensual, whereas Astaire is graceful and largely sexless. However, it could be claimed for Kelly that he has been the single most important influence on the movie musical as a star, choreographer and director.

Kelly became a star on Broadway playing *Pal Joey*, then he went to MGM and made *For Me and My Gal* with Garland. *Cover Girl* with his choreography for his alter-ego dance marked a breakthrough for Kelly and he went on to star in, and co-direct with Stanley Donen, *On the Town*, *Singin' in the Rain* and *It's Always Fair Weather*. In between he was directed by Vincente Minnelli in

The Pirate, *An American in Paris* and *Brigadoon*. The *Singin' in the Rain* number in the movie of that name has become one of the most famous movie sequences of all time. Kelly's Irish-American charm and his grin that 'could melt stone' endeared him to audiences, until the musical bubble burst and he was set free by MGM. His career went into reverse until he was given the chance to direct *Hello Dolly!* in 1969. Since then his reputation as the most creative star-director-choreographer in the history of the movies has been firmly established. A Hollywood original.

Judy Garland
. . . .

Garland is another icon of the movie musical. A child prodigy, Garland was overworked by her studio, MGM, in a series of musicals with Mickey Rooney. She was also Dorothy in *The Wizard of Oz*. Graduating from teen musicals, she made *Meet Me in St Louis* in which she was directed by Vincente Minnelli who shortly afterwards married her. This coupling produced Liza Minnelli. Garland starred with Gene Kelly in three movies: *For Me and My Gal*, *The Pirate* and *Summer Stock*. She made *Easter Parade* with Astaire, by which time she was in serious trouble with the studio and herself. Addicted to pills of various kinds, she blamed MGM for exploiting her and not using her talent intelligently, but when she failed to turn up for the shooting of *Annie Get Your Gun*, MGM sacked her. Her comeback film was the classic *A Star is Born* in which she co-starred with James Mason. Her film appearances after that were few and far between. She resumed her concert career, but stories of her drinking and broken marriages dogged her and she finally died in 1969. Around Garland arose a legend of the kind that only show business could create and her fans are among the most loyal of all, even twenty-odd years after her death.

Bing Crosby

. . . .

The 'Old Groaner' got by on a voice that was pleasant and a personality that smacked of good humour and easy-going ways. Off screen, he was a tyrannical father and mean with a buck. He always knew he was a very lucky man, and he was certainly fortunate to team up with Bob Hope in the series of 'Road' movies they made. He also co-starred with Astaire in *Holiday Inn* and *Blue Skies*. Crosby used that Irish charm of his in two schmaltzy movies about priests, *Going My Way* and *The Bells of St Mary's*. He also tried his hand at straight acting in *The Country Girl* and the remake of *Stagecoach*, in which he played the drunken doctor part. One of his best musicals was *High Society* with Frank Sinatra. Crosby was notoriously reluctant to do retakes, preferring to spend his time on the golf course. This laid-back approach to his work comes over on film.

Frank Sinatra

. . . .

Sinatra's movies range from musicals to westerns to straight dramas. Indeed, he won an Oscar for Best Supporting Actor in *From Here to Eternity*. But 'the Voice' naturally started out in musicals, all of which were entirely forgettable until *Anchors Aweigh*, *Take Me Out to the Ball Game* and *On the Town* gave him some kind of screen respectability. However, a series of terrible films made him box-office poison for a while until he begged to play Maggio in *From Here to Eternity*. From then on, he could choose his roles. Among the musicals were *Young at Heart*, *Guys and Dolls* and *High Society*. Sinatra has become the most famous entertainer in the world, partly because of his dubious off-screen acquaintances, but too many of his movies have been utterly worthless, particularly the 'home movies' he made with his gang, the Rat Pack, in the sixties.

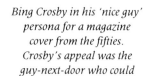

BELOW

Bing Crosby in his 'nice guy' persona for a magazine cover from the fifties. Crosby's appeal was the guy-next-door who could croon a little and make the spectator feel he was just like the rest of us.

PAL JOEY

LEFT
The Sinatra image was exploited to the hilt in Pal Joey *(1956). Here he is flanked, as ever, by two beautiful women, Kim Novak (right) and Rita Hayworth (left). The part of Joey was played first by Gene Kelly in the 1940 stage production, but when they filmed it, the role had to be adapted for the Sinatra talents, which meant there was no hoofing.*

Barbra Streisand

Streisand had a great success as Fanny Brice in *Funny Girl* then had two flops in a row with *Hello Dolly!* (in which she was miscast) and *On a Clear Day You Can See Forever*. However, her screen career recovered with *What's Up, Doc?* and *The Way We Were*. She made *Funny Lady* in 1975 and *A Star is Born* in 1976. She wanted to control her own career and managed to co-write, co-produce and direct *Yentl* in 1983. She has a reputation for egomania, but it is difficult to know how accurate this charge is or how much it is the reaction of chauvinists to a powerful woman in the movie industry.

LEFT

Barbra Streisand looks as uncomfortable as she must have felt in Hello, Dolly!, *an unusual flop amongst her films.*

BELOW

Barbra Streisand overhears some dodgy information about husband Robert Redford in The Way We Were *(1973). Streisand has also gone on to direct films, with* Yentl *and* The Prince of Tides.

THE NEW WOMEN

Women's roles on screen have been too often geared to male fantasies and too seldom reflect the reality of women's lives. However, the changing roles of men and women in real life have gradually been reflected in the range and depth of parts female stars are offered.

Katharine Hepburn

Hepburn has largely played emancipated, strong-minded women, albeit often with a quivering voice and trembling lip. Early Hollywood successes with *Morning Glory* and *Little Women* were followed by less commercially successful movies such as *Alice Adams*, *Sylvia Scarlett* and *Mary of Scotland*. Labelled 'box-office poison' by distribu-

BELOW

Katharine Hepburn might even be saying 'The calla lilies are in bloom again,' in this pose (she said it in Stage Door; 1937), but this is in fact merely a publicity pic. At her best when she played spunky women who were fast-talking and witty, Hepburn could also descend into a quivering emotionalism that was embarrassing to watch.

tors, she hit back in comedies such as *Bringing up Baby*, *The Philadelphia Story* and *Woman of the Year*, the latter with Spencer Tracy with whom she had a long relationship and made several notable movies including *Keeper of the Flame*, *Adam's Rib*, *Pat and Mike* and *Guess Who's Coming to Dinner?*. She played spinsters in *The African Queen*, *Summer Madness* and *The Rainmaker*. Never an actress to underplay, opinions divide over her performances in movies such as *Suddenly Last Summer*, *The Lion in Winter* and *The Madwoman of Chaillot*.

Her upper-class New England manner was best suited to her early roles when she symbolised a new kind of female star who depended hardly at all on physical allure.

ABOVE

Jane Fonda in her unreconstructed pre-feminist phase as Barbarella *(1968), directed by her then-husband, Roger Vadim. Soon after, Fonda left these glamour girl roles behind her and went on to be the conscience of the nation in movies such as* A Doll's House *(1974),* Julia *(1977) and* The China Syndrome *(1979).*

Jane Fonda

Fonda has had to work hard to be taken seriously in serious roles, partly because of her glamorous appearance and partly because her early film career landed her with decidedly unliberated parts such as those in *Cat Ballou* and *Barbarella* (with her then-husband Roger Vadim directing). Her first real success was in *Klute* for which she won an Oscar and this was followed by more overtly feminist roles in *A Doll's House*, *Julia* and *The China Syndrome*. In 1981 she appeared with her father, Henry, in *On Golden Pond*, playing a daughter having difficulties with her father, which apparently she had always had in real life with Henry until they were reconciled. She had a popular success in *Nine to Five* but has also played in some flops, *Rollover* and *Agnes of God*, for example. She co-starred with Jeff Bridges in *The*

Morning After and with De Niro in *Stanley and Iris*. Her liberal politics made her hated by many Americans during the Vietnam war, but she has been better known in latter years for the exploitation of her own image in promoting her health and beauty business.

Meryl Streep

Streep's quest for variety in her roles has led to her being identified with parts demanding yet another accent. She was British in *The French Lieutenant's Woman* and *Plenty*, Polish in *Sophie's Choice*, Danish in *Out of Africa* and Australian in *Cry in the Dark*.

Streep first came to prominence as De Niro's lover in *The Deer Hunter* and they appeared together again in *Falling in Love*. She played unsympathetic women in *Manhattan* and *Kramer*

'Yes, I said syphilis!' Karl-Maria Brandauer breaks the bad news to wife Meryl Streep in the 1986 Oscar-winner Out of Africa, *directed by Sidney Pollack. This was one of the numerous movies in which Streep tested out her capacity for foreign accents. In this one she was Danish, in* Sophie's Choice *(1982) she tried on Polish, and in* Plenty *(1985) she was immaculately English.*

vs. Kramer, whilst in *Silkwood* she played the tough, working-class rebel Karen Silkwood who was bumped off for exposing secrets of the American nuclear industry. She has had her bad reviews, notably for *Ironweed* and *She-Devil*. Streep is known to prepare meticulously for her roles and there may be an element of clinical overkill in her acting that prevents her from achieving real presence on screen.

Jessica Lange
. . . .

Lange's acting talents were hardly used in the 1976 remake of *King Kong*, for which she was taken from near obscurity to play the female lead. The film was not a success, but she fared better in *All That Jazz*, *The Postman Always Rings Twice* and *Frances* in which she played the role of Frances Farmer, the thirties star destroyed by a combination of Hollywood and her own self-destructive tendencies. Lange now chooses her roles with care and makes movies that 'say something'. Even the comedy in which she starred opposite Dustin Hoffman, *Tootsie*, reflected something about men-women relationships, whilst *Country*, *Sweet Dreams*, *Crimes of the Heart* and *The Music Box* all attempt to reflect aspects of contemporary society.

Sigourney Weaver

Weaver achieved star status in her role of Ripley in *Alien* and again played the feminist hero in the sequel, *Aliens*. She starred opposite Mel Gibson in *The Year of Living Dangerously* and had a great success in *Ghostbusters*. She played the baddie in *Working Girl* and the goodie in *Gorillas in the Mist*. Weaver has looks, intelligence and strength on screen – a major star.

Kathleen Turner

Turner combines a 'new woman' persona with the allure of the old-time Hollywood beauty queens. She made her first big impression in *Body Heat* playing a spider woman who frames William Hurt, in a virtual remake of *Double Indemnity*. Then she went against image and starred as the overweight romantic novelist in *Romancing the Stone*. In *Prizzi's Honor* she played a rather unconvincing ruthless hit-woman, whilst in the Ken Russell-directed *Crimes of Passion*, she was a career-woman-turned-prostitute. She reluctantly made *Jewel of the Nile*, the sequel to *Romancing*, and then appeared in the title role in *Peggy Sue Got Married*. She actually lost husband William Hurt in *The Accidental Tourist* to Geena Davis, which seemed almost unbelievable, and managed to more or less destroy her fictional husband in *Wars of the Roses*. Another strong role for her came along when she played the private detective, *V.I. Warshawski*.

Debra Winger

A spiky, off-the-wall image has been created for Winger in movies such as *An Officer and a Gentleman* and *Terms of Endearment*. She is usually allowed to be unglamorous in her roles, although the dowdy young woman at some point in the screenplay usually turns into the beautiful princess, as in *Officer* and *Black Widow*. Playing Shirley MacLaine's daughter in *Terms of Endearment* did not seem to harm her career, although the bombing at the box-office of *Legal Eagles* in which she co-starred with Robert Redford dented her record of being associated with hit films.

ABOVE
Sigourney Weaver and Bill Murray in the 1984 hit Ghostbusters.

LEFT
Debra Winger in Black Widow *(1987).*

FAR LEFT
Kathleen Turner sets the trap for eager sap, William Hurt, in Body Heat *(1982).*

Susan Sarandon in an early screen role as Cathy in The Other Side of Midnight, *a hilarious over-the-top melodrama of 1977. Since then Sarandon has graced movies such as* Atlantic City (1980), White Palace (1990) *and* Thelma and Louise (1991).

Jody Foster in Bugsy Malone, *Alan Parker's pastiche of the gangster genre. She has gone on to play strong roles in* The Accused *and* Silence of the Lambs.

Diane Keaton

A rather more 'whiny' and 'kookie' version of Hollywood's new women, Keaton was associated with Woody Allen in the earlier part of her screen career. She was *Annie Hall*, for example, and also appeared in *Love and Death, Interiors* and *Manhattan*. She took on 'tougher' roles in movies that were not directed by Allen: the three *Godfather* movies, in which she played the wife of Michael Corleone, *Looking for Mr Goodbar, Reds, Shoot the Moon, The Little Drummer Girl* and *Crimes of the Heart*. Keaton is a 'mannered' actress, and it remains to be seen whether her screen persona of the slightly eccentric and suffering arty type ensures that she remains a leading star in the nineties.

Susan Sarandon

Two films in the late seventies for the French director, Louis Malle, *Pretty Baby* and *Atlantic City*, helped to establish Sarandon as a sensitive and powerful actress. She did not have a major success after that until *The Witches of Eastwick*, which she followed up with portrayals of sadder-but-wiser 'older women' in *White Palace* and *Thelma and Louise*. Her usual persona is the tough, worldly-wise, attractive working woman. One of the most effective of current female stars.

Jodie Foster

Foster came to prominence as a 'child star' in two Martin Scorsese movies, *Alice Doesn't Live Here Anymore* and *Taxi Driver*, in which she played the twelve-year-old prostitute Iris. After a Disney film *Freaky Friday* and a teen angst pic *Foxes*, she made her mark again in *Hotel New Hampshire* before she won an Oscar for her role in *The Accused*, in which she played a rape victim. However, it was *The Silence of the Lambs* in which she gained the status of major star (and the 1992 Best Actress Oscar); she played Clarice Starling, an FBI agent who tracks down a serial killer with help from one Hannibal Lecter. Foster claims that her character was not just a female version of a male hero, but many disagree with her.

> ◆◆*If you really don't like publicity you don't decide to become an actress. It goes with the territory.*◆◆
>
> **DIANE KEATON**

BELOW

Diane Keaton as the uptight schoolteacher who cruises the singles bars looking for one-night stands in Looking for Mr Goodbar.

STARS

THE STREETWISE STARS

There is a group of stars whose screen persona is hard to categorise, because of the range of parts they take on. These seven male stars emerged from the sixties and after, and all have varying degrees of 'street wisdom'. They represent characteristics of the time and their roles usually involve them in moral dilemmas of a specifically contemporary nature.

Warren Beatty

Beatty first came to prominence playing an angst-ridden teenager in Elia Kazan's *Splendor in the Grass*. His 'pretty boy' image was enhanced when he played a gigolo to middle-aged Vivien Leigh in *The Roman Spring of Mrs Stone*. His first huge success was as Clyde Barrow in *Bonnie and Clyde* in 1967 which he also co-produced.

Beatty's looks and off-screen reputation for womanising meant he had to fight to get roles that stretched him as an actor. *The Parallax View* and *Shampoo*, which he also co-wrote, both attempted to comment on contemporary American society, but it was *Reds* in 1981 which he starred in, produced, co-wrote *and* directed that finally freed him from the charge of being 'lightweight'. In *Reds* he played a left-wing American journalist, John Reed, who was also a communist. Hollywood, anticipating a thaw in the relations between the superpowers, gave Beatty an Oscar for his direction. Since then, Beatty has had to survive the 40-million-dollar flop that was *Ishtar*. *Dick Tracy* brought him another success. Beatty is the brother of Shirley MacLaine.

Jack Nicholson

If 'streetwise' describes Nicholson's screen persona in his earlier films, in relation to his later films, the adjective 'demonic' would certainly have to be added. Nicholson had small parts in some of Roger Corman's horror films of the early sixties and then had a huge success as the alienated and drug-addicted lawyer in *Easy Rider*.

In *Five Easy Pieces, Carnal Knowledge* and *The King of Marvin Gardens* Nicholson played loners imbued with self-dislike, alienated from their roots and out of touch with their feelings. A succession of 'streetwise' roles followed in *The Last Detail, Chinatown, Tommy, One Flew Over the Cuckoo's Nest, The Missouri Breaks* and *The Last Tycoon*. His demonic side first appeared in *The Shining*, was reprised in part in *Terms of Endearment* and replayed in full for *The Witches of Eastwick*. His best performances were in the early seventies when he seemed· to symbolise the restless alienation and cynicism of Nixon's America.

ABOVE

Warren Beatty in the title role of Dick Tracy *(1990). Beatty has had to fight to be taken seriously as an actor, partly because of his good looks and partly because of his Don Juan reputation.*

RIGHT

Jack Nicholson as Daryl Van Horne, aka the Devil, in The Witches of Eastwick *(1987).*

© Touchstone Pictures

Al Pacino

Of New York-Sicilian descent, Pacino became a major star after *The Godfather* and *The Godfather Part II*, playing Michael Corleone. He has balanced powerful roles as a Mafia chieftain with a penchant for outsider parts, such as in *Scarecrow* and *Dog Day Afternoon*. He has played a lawyer defending no hopers in *And Justice for All* and a cop who blows the whistle on police corruption in *Serpico*. His aura of suppressed violence was used in *Cruising* and *Scarface* while a softer, more humane face was revealed in *Bobby Deerfield* and *Author! Author!* Pacino has made comparatively few films because he returns to the theatre frequently, but his name above a film's title usually ensures box-office success, although not with *Revolution* in 1986.

Michael Douglas

Son of Kirk Douglas, Michael first came to prominence in the television cop series *The Streets of San Francisco*. Being second-generation Hollywood probably gave him an early insight into the movie business and he followed in his father's

ABOVE
Al Pacino as Scarface in the 1983 movie of the same name, directed by Brian De Palma. Pacino alternates between 'animalistic' roles and lovable oafs, as in Frankie and Johnny *(1992). He made his reputation as Michael Corleone in the* Godfather *movies.*

footsteps by becoming a major star, but he also became a producer. He co-produced *One Flew Over the Cuckoo's Nest* and then achieved success as an actor in *Coma, The China Syndrome, Romancing the Stone* and *A Chorus Line*. In 1987 he really hit the jackpot with two major hits, *Fatal Attraction*, where he played an errant husband who pays heavily for his adultery with Glenn Close, and *Wall Street*, in which he played a very rich but unscrupulous dealer in junk bonds. In *The Wars of the Roses* he was again in the midst of marital trouble. For many, Douglas *fils* lacks the charisma of his dad, but there is no doubting his talent as a star-entrepreneur.

Jeff Bridges

Son of Lloyd Bridges, Jeff's first major film was *The Last Picture Show*, directed by Peter Bogdanovich. He often plays charming rogues as in *Bad Company, Thunderbolt and Lightning* and *Stay Hungry*. That charm can also be used to suggest hidden pathological intent as in *Jagged Edge* and *The Morning After*. Bridges is a very physical actor and also has a talent for communicating worldweary cynicism.

Richard Gere
. . . .

Gere came to prominence with *Days of Heaven* and *Yanks*. His good looks and the impression of overt narcissism were used to good effect in *American Gigolo* and *An Officer and a Gentleman*, the latter confirming his star status. A series of failed films (*Breathless*, *The Cotton Club*, *King David* and *No Mercy*) did his career no good, but *Internal Affairs* and *Pretty Woman* were hits for him.

ABOVE LEFT

Michael Douglas starred with Kathleen Turner in the 1986 The Jewel of the Nile. *Douglas sometimes plays the nice guy, but can play ruthless types like Gordon Gecko in* Wall Street.

ABOVE

Richard Gere was marketed as a male sex object, but recently he has shown signs of breaking free from that stereotype.

LEFT

Jeff Bridges starred with Jane Fonda in the 1986 The Morning After.

Tom Cruise

· · · · · · · · · ·

Cruise plays the brash All-American kid on the make. He appeared in *Taps* and *All the Right Moves* before Coppola used him in *The Outsiders* along with Matt Dillon and Patrick Swayze, both of whom have also gone on to become major stars. *Risky Business* did good business at the box-office, whilst *Top Gun* shot Cruise to major star status.

Scorsese's sequel to *The Hustler*, *The Color of Money*, was one of that director's failures, but it did Cruise's image as the hard-nosed street kid no harm. *Far and Away*, co-starring his wife, Nicole Kidman, was another winner for the young star, who can probably look forward to many years at the top if he can develop his screen persona beyond the ambitious, ruthless-young-man image he has created so far.

ABOVE

Tom Cruise poses heroically in the cockpit for Top Gun *(1985). Cruise has broken out of bone-headed hero parts to play Hoffman's* cynical brother in Rain Man *(1990) and the paraplegic Vietnam veteran in Oliver Stone's* Born on the Fourth of July *(1990).*

THE TOUGH GUYS

James Cagney
. . . .

Cagney played a succession of gangster roles in movies such as *Public Enemy*, *Angels with Dirty Faces*, *The Roaring Twenties*, *White Heat* and *Love Me or Leave Me*. So convincing was he in these roles that much of his fan mail reputedly came from men in prison. However, Cagney continually chafed against type-casting and won his case by winning an Oscar for his portrayal of Irish-American hoofer, George M. Cohan, in *Yankee Doodle Dandy*. Cagney was also one of those actors who disdain the profession that brings them fame and wealth; but his power and cockiness on screen, where he dominated the frame in a succession of psychopathic roles, won him a huge following. Cagney snarling 'You dirty rat!' is an essential part of any mimic's repertoire.

ABOVE

James Cagney menaces his childhood friend, Pat O'Brien, who has had the bad taste to grow up to be a priest in Angels with Dirty Faces *(1938).*

RIGHT

Cagney was never as convincing as a cowboy as he was as a gangster.

John Wayne

For some reason known as 'The Duke', Wayne evoked strong responses among moviegoers and non-moviegoers. Fans loved him for his stature and presence on screen; detracters hated him for his over-emphatic macho image and his extreme right-wing views. No-one could deny his box-office impact, however; after *Stagecoach* (1939) established him as a star, he became Hollywood's most bankable asset in a succession of movies, most of which were far from memorable. His best work was done for two directors: John Ford and

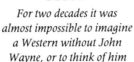

BELOW

For two decades it was almost impossible to imagine a Western without John Wayne, or to think of him without his cowboy boots on.

Howard Hawks. Ford directed him in *Stagecoach*, *The Long Voyage Home*, *Three Godfathers*, *Fort Apache*, *She Wore a Yellow Ribbon*, *Rio Grande*, *The Quiet Man*, *The Searchers*, *The Man Who Shot Liberty Valance* and *Donovan's Reef*; Hawks in *Red River*, *Rio Bravo* and *El Dorado*. Wayne won an Oscar for his role as Rooster Cogburn in *True Grit*, but it is the movies he made with Ford and Hawks he will be remembered for.

Wayne's political views led him to support the persecution of liberals and lefties in Hollywood during the McCarthyite investigations. There was even talk of his standing as Goldwater's vice-presidential candidate in the 1964 election, but that might not now appear any more risible than the fact that America twice elected Ronald Reagan to the Presidency!

Humphrey Bogart

Bogart, or 'Bogey', has a cult status close to that of Monroe and Dean. He symbolised the tough guy with integrity, the kind of guy whom you'd want around if things turned ugly, but on whom you could also count to do the decent thing. These characteristics made him a natural for the part of Philip Marlowe in *The Big Sleep* and Sam Spade in *The Maltese Falcon*. His role as Rick in *Casablanca* also reflected the 'Bogey' persona: tough, cynical, worldly but with a heart of gold under that veneer of nihilism. When Woody Allen is having difficulties with women in *Play It Again, Sam* he turns to Bogart (or an actor impersonating Bogey) for advice.

The Bogart persona is a favourite with most professional and amateur impersonators: dressed in a fairly shabby raincoat, with the ever-present cigarette, the imitation Bogart usually does an abbreviated version of his speeches in the famous last scene of *Casablanca*: 'It doesn't take a genius to figure that the problems of three little people don't amount to a hill of beans in this crazy world . . .'. Bogart was married four times; his last marriage to Lauren Bacall, with whom he made *To Have and Have Not*, *The Big Sleep* and *Key Largo*, was by far the most successful. Happiness with Bacall coincided with later film triumphs such as the Oscar he won for his role in *The African Queen* and his performance as Captain Queeg in *The Caine Mutiny*. However, cancer cut short his life in 1957, probably because of the accumulative effect of too much smoking and drinking. But the Bogart persona lives on.

Alan Ladd
. . . .

Ladd became a star after *This Gun for Hire* (1942); his co-star was Veronica Lake and he went on to make *The Glass Key* and *The Blue Dahlia* with her. Raymond Chandler wrote that Ladd was a small boy's idea of a tough guy, and certainly Ladd suffered from 'sizist' jokes all his career because of his diminutive stature. But at the peak of his career he was enormously popular, partly because of his brooding, choirboy features that suggested imminent violence. His best part was Shane in the western of the same name. Despite this huge success, Ladd continued to feel insecure and he became an alcoholic. He died in 1964 at the age of forty-seven. In *Rebel without a Cause*, there is a scene where the tiny teenager, Sal Mineo, opens his high school locker and we see a picture of Alan Ladd stuck on the inside of the locker door. Yes, indeed, a small boy's idea of a tough guy.

Burt Lancaster
. . . .

Lancaster is hard to categorise but many of his roles have involved him in 'tough guy' antics. His first film *The Killers* had him as an ex-gangster waiting stoically for his own demise at the hands of two goons. He played a very tough guy indeed in *Brute Force*, a liberal prison movie directed by Jules Dassin. Lancaster had been a circus acrobat before becoming an actor and he employed these talents in the swashbucklers *The Flame and the Arrow* and *The Crimson Pirate*. But he has always sought to play a broad range of parts and this is reflected in the variety of movies he made in the fifties: *From Here to Eternity*, *Come Back Little Sheba*, *The Rainmaker*, *Vera Cruz*, *Sweet Smell of Success*, *Gunfight at the OK Corral* and *Separate Tables*. He followed these with *Birdman of Alcatraz* and *The Leopard*, which was directed by Luchino Visconti.

Thrillers such as *Seven Days in May* and *Executive Action* suggest Lancaster's politics lean towards the liberal, and he has always been interested in playing people from ethnic minorities, such as *Apache*, *Jim Thorpe – All-American* and *Valdez is Coming*. He had two successes in the eighties: *Atlantic City* and *Local Hero*. He also played Moses for television, and so Lancaster, if he is a tough guy actor, is certainly a versatile tough guy . . .

Kirk Douglas
· · · · · · · · · ·

LEFT
Burt Lancaster looks steely-eyed and determined in The Kentuckian.

Douglas was at one time dubbed 'the most hated man in Hollywood' because of his reputation for aggressiveness and egomania. Another jibe thrown at him has been that he has always wanted to be Burt Lancaster. Certainly their careers have often coincided (*Gunfight at the OK Corral*, *The Devil's Disciple*, *The List of Adrian Messenger*, *Seven Days in May*, *Tough Guys*). Douglas's forte is portraying obsessed, self-destructive loners, which he showed in films such as *Champion*, *Ace in the Hole*, *Detective Story*, *The Bad and the Beautiful*, *Lust for Life* (as Vincent Van Gogh) and *Two Weeks in Another Town*. But he has also played various larger-than-life heroic roles, in particular in *Spartacus*, *Twenty Thousand Leagues Under the Sea*, *Paths of Glory*, *In Harm's Way* and *Cast a Giant Shadow*. His best part? Not everyone will agree, but my vote for this goes to his role in *Lust for Life*.

ABOVE
Kirk Douglas has always had to live down the crack that he's always wanted to be Burt Lancaster. In fact, Douglas is his own man, his forte being the obsessive loner who won't lie down.

LEFT
Alan Ladd said of himself: 'I have the face of an ageing choirboy and the build of an undernourished featherweight. If you can figure out my success on screen, you're a better man than I am.' But success he certainly had in the forties with films such as This Gun for Hire (1942) and The Blue Dahlia (1946).

The Cincinnati Kid (1965) provided Steve McQueen with one of his quinessential roles – a young gambler pretending to the throne of the King himself, played by Edward G. Robinson. McQueen was the screen loner, cold, ambitious and isolated.

Clint Eastwood (right) and Eli Wallach in The Good, the Bad and the Ugly (1966), one of the Italian 'spaghetti' westerns that shot Eastwood to major stardom.

Steve McQueen

McQueen was a macho star who insisted very often on doing his own stunts. In the famous car chase in *Bullitt* he drove the car himself and in the motor-bike escape section in *The Great Escape* he not only rode his own motor-bike but the bike of his supposed pursuer as well. McQueen had an icy quality on screen, which many people liked and which just as many disliked. But enough movie-goers flocked to his films to make him a very big star indeed. His hits include *The Magnificent Seven*, *The Cincinnati Kid*, *The Thomas Crown Affair* and *The Getaway*. He died of cancer at the age of fifty in 1980.

Clint Eastwood

Eastwood was the major macho star of the seventies and eighties. He made his name in the spaghetti westerns, *A Fistful of Dollars*, *For a Few Dollars More* and *The Good, The Bad and The Ugly*. He then struck another goldmine with a series of films in which he played psychopathic cop Harry Callahan: *Dirty Harry*, *The Gauntlet*, *Sudden Impact*. In between he has made action movies such as *Where Eagles Dare* and *The Eiger Sanction*. He sang disastrously in *Paint Your Wagon* but other attempts to break the Eastwood mould have been more successful, notably in *Bronco Billy* and *Honky Tonk Man*.

Eastwood's acting style belongs, as someone once said, to 'the Mount Rushmore school of acting' but audiences and critics seemingly approve. He has branched out into directing with films such as *Play Misty For Me*, *The Outlaw Josey Wales* and *Bird*. Surprisingly, some critics rate him as a director, but it is likely he will be best remembered for his portrayal, if that is not too extravagant a description, of The Man With No Name in the Sergio Leone westerns, and the maniacal Harry Callahan.

ABOVE

*Sylvester Stallone as Rambo
in the 1985 film of the same
name. The Rambo character
made his first appearance in
First Blood (1982), and
Stallone has gone on playing
either Rambo or Rocky in
almost all of his pictures. An
unreconstructed macho star.*

Sylvester Stallone

. . . .

Stallone has specialised in characters whose
biceps are infinitely bigger than their brains. His
brand of over-the-top masculinity is in danger of
giving machismo a bad name. His first and
greatest success was with *Rocky*, which he wrote
for himself to star in. There have been several
sequels and a nightmare vision of the future
would have *Rocky 32* opening in 2010. Another
'character' Stallone has spawned is Rambo, a
vigilante psychopath who has murdered hun-
dreds in his several screen appearances. Stallone
often appears on the front pages of the tabloids,

which delight in deflating the overblown star by
exposing his marital and amatory failures. Stallone is now so rich that it is likely he will be able
to go on making more bloodbath films, at least
until the public decide enough is enough and
refuse to pay good money to see such fare.

Arnold Schwarzenegger

. . . .

Schwarzenegger was a Mr Universe before he
started 'acting'. His first films featured him in his
real-life role as a muscle-man: *Stay Hungry* and
Pumping Iron, but soon he was playing character
roles such as *Conan the Barbarian* and *Conan the*

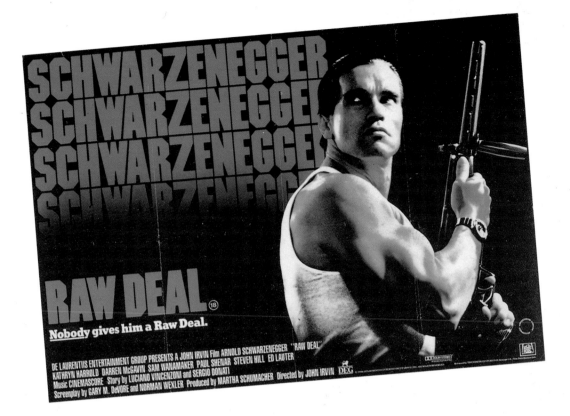

LEFT

Arnold Schwarzenegger is Stallone's main rival in the bone-headed hero stakes, and indeed has outstripped Stallone lately. However, some attempts have been made to soften Arnie's screen image.

BELOW

Mel Gibson in the 1988 thriller Tequilla Sunrise. *Hollywood has used him in macho roles for the most part, but* Hamlet *(1991) shows that the actor is not content to be restricted to stereotypical parts.*

Destroyer. The Terminator, Commando, Red Sonja, Raw Deal, Predator and *Total Recall* have made him the favourite of the Saturday-night video-and-takeaway-Tandoori circuit. He was also encouraged to show off his softer side in the truly cynical *Kindergarten Cop*. He is not as mindless as his roles might suggest; he was in the comedy *Twins*, with Danny De Vito playing his unlikely twin. Married to one of the Kennedy clan, Schwarzenegger is rumoured to have political ambitions. Conan for President in the year 2000?

Mel Gibson

Gibson has now become a Hollywood star and has adapted his Aussie accent accordingly. He has been sold to the cinema-going public on the basis of his boyish good looks and his reputation as a man of action on and off the screen. However, he is definitely a better actor than he has been credited for; he played Hamlet in the 1990 Zefferelli-directed movie and did a creditable job.

He first came to prominence in the *Mad Max* movies, which helped to put him and the new Australian cinema on the cinema map. He was also very effective in Weir's *Gallipoli* and *The Year of Living Dangerously*, and in the Fletcher Christian part in *The Bounty*. However, the movies that really catapulted him to world stardom were the *Lethal Weapon* duo. *Birds on a Wire* with Goldie

Hawn flopped at the box-office, but there is no doubt that Gibson is now established as a major world star. Having proved he can act, perhaps he can consolidate that reputation by working with the better Hollywood directors and making fewer mindless, violent action movies.

THE COMEDY ACTORS

Comedy actors are a different breed from comics like Chaplin and Keaton. Comedy actors are not really professional clowns, they play ordinary people who find themselves in difficulties, and comedy arises as they try to extricate themselves from their predicaments.

William Powell

· · · · · · · · ·

Debonair is the adjective most over-used about Powell, but he was an accomplished comedy actor in movies such as *My Man Godfrey, Love Crazy, Life with Father,* and in the *'Thin Man'* series with co-star Myrna Loy.

Carole Lombard

· · · · · · · · ·

Lombard was an intelligent, tough comedy actress who was killed in an air crash in 1942, leaving Clark Gable a widower. She showed her prowess in *Twentieth Century, My Man Godfrey, Nothing Sacred, They Knew What They Wanted, Mr and Mrs Smith* and *To Be Or Not To Be.*

Rosalind Russell

· · · · · · · · ·

Russell was at her best in comedies such as *The Women, His Girl Friday, My Sister Eileen* and *The Velvet Touch.* She also played dramatic roles in *Night Must Fall, Sister Kenny* and *Picnic.* She was the screen's *Auntie Mame.*

Cary Grant

· · · · · · · · ·

British-born Archie Leach became Cary Grant and went on to become one of Hollywood's greatest stars. Picked by Mae West for *She Done Him Wrong* (1933), Grant was soon a comedy actor in demand in movies such as *The Awful Truth, Bringing Up Baby, His Girl Friday* and *The Philadelphia Story.* His dark good looks also qualified him for straight roles in *Gunga Din, Only Angels Have Wings* and *Suspicion,* the latter directed by Hitchcock who saw something more sinister behind those handsome features, which

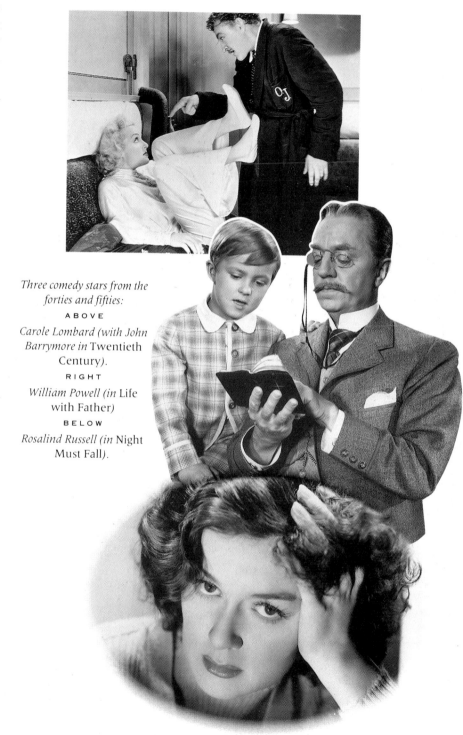

Three comedy stars from the forties and fifties:
ABOVE
Carole Lombard (with John Barrymore in Twentieth Century*).*
RIGHT
William Powell (in Life with Father*)*
BELOW
Rosalind Russell (in Night Must Fall*).*

Jack Lemmon as the gendarme in Billy Wilder's 1963 movie Irma La Douce. *Lemmon and Wilder have repeatedly worked together.*

'This is another fine mess you got me into,' Lemmon seems to be saying to Matthau in this scene from The Front Page (1974). *In Lemmon–Matthau films, Lemmon plays the fall guy to Matthau's con-man.*

Walter Mathau as the irascible half of a geriatric comedy duo in The Sunshine Boys (1975). *The slob-with-the-heart-of-stone is his normal screen image, although all the time Mathau is working hard at being thought lovable by the audience.*

he exploited later in *Notorious*. Other important comedies were *I Was a Male War Bride*, *Monkey Business* and *Operation Petticoat*, which he mixed with straight roles in *North by Northwest*, *An Affair to Remember*, *Indiscreet* and *Charade*. Grant symbolised sophistication for many film-goers, but he was not afraid to show himself as ridiculous in his comedies. Married five times, Grant retired from movies in 1966 to devote himself to promoting cosmetics for an internationally known firm. He died at the age of 84 in 1986 after weathering the passage of time remarkably well.

Jack Lemmon

Lemmon has often been accused of working too hard at the comic effects he aims to achieve, and certainly he could never be said to underplay, but he has been very effective in some movies such as *Some Like It Hot*, *The Apartment*, *How to Murder Your Wife*, *The Fortune Cookie*, *The Odd Couple* and *The Front Page*. Lemmon has been particularly associated in the public's mind with characters in Neil Simon comedies such as *The Out-of-Towners* and *The Prisoner of Second Avenue*. In these movies he plays the harassed American middle-class male, beset by problems of urban violence, bureaucratic red tape and the general hassle of twentieth-century life. He has also played straight roles in *Days of Wine and Roses*, *Save the Tiger*, *The China Syndrome* and *Missing*. His speciality is the decent, average middle-class man all at sea in a world of dishonesty and brutality.

Walter Matthau
· · · · · · · · · ·

A great buddy of Lemmon's, Matthau achieved star status comparatively late in life. Matthau's speciality is the cynical slob, and he has played variations of this stereotype in *The Fortune Cookie*, *The Odd Couple*, *Plaza Suite*, *Kotch*, *The Sunshine Boys*, *The Bad News Bears*, *House Calls* and *California Suite*. He has also played assorted villains in various movies and had the misfortune to play opposite Streisand in *Hello Dolly!*. His critical and sarcastic comments about her indicated that his on-screen persona may reflect a lot of his own personality.

BELOW

A great British comedy actor who never quite realised his potential in films, Peter Sellers in The Mouse that Roared *and as his most popular creation, Inspector Clouseau, from the* Pink Panther *films.*

Peter Sellers
· · · · · · · · · ·

Sellers made his name in the *Goon Show* on British radio, then graduated to British movies such as *The Lady Killers*, *The Smallest Show on Earth*, *I'm All Right, Jack* and *Only Two Can Play*. When he went to Hollywood, his early films such as *Lolita*, *Dr Strangelove* (in which he played three parts) and *The Pink Panther* held promise of a great international career. But his emotional problems and a disastrous run of bad films put his career into reverse. A near-fatal heart attack in 1964 seemed to increase his sour view of life, but he found steady work and success in the series of Inspector Clouseau films that followed *The Pink Panther* after a ten-year gap, although they scarcely stretched him as a comedy actor. One last worthwhile film before he finally succumbed to his heart condition was *Being There* (1979). Sellers once said revealingly, 'If you ask me to play myself, I will not know what to do. I do not know who or what I am.' Sellers was a man who hid behind funny voices.

Danny De Vito

Of diminutive stature, De Vito has become a major comedy star in the eighties in movies such as *Ruthless People*, *Wise Guys*, *Throw Momma from the Train*, *Twins*, *Tin Men*, *The Wars of the Roses* and *Other People's Money*.

Steve Martin

Martin is a talented ex-nightclub comic who first made an impact in *The Jerk*. The commercial disaster that was *Pennies from Heaven* did not sink him, but it took successes such as *Dead Men Don't Wear Plaid* and *Roxanne* to make him a bankable star. *Dirty Rotten Scoundrels* in which he co-starred with Michael Caine was a remake of the Brando-Niven *Bedtime Story*. *Parenthood* starred him with Mary Steenburgen.

TOP
Danny De Vito and Helen Slater in the 1986 comedy Ruthless People. *De Vito first came to prominence in* One Flew over the Cuckoo's Nest *(1976).*

ABOVE
Steve Martin in Roxanne *(1986), an updated version of* Cyrano de Bergerac.

THREE GREAT STARS

Marlon Brando, George C. Scott and Robert De Niro qualify for the accolade of all-time greats but they defy categorisation, although some critics have tried to pigeon-hole them.

Marlon Brando

Born in 1924 in Omaha, Nebraska, Brando played Stanley Kowalski in *A Streetcar Named Desire* on Broadway before starring in Elia Kazan's film version. This part created the Brando stereotype: the incoherent, primitive and rapacious male animal. However, the tabloids who peddled that stereotype conveniently ignored the range of parts that the 'Method' actor undertook: the paraplegic in *The Men* (1950), his first movie, the Mexican revolutionary in *Viva Zapata*, Mark Antony in *Julius Caesar* and the motor-bike gang leader in *The Wild One*. His most memorable part in the early part of his film career was in *On the Waterfront*. Again he played an incoherent, potentially violent man, but Brando revealed reserves of tenderness and vulnerability in the character, thereby creating one of the all-time great screen performances.

Brando has never really hidden his contempt for his profession; perhaps his contempt is reserved more for the business end of the film business than for film acting itself, but his lack of care has led him into making some movie stinkers: *Desiree*, *The Teahouse of the August Moon*, *Sayonara*, *Bedtime Story* and *Candy*. But his range is staggering: from Shakespeare to musicals, from intense drama to comedies. He was a charming Sky Masterson in *Guys and Dolls* and an effete Fletcher Christian in *Mutiny on the Bounty*. It was *Bounty* that marked a break with the Hollywood moguls who complained about long delays in the shooting of the film because of Brando's whims. How much of that is true and what the Brando version of events is lies in obscurity, because the actor has gradually withdrawn from the public eye and now lives in Hawaii for the most part (though an autobiography is promised).

BELOW

Marlon Brando. Brando has always resisted the marketing ploys of Hollywood, insisting on being his own man and even refusing an Oscar along the way. However, when he does deign to make a movie, this does not prevent him insisting on huge fees.

He directed *One Eyed Jacks* in 1960, starred in *The Chase* and *Reflections in a Golden Eye* in the sixties, the only two decent movies he made in that decade, and then appeared as Don Corleone in *The Godfather* in 1972. When the Academy awarded him an Oscar, he sent an Indian woman to collect it in order to draw attention to the plight of contemporary Indians in America. Increasingly Brando has devoted himself to causes and his later films have reflected his political leanings: *Queimada*, *Roots: the New Generation* (for television), *Apocalypse Now*, *The Formula* and *A Dry White Season*. Brando has now left behind the tag of Method actor and the image of Stanley Kowalski, and won himself a unique position in this profession of acting which he so despises.

George C. Scott

Scott is another great screen actor with a contempt for his profession. His self-loathing, by his own testimony, brought him to the brink of total breakdown on numerous occasions and he has had to fight periods when he just wanted to lose himself in a bottle. Yet on screen he is one of the most powerful presences ever seen.

He was first noticed as the prosecutor in *Anatomy of a Murder*, but really made his mark as the smooth but ruthless gangster in *The Hustler*. Scott's range as an actor was reflected in his comic portrayal of Buck Turgidson in *Dr Strangelove*, one of his greatest screen performances. A series of indifferent movies followed, but he hit the jackpot with his portrayal of George S.

Patton in *Patton* (1970). Awarded an Oscar, he refused the honour, stating that he disagreed with actors being judged in competition with one another. Solid performances in *The Last Run* and *The Hospital* followed, but again Scott seemed fairly indifferent to the movies he appeared in. *The Day of the Dolphin* (1973), *Islands in the Stream* and *Movie Movie* were the best of the seventies. In *Movie Movie* he again showed his talent for comedy, while in Paul Schrader's *Hardcore* he played a religious man looking for his lost daughter in a pornographic underworld. Scott has since contented himself with appearing in television movies, thereby paying his bills for tax and alimony. The fact that he has made so few good movies is a matter of regret, although he would almost certainly refute that.

BELOW

George C. Scott in his most famous role as General Patton in Patton *(1970). Scott's screen presence is powerful. He has the voice, the rugged looks and the authority to take on the big parts, but too often his disdain for the craft of acting has led him to mark time in lesser roles.*

Robert De Niro
· · · · · · · · ·

De Niro first came to real prominence with his performance as Johnny Boy in Martin Scorsese's *Mean Streets*. Scorsese encouraged his actors to improvise and use aspects of their own personalities; this approach paid off particularly in the scenes between De Niro and Harvey Keitel. Keitel and De Niro again appeared together in Scorsese's *Taxi Driver*, surely the best American film of the seventies, and once more their improvisational technique paid off in terms of the realism of the scenes between them. In between these two movies, De Niro starred in *The Godfather Part II* in which he played the younger Don Corleone, Brando's part in *The Godfather*.

It was appropriate that De Niro played Corleone as a younger man because in many ways he is Brando's natural successor in Hollywood. He has the same range of abilities: he is expert at comedy (*New York, New York, King of Comedy, Brazil, Midnight Run*); can play romantic roles

(*Falling in Love*); exudes repressed and expressed violence (*Raging Bull, The Deer Hunter, Once Upon a Time in America, The Mission, The Untouchables*) and plays straight intense dramatic roles (*True Confessions, Angel Heart* and *Stanley and Iris*). De Niro goes to excessive lengths to prepare for his roles, for example adding 60 extra pounds to his frame to play Jake La Motta in *Raging Bull*; it may be that, like many actors, De Niro hides from himself in the parts he plays. Whatever the explanation for what makes De Niro tick, he remains a great star.

> ♦♦*There's nothing so offensive to me as watching an actor with his ego.*♦♦
>
> **ROBERT DE NIRO**

ABOVE
Robert De Niro as Travis Bickle in Taxi Driver *(1976). De Niro can play psychopaths with disturbing authenticity, as he displayed in this and other Scorsese-directed films, including* Goodfellas *(1990) and* Cape Fear *(1992). However, he can play comedy too, as in* New York, New York *(1977) and* King of Comedy *(1984), again both directed by Scorsese.*

CHILD STAR

Shirley Temple
. . . .

Of all the Hollywood child stars, Temple was the most popular. Jackie Coogan and Jackie Cooper pre-dated her as big box-office draws, but they could not rival her popularity in the thirties when she topped the 'most popular stars' list year after year. *Little Miss Marker*, *Baby Takes a Bow*, *The Little Colonel*, *Curly Top*, *The Littlest Rebel*, *Dimples*, *Wee Willie Winkie* and *The Little Princess* were some of her box-office winners, a record of success that made Louis B. Mayer green with envy and desperate to get Temple for the role of Dorothy in *The Wizard of Oz*. Fortunately, the part went to Judy Garland, and the world was saved from the sight and sound of the entirely resistible Temple singing 'Over the Rainbow'. When adult life came, she was unable to carve herself out a new career, unlike the leading child star of the next decade, Elizabeth Taylor. Her only real rival at the box-office was Margaret O'Brien, MGM's answer to Temple. The adult Shirley Temple became US Ambassador to the United Nations. Well, Ronald Reagan became President. What's so strange about that?

LEFT

A studio portrait of the 'adorable moppet', Shirley Temple. It is difficult to see why Temple was at the top of the box-office league in the thirties. However, as some wag said, no one ever went broke by underestimating the taste of the general public.

THE BRITISH

It may seem disproportionate to give a section over to British stars who have made it internationally, but those who appear here are difficult to categorise in terms of Hollywood archetypes. Each of them, with one exception, started in British films and then made it in Hollywood — but remained essentially British in the parts they played.

James Mason

Mason made his name in a series of Gainsborough melodramas such as *The Man in Grey*, *The Seventh Veil* and *The Wicked Lady*. He gave a fine performance as an IRA gunman in *Odd Man Out*, then went to Hollywood and starred in *Caught*, *Pandora and the Flying Dutchman* and as Rommel in *The Desert Fox*. He was Brutus in *Julius Caesar* and the self-destructive star in *A Star is*

Born, one of his finest performances. He was the villain in Hitchcock's *North by Northwest* and Humbert Humbert in *Lolita*. Excellent performances followed in *The Pumpkin Eater*, *The Deadly Affair*, *Autobiography of a Princess* and *The Shooting Party* (1984), his last film. Mason was one of the most accomplished screen actors Britain has ever produced.

Deborah Kerr

Scots-born Kerr made *The Life and Death of Colonel Blimp*, *I See a Dark Stranger* and *Black Narcissus* before going to Hollywood and starring in *King Solomon's Mines*, *Quo Vadis*, *From Here to Eternity*, *The King and I*, *Tea and Sympathy*, *Heaven Knows, Mr Allison* and *Separate Tables*. In the sixties she found good roles harder to come by and resorted to television and stage appearances.

BELOW
James Mason as Brutus in Julius Caesar (1953). Mason struggled to gain roles worthy of his talents, both in his early years in Britain and then in Hollywood. An actor rather than a star, Mason did succeed in leaving numerous fine performances on film for us to remember him by.

RIGHT

Vivien Leigh as Lady Hamilton in the 1941 movie of that name. Her outstanding beauty meant critics could not see her acting talent beneath the looks. She will always be remembered for her Scarlett O'Hara, however.

Vivien Leigh

Blessed with outstanding beauty, Leigh also found her looks somewhat of a handicap when it came to being taken seriously as an actress. Married for many years to Laurence Olivier, she may also have suffered from being perceived as 'Mrs Olivier'. However, she was excellent as Scarlett O'Hara in *Gone with the Wind* and had successes in *Waterloo Bridge* and *Lady Hamilton*. Her more serious film roles in *Caesar and Cleopatra* and *Anna Karenina* did not bring her critical praise. Her last important screen role was as Blanche Dubois opposite Brando in *A Streetcar Named Desire*. Ill-health shortened her life and she died at the age of 54 in 1967.

Trevor Howard

Howard had a powerful screen presence that very few other British actors have possessed. He was excellent in *Brief Encounter* and *The Third Man*, but his performances in *Outcast of the Islands* and *The Heart of the Matter* are two of the best ever in British films. He made some Hollywood movies, notably as Captain Bligh in the Brando *Mutiny on the Bounty*, but he never became a Hollywood star.

Jean Simmons

Simmons's best-known British films are *Great Expectations* (as Estelle), *Black Narcissus* (as an Indian girl), *The Blue Lagoon* (shipwrecked on a desert island with Donald Houston) and *Hamlet*, Olivier's choice for his Ophelia. Hollywood gave her a string of atrocious parts until *Guys and Dolls*, *The Big Country*, *Elmer Gantry*, *Spartacus* and *The Grass is Greener*. Then her career

AUDREY HEPBURN
and GREGORY PECK

her start in British pictures such as *Laughter in Paradise* and *The Lavender Hill Mob*. *Roman Holiday* made her a star in Hollywood and this success was followed by a string of important films: *Sabrina, War and Peace, Funny Face, The Nun's Story, Breakfast at Tiffany's, Charade* and *My Fair Lady*. She usually played child-women, an archetype that won her many ardent fans but which made it more difficult for her to get worthwhile parts in the seventies and eighties. She played the angel in *Always*, Spielberg's 1990 remake of *A Guy Named Joe*.

Julie Andrews

Andrews made her name in the stage version of *My Fair Lady* but lost out to Audrey Hepburn when the film came along. She has tried hard to cast off the squeaky-clean image she then gained from *The Sound of Music* and *Mary Poppins*, determinedly trying to create a sexual image for herself in *The Americanisation of Emily, Darling Lili, 10, S.O.B., Victor/Victoria* and *The Man Who Loved Women*. However, her essential scrubbed English nanny persona has never really deserted her. She has appeared in several movies directed by her husband, Blake Edwards.

Richard Burton

At times Burton was more famous for his off-screen antics than his on-screen performances: his drinking bouts, his marriages to Elizabeth Taylor, his conspicuous consumption of luxury goods. After appearing in a number of forgettable British films, Burton made *My Cousin Rachel* in Hollywood, then the first CinemaScope film *The Robe*, followed by *The Desert Rats, Alexander the Great* and *Bitter Victory*. His career took an upturn with *Cleopatra* and his marriage to Taylor – he then became the male half of the Taylor-Burton industry. But decent movies were still few and far between. Possible exceptions, depending on taste, were *Who's Afraid of Virginia Woolf, The Spy Who Came in from the Cold, The Taming of the Shrew* and *The Comedians*. He played the hero in *Where Eagles Dare* opposite Eastwood, hammed it up as Henry VIII in *Anne of the Thousand Days*, and was awful in awful movies such as *Blackbeard, Exorcist II* and *The Wild Geese*. His last film, *1984*, gave him a decent part and he was effective in it. His was a lost talent.

seemed to stagnate and lately she has made very few films. Husbands include Stewart Granger and Richard Brooks, the director.

John Mills

Mills never made it in Hollywood, probably because he is so irretrievably British. A succession of war movies established him as the archetypal British officer, stiff upper-lip and terribly, terribly decent: *In Which We Serve, We Dive at Dawn, The Way to the Stars, Morning Departure, The Colditz Story, Above Us the Waves, Dunkirk* and *Ice Cold in Alex*. He was also a military man in *Tunes of Glory* and *Oh What a Lovely War*. In between war heroics, he played *Scott of the Antarctic* and Mr Polly in *The History of Mr Polly*. Hollywood movies include *War and Peace, King Rat, Ryan's Daughter* (playing a deaf mute, for which he won an Oscar) and *Oklahoma Crude*. But for many film fans he will be remembered as the secret weapon the Gerries never had.

Audrey Hepburn

Actually, strictly speaking, Hepburn was Belgian-born and of Irish-Dutch parentage, but she made

ABOVE

Audrey Hepburn looks up to Gregory Peck in the 1953 romance Roman Holiday. *'Elfin' is one of the cliché adjectives used to describe Hepburn, but 'elfinness' soon reaches its 'sell-by' date, which may account for the fact that Hepburn's roles have been few and far between since the mid-seventies.*

Laurence Olivier
. . . .

Olivier was a great stage *and* screen actor. One of the few actors to master both mediums, he appeared in British movies such as *Fire over England* and *The Divorce of Lady X* before going to Hollywood to star in *Wuthering Heights* (during the shooting of which Sam Goldwyn complained about this 'dirty British actor'). Hollywood, or Greta Garbo, had already rebuffed him by turning him down for a part in *Queen Christina*. He played Max De Winter in *Rebecca* and Darcy in *Pride and Prejudice*, then he starred in, and directed, *Henry V* and *Hamlet*. Later film triumphs included *Carrie*, *Richard III* (which he also directed), *Spartacus* and *The Entertainer*. *Sleuth* and *Marathon Man* were the best of the movies he made in the latter part of his movie career, when he tended to take parts for the money, including playing Neil Diamond's father in *The Jazz Singer*. Olivier could have remained a matinee idol, because he had the looks and style for that role, but he wanted to be much more than that.

Sean Connery
. . . .

There is a lot more to Sean Connery than the James Bond tag. Incomparably the best of the Bond actors (although when you consider the

ABOVE

Laurence Olivier in Richard III. *Olivier was one of the few actors to master both the stage and the screen. Recent attempts to debunk his reputation have failed to destroy his status. Yes, he could be bad on screen* (Othello; 1965 and The Jazz Singer; 1981 for example)*, but he also gave many fine performances.*

competition, that's not saying much), Connery has also worked for Hitchcock in *Marnie*, for Martin Ritt in *The Molly Maguires* and John Boorman in *Zardoz*. He played an Arab chieftain in *The Wind and the Lion* where he got away with his Scottish brogue in the desert, and was an elderly Robin Hood in *Robin and Marian*. He returned to the Bond part in 1983 (*Never Say Never Again*), but his career has had a great boost lately with *The Name of the Rose*, *The Untouchables* and *Indiana Jones and the Final Crusade*, in which he played Harrison Ford's dad. One of the few Scottish actors to make it internationally, Connery has ploughed some of his money back into helping deprived Scottish youth get a decent start in life. Even when playing tough, Connery has a likeable quality that gains him fans who normally do not respond to machismo.

Peter O'Toole
. . . .

O'Toole is another of those British actors famous for their drinking and generally self-destructive ways. He became a star after playing Lawrence of Arabia in David Lean's film, then played Henry II to Burton's Becket in *Becket*, but also appeared in some stinkers such as *What's New, Pussycat?*, *Casino Royale* and *Goodbye Mr Chips*. *The Lion in Winter* was one of his more notable films, but a

Sean Connery first played James Bond in Dr No *in 1962, and it seemed for a while after that he would never escape the straitjacket of the role. However, in the last decade his career has taken a remarkable new direction and he is once again a major international star.*

success was as Albert Seaton in *Saturday Night and Sunday Morning*, the archetypal working-class rebel figure. He was the first of the British stars who could play working-class men with authenticity; hitherto we had to suffer Johnny Mills or Stewart Granger going downmarket. Finney had a popular success with *Tom Jones*, but none of his other sixties movies made much of a mark, including the underrated *Charlie Bubbles* which he directed himself. He was amusing in *Gumshoe*, excruciating as Hercule Poirot in *Murder on the Orient Express*, but compelling in *Shoot the Moon* and *The Dresser*. Too many movies like *Scrooge*, *Annie* and *Under the Volcano* have restricted the number of decent performances he has given on screen. Finney is a physical actor of great screen potential; a few times that potential has been tapped.

Julie Christie

Christie came to prominence in the 1963 *Billy Liar* and then won an Oscar for her performance in the lamentable *Darling*. Her career reached something of a peak with *Doctor Zhivago*, but she was woefully miscast in *Far from the Madding Crowd*. Two better roles came her way in *Petulia* and *The Go-Between*. She co-starred with Warren Beatty in *McCabe and Mrs Miller*, definitely one of her better films, as was Nicholas Roeg's *Don't Look Now*. *Shampoo* and *Nashville* were two further hits for her, but she now chooses to work only occasionally when a film really interests her; of her subsequent films only *Heat and Dust* has caused much interest.

succession of box-office failures, together with his reputation for boozing, put his film career in jeopardy. On stage he was so bad as Macbeth at the Old Vic that people queued to see him go over-the-top every night. His film career was rescued to a certain extent by *The Stunt Man* and *My Favourite Year*. Omar Sharif has called him 'the prototype of the ham' and this is an accurate summation, except to say that haminess sometimes works in particular roles on screen.

Julie Christie as Bathsheba in Far from the Madding Crowd *(1967). Unfortunately, she seemed too much of a sixties person for that nineteenth-century tale, but she has been more successful in movies set in modern times, such as* Shampoo *(1975).*

♦♦*I was sort of Vanessa Redgrave of the fifties.*♦♦
PETER O'TOOLE

Albert Finney

Finney's stage and screen career has been inconsistent because he has decided that there are more things to life than being a successful and famous actor. Hence, his screen appearances have been spasmodic, although some of his performances reveal that he has what it takes to be a really expert movie actor. His first big

THE FRENCH

Jean Gabin

. . . .

Jean Gabin could play proletarian heroes, tough guys and members of the officer class. He starred in some of the great French classics: *La Grande Illusion*, *Quai des Brumes*, *La Bête Humaine* and *Le Jour Se Lève*. He frequently played gangsters in movies such as *Touchez pas au Grisbi* and *The Sicilian*. He also played Inspector Maigret in a series of movies, but there is no doubt that it will be for the pre-war movies that Gabin will be best remembered, when he seemed to typify something essentially French: style, toughness mixed with tenderness, honesty and a romantic aura.

Yves Montand

. . . .

Gabin's natural successor, Montand started as a singer, then graduated to serious roles. He first came to international prominence in *Wages of Fear* (1953). He made *Let's Make Love* (1960) with Marilyn Monroe and had a much-publicised affair with her. However, his Hollywood career did not take off and he returned to Europe to make films such as *The War is Over*, *Vivre Pour Vivre*, *The Red Circle* and *Le Sauvage*. He returned to Hollywood in 1970 to make *On a Clear Day You Can See Forever* with Streisand and Vincente Minnelli. In the latter part of his career he had great success with *Jean de Florette* and *Manon des Sources*.

Montand died in 1991 at the age of seventy. The French mourned him deeply; most remembered him as the young protégé of Edith Piaf, the errant but loving husband of Simone Signoret and as a French Bogart.

Simone Signoret

. . . .

One of those French actresses who seemed to symbolise something eternally French, Signoret had a long and distinguished career in French movies from 1942 to 1981. Her best-known films are *La Ronde*, *Casque d'Or*, *Les Diaboliques* and *Le Mort en Ce Jardin*. Foreign films included *Room at the Top*, *Ship of Fools*, *The Deadly Affair* and *Games*.

ABOVE

Yves Montand hands it out in one of his most famous roles, Wages of Fear *(1953). When Montand died in 1991, France went into mourning: he symbolised something significant to the French, although he was actually of Italian origin.*

LEFT

Brigitte Bardot was the 'sex-kitten' of the fifties, created by her then-husband Roger Vadim, who would later try to do the same thing with Jane Fonda. Bardot eventually tired of sexual stereotyping and gave up on her film career. Who can blame her?

Brigitte Bardot

Bardot became a sex symbol in the fifties, largely due to her roles in movies directed by her then-husband, Roger Vadim: *And God Created Woman* and *Heaven Fell That Night*. Dubbed a 'sex kitten' Bardot never managed to break free from that stereotype, although she tried in movies such as *The Truth*, *Contempt* and *Shalako*.

Philippe Noiret

Noiret has become better known internationally through performances in recently successful films, *Life and Nothing But* and *Cinema Paradiso*, but he has had a screen career spanning four decades. He was in *La Grande Bouffe* (*Blow Out*), Francesco Rosi's *Three Brothers* and Tavernier's *The Clockmaker*. He has appeared in Hitchcock's *Topaz*, *Justine*, *Murphy's War* and *Round Midnight*. He has become almost as recognizable a symbol of Frenchness as Gabin in his day.

BELOW
Catherine Deneuve in Belle de Jour *(1966), directed by Luis Buñuel. Blessed with classic good looks, Deneuve scarcely had to do more on screen than flesh out many a male fantasy.*

Jeanne Moreau

Moreau came to prominence with *Les Amants* (1959) and *Les Liaisons Dangereuses* (1960). Antonioni used her beautiful but ravaged features in *La Notte* and Truffaut saw her as a symbol of femininity in *Jules et Jim*. She worked with Luis Buñuel in *Diary of a Chambermaid* and Orson Welles in *Chimes at Midnight*.

Gerard Depardieu

Depardieu has graduated from animalistic parts to portraying more sensitive men in *Le Dernier Metro*, *The Woman Next Door*, *Danton*, *Jean de Florette*, *Trop Belle Pour Toi*, *Cyrano de Bergerac*, *Green Card* and *Uranus*. Indeed, the hulk has turned out to be a fine screen actor.

Catherine Deneuve

Deneuve became a symbol of French beauty in art-house movies such as *Les Parapluies de Cherbourg*, *Les Demoiselles de Rochefort*, *Mayerling* and *The Hunger*. Polanski used her rather differently in *Repulsion*. Luis Buñuel also gave her more opportunity than usual in *Belle de Jour* and then in *Tristana*, while François Truffaut starred her in *Le Sauvage* and *Le Dernier Metro*.

Isabelle Huppert

Huppert emerged as one of the leading screen actresses in France in the seventies and eighties. Her first big success was as the victim heroine of *The Lacemaker*, then she had a change of pace as the murderer, *Violette Nozière*. Cimino followed this change of style by casting her as the gun-toting madame in *Heaven's Gate*. Her lack of classical beauty and her limited English may mean that international stardom will elude her, but she still commands strong parts, as she showed when she played the title role in Claude Chabrol's version of Flaubert's classic novel, *Madame Bovary*.

THE ITALIANS

Anna Magnani

Magnani played powerful, passionate women to the hilt. There was never underplaying when she was on screen, but she was highly effective in Rossellini's *Open City* and De Sica's *The Miracle*. Hollywood tried to make an international star of her in movies such as *The Rose Tattoo*, *Wild is the Wind* and *The Fugitive Kind* (with Marlon Brando), but she could never really be fitted into the Hollywood mould. After her Hollywood efforts, she failed to regain her former status in her domestic industry and died at the comparatively early age of 66.

Gina Lollobrigida

'La Lollo', as she was known, was, unlike Magnani, never accused of overacting; indeed, the debate was whether she ever acted at all. She played mindless, busty and plastic beauties in a succession of movies of which *Fanfan la Tulipe*, *Belles de Nuit*, *Bread, Love and Dreams*, *Beat the Devil*, *Trapeze*, *Solomon and Sheba* and *Woman of Straw* were the most successful. Her screen image must have set back the cause of the liberation of Italian women for many years.

RIGHT

Gina Lollobrigida showing what made her famous in the Italian-made film that secured her fame, Pane, Amore e Fantasia *(Bread, Love and Dreams; 1954).*

Sophia Loren
· · · · · · · · · ·

La Loren has her supporters who say she is a talented actress. These fans cite movies such as *Desire under the Elms*, *Two Women* and *The Condemned of Altona* as evidence of this. But the public remember her mostly for her exposure in movies such as *Boy on a Dolphin*, *Heller in Pink Tights*, *El Cid*, *The Millionairess*, *Arabesque* and *Man of La Mancha*. Married to producer Carlo Ponti, Loren has had her difficulties with the Italian tax authorities, spending a short spell in jail. She has a cold quality on screen which prevents her, for some, from being watchable. However, she was an international star for a number of years.

LEFT
Sophia Loren – a charismatic presence, although the critics are divided on her acting abilities. Her best roles were in Two Women *(1961), which was directed by Vittorio de Sica, and* The Millionairess *(1961), directed by Anthony Asquith.*

Marcello Mastroianni
· · · · · · · · · ·

A handsome star who is also an intelligent actor, Mastroianni has worked with Fellini in *La Dolce Vita* and *8½* and Antonioni in *La Notte*. Other important films have included *The Stranger*, *Yesterday, Today and Tomorrow*, *Casanova '70 La Grande Bouffe* and, with Fellini again, *Fred and Ginger*. Undoubtedly Mastroianni has occasionally taken roles that he can amble through, but generally he has brought a skilful technique to his many screen appearances.

RIGHT
Marcello Mastroianni as a modern-day Casanova, in Casanova '70, *directed by Mario Monicelli. Mastroianni's best work was done for directors Michelangelo Antonioni and Federico Fellini.*

THE
MOVIE
WORLD

INSET

Mel Gibson in Mad Max II. *The combination of comic-strip inspired plot and post-apocalypse setting drew large crowds and produced three films in the series.*

LEFT

A vast battery of lights floods the huge, almost empty stage during the making of Federico Fellini's Fellini Satyricon (1969). *This is all part of the 'cinematic apparatus', the means by which filmmakers turn their fantasies into our fantasies (that is, if we allow that to happen). Cinema is a technological art, the only art that was created from scratch during this century.*

> ◆◆*Give me any two pages of the Bible and I'll give you a picture.*◆◆
>
> CECIL B. DE MILLE

IN HIS EXCELLENT book, *America in the Dark*, David Thomson writes about 'Hollywood and the gift of unreality'. His argument is that Hollywood created a separate reality, indeed an alternative reality, which obeyed different rules from the reality of everyday life. Indeed, the prime function of the movies was to create unreality for the masses. Whenever films did touch on social issues or life as we know it, Hollywood managed to distort the reality of things to provide reassuring messages and re-solutions. In life, there may be a few happy endings; in Hollywood, there is *always* a happy ending. Its staple fare is the 'feel good' movie. It sells hope and solace. From Busby Berkeley musicals to Steve Martin comedies, from Bette Davis melodramas to Bette Midler farces, the message has remained much the same: trust in the American Way of Life and, even though things may appear hopeless, a happy ending will somehow be conjured up for you.

However, not even Hollywood can provide endlessly carefree movies of the Andy Hardy and *Lassie Come Home* variety. There have to be bumpy rides along the way before the uplifting chords of the final reprise of the score usher us out of the cinema to face real life again. You can fool most of the people a lot of the time, but not all of the customers all of the time, so signs of social conflict or contradictions must be repre-sented in some movies. And that is where genre movies come in: the westerns, the musicals, the gangster movies, the horror flicks, the science fiction epics, the adventure films, the swash-bucklers, the screwball comedies, the war pic-tures, the epics, the social issue movies.

Genres made commercial sense because the studios could sell an easily identifiable product to a mass audience accustomed to buying that product. However, genre movies were also a useful means of representing a conflict within society, often between an individual and the community, and reaching a compromise resolu-tion that reinforced the values of the commun-ity. Thus, a western such as *Shane* could show the conflict between a greedy rancher and small

BELOW

Mickey Rooney explains his latest business scheme to an impressed group of real adults in the last of the Andy Hardy series, Andy Hardy Comes Home *(1958). Small-town values and respect for authority permeated this MGM series, raising the question: did the Hardy movies reflect small-town America, or did small-town America model itself on Andy Hardy movies?*

homesteaders, and resolve the conflict through the figure of Shane, the buckskin-clad, loner hero (Alan Ladd), who has to move on when he, through his special skills as a gunman, has made the valley safe for the homesteaders to grow their families and crops. Message: you need a professional, specially skilled military to defend the rights of ordinary citizens against bullies of one kind or another (perhaps a particularly useful message for the Cold War era). Courtroom dramas are almost a separate genre of their own; in *Twelve Angry Men* Henry Fonda plays the classic role of the liberal in the cream suit who gently persuades his fellow jurors that they are wrong to find a Hispanic youth guilty of murder, thereby condemning him to the electric chair. In the movie, all the conflicts and dissensions among the jury members are smoothed over and the American system of justice has been triumphantly vindicated by the end of the film. The issue of the rights and wrongs of capital punishment is not even addressed. However, the audience feels reassured and, indeed, grateful to such a wonderful judicial system and leaves the cinema with the thought that there will always be a Henry Fonda around to prevent injustice. Oh, yeh? Well, it only happens in the world of the movies, that world of unreality . . .

Hollywood, someone once said, is a state of mind rather than a place. However, it is a place as well, although only one studio, Paramount, now physically remains there. Every year the workers and executives of this mythical or real place, depending on your point of view, come together to present prizes to one another in the Oscars ceremony. As usual with Hollywood, the business end of things is the driving force behind the hype of this orgy of mutual congratulation. The Oscars achieve massive publicity for the American film industry, and the winning actors, directors and movies find their value in the market place has increased considerably. However, the massive publicity that Hollywood courts and actively co-operates with also has its down side, and that is the possibility of scandal. The publicity hounds who eat up Hollywood hype can also bite the hands that feed them, and many a star or film personality has succumbed to the pressures of living their lives in the endless limelight of notoriety. Hollywood may try to arrange itself and its movies to convey a rosy and wholesome image, but occasionally superman is found without his cape on and looks like a sleazy creature from the sewers.

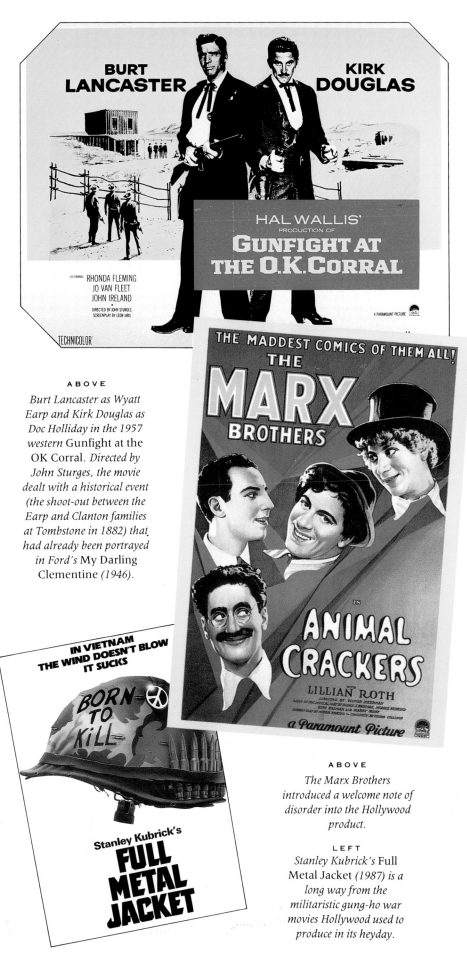

ABOVE

Burt Lancaster as Wyatt Earp and Kirk Douglas as Doc Holliday in the 1957 western Gunfight at the OK Corral. *Directed by John Sturges, the movie dealt with a historical event (the shoot-out between the Earp and Clanton families at Tombstone in 1882) that had already been portrayed in Ford's* My Darling Clementine *(1946).*

ABOVE

The Marx Brothers introduced a welcome note of disorder into the Hollywood product.

LEFT

Stanley Kubrick's Full Metal Jacket *(1987) is a long way from the militaristic gung-ho war movies Hollywood used to produce in its heyday.*

THE
SILENT YEARS

IRVING THALBERG IS quoted as saying there never was any such thing as a silent movie. He described how at MGM in the pre-sound days he would sit with other executives in the screening room and watch MGM's latest offering in despair at what he saw, wondering what kind of product they had to sell to the public. Then they would put the movie into a cinema, either with a fully-fledged orchestra or pianist to provide musical accompaniment, and suddenly there was drama, excitement and magic up there on the screen. The sound of the music more than just underscored the narrative the audience was seeing on the screen, it told them what to feel and how to react. Thus, when we talk about 'the silents' we should always bear Thalberg's dictum in mind. Indeed, when silents are revived now for theatrical showings, they usually have an added soundtrack of specially written music.

However, when Georges Méliès, theatre-owner in Paris at the end of the nineteenth century, began making and showing films, musical accompaniment was not part of his plans. He merely saw film as an extension of his skill as an illusionist. But the movies he made caught on and in 1900 he filmed the story of Cinderella. Along the way he discovered the use of fades and dissolves, slow (and fast) motion and animation, especially in his science fiction films, *A Trip to the Moon* and *An Impossible Voyage*. The first real 'movie' is generally reckoned to be

The Great Train Robbery. It was made by Edwin Porter, one of a group of American pioneers who were inspired by the likes of Méliès to use the new invention as a means of narrative. Porter's films became regular features in the fare served up by the nickelodeons.

In the beginning films were photographed with a stationary camera, which recorded what happened in front of it in an unbroken sequence. Movies did not seem all that different from stage plays, except the actors were not actually performing there in the theatre. Close-ups and editing techniques were slow to come, until Griffith got to work moving the technique of the motion picture towards what we recognise as the art of the cinema nowadays. His use of close-ups, editing techniques, cross-cutting and composition within the frame was to reach its apotheosis in *Birth of a Nation*. The cinema would never be the same again.

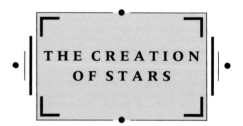

THE CREATION OF STARS

The actors who appeared in those early movies were largely anonymous, until a certain Florence Lawrence broke the barrier because of her popularity with audiences. She became known as 'the Biograph girl' – a star had been born and producers began to realise you could sell movies by association with big names. Famous stars would provide what producers desperately needed: 'product identification', and competition for the hottest new properties increased dramatically. Mary Pickford, for example, who joined Biograph in 1909, became a favourite of the masses, was dubbed 'the world's sweetheart' and ended up earning more than half-a-million dollars a year from Paramount.

LEFT
Georges Méliès dealt in cinematic magic, as this shot of the moon getting one in the eye demonstrates. 2001 it isn't, but to turn-of-the-century audiences coming fresh to this new art, this was spectacle indeed.

Movies were now attracting famous stars from the stage and vaudeville, including John Barrymore, Walter Hampden, Gaby Deslys the opera star, Geraldine Farrar and W.C. Fields. Mary Pickford was the highest-paid, but sweetness was not the only draw: Theda Bara became the first screen 'vamp', a sort of female vampire who devoured men. Charlie Chaplin also shot to fame from a debut in a Keystone comedy; he was shortly signed by the Essanay company for a salary of $1250 a week.

Douglas Fairbanks became an instant star with his first film *The Lamb*, and William S. Hart, a rather lugubrious fellow, was the first screen western hero. The sisters, Lillian and Dorothy Gish, were also major stars. Lillian starred in Griffith's post *Birth of a Nation* epic, *Intolerance* (1916), which was received coolly by critics and public alike.

SILENT COMEDY

What most people remember from the silent years are the comedies: the Mack Sennett Keystone Kops series, Charlie Chaplin, Buster Keaton, Fatty Arbuckle, Harold Lloyd, Ben Turpin and Laurel and Hardy.

Sennett's comedies comprised mad chases, wild mayhem and surreal slapstick involving violence that never seemed to hurt anyone. Indeed, these movies resembled crazy, out-of-control dream sequences where everyday stability was turned upside down. Their function was eventually taken over by cartoons. By way of contrast, the slapstick in Chaplin's silent comedies was minimised. His main talents were as a mime and a kind of comic ballet dancer. His character as the 'little tramp' or vagabond was milked for every drop of pathos. The other great comedian of the twenties, Buster Keaton, was less interested in making his audiences feel sorry for the incompetents and unfortunates he impersonated, and instead specialised in amazing stunts and acrobatics. All the same, 'Old Stoneface' as he was known, gained the audience's sympathy by more subtle means.

ABOVE
Stars of the silent screen:
Theda Bara, Florence
Lawrence, Mary Pickford
and Douglas Fairbanks.

RIGHT

Charlie Chaplin and Jackie Coogan co-starred in The Kid *(1920), with Chaplin himself directing with his usual taste for mixing comedy and mawkishness. The film elevated Coogan to major stardom, and he became one of the most famous child stars in movie history.*

BELOW

Buster Keaton has some difficulties with the box-office in The Playhouse *(1922).*

♦♦ *Charlie Chaplin is no businessman – all he knows is he can't take anything less.* ♦♦

SAMUEL GOLDWYN

Fatty Arbuckle was nearly as big a star as Chaplin at the time of his downfall (see 'Hollywood Scandals and Tragedies'). Harold Lloyd made a living out of appearing to hang out of tall buildings, whilst Ben Turpin's cross-eyed comedian act made up in gusto for what it lacked in comic nuance. Many people see Laurel and Hardy as effectively silent comedians, and among the very greatest of them; even though most of their films were talkies they are still basically visual comedians.

Nothing dates faster than comedy, but many of these silent comedies and actors stand the test of time, principally because they *are* silent. Perhaps visual comedy is more timeless than comedy that depends on dialogue or the witty one-liner. At any rate, television regularly shows compilations of the best sequences from the Hollywood silent comedies, and the sales of videos of some of the best of the silent comedies reflect a continuing public interest. It is interesting to note that only silent comedies made by Hollywood survive to this day. No other national cinema rivalled the American film industry in making the world laugh at the antics of these mute lunatics on the screen.

THE EUROPEANS

However, when it came to artistic advances the real progress was taking place in Europe, particularly in Germany, Russia, France and Scandinavia. In Germany the Expressionist movement strongly influenced directors such as Fritz Lang in *The Niebelungs* (1923–1924), *Metropolis* (1926) and *Spies* (1928). Similarly, Robert Wiene's *The Cabinet of Dr Caligari* (1919) showed the influ-

ence of Cubist painting. F.W. Murnau, another distinguished German director, made important films in *The Last Laugh* (1924) and *Faust* (1926).

In Russia, the leaders of the Revolution soon realised the propaganda value of the infant medium. Sergei Eisenstein became the most famous director in the world, and an important film theoretician as well. His films, *Strike* (1924), *Battleship Potemkin* (1925) and *October* (1928), reflected his belief in the power of montage sequences – the editing of film in a succession of closely controlled shots to produce a specific effect on the cinema audience.

In France, Abel Gance produced *Napoleon* (1927), a film which was shot for multiple projectors throwing images on a triple screen. Jean Renoir, the son of the famous painter, began his long film career with *The Water Girl* (1924) and *Nana* (1926). Mauritz Stiller in Sweden made *The Emigrants* (1921), *Gunnar Hedes Saga* (1922) and *Gosta Berling Saga* (1922) – which launched the film career of a rather chubby young woman, Greta Garbo. In Denmark, Carl Dreyer became known world-wide for his movies *The Minister's Wife* (1921), *Master of the House* (1925) and *The Passion of Joan of Arc* (1928).

> ♦♦*A collar button under a lens and thrown on a screen may become a radiant planet.*♦♦
>
> SERGEI EISENSTEIN

ABOVE
A famous shot from Eisentein's The Battleship Potemkin *(1925).*

RIGHT
One of the great silent stars, Louise Brooks, appeared in German director G.W. Pabst's Pandora's Box *(1929). But her career did not survive long into the sound era.*

RIGHT
Abel Gance was a French director who thought big, and if he had been alive in the fifties, he would have been handed many an epic to direct. Napoleon *is still regularly revived today. Note the 'Francis Coppola presents' heading for this re-release.*

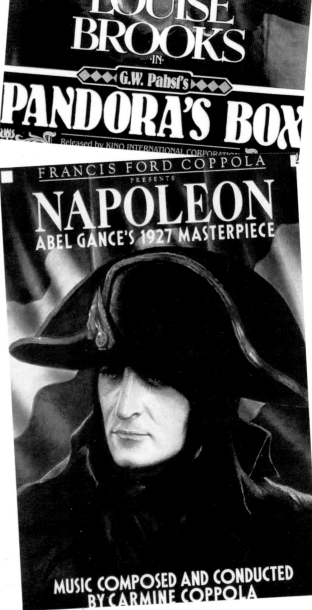

THE SILENT TWENTIES IN HOLLYWOOD

Hollywood was producing its own masterpieces in the last years of the silents. Erich Von Stroheim was a highly extravagant, maverick director who eventually found it impossible to operate within the Hollywood system which put such a premium on making a cost-effective product with an assembly-line production method. Before his directorial career was eclipsed,

however, he made *Foolish Wives* (1921), *Greed* (1923) and *The Wedding March* (1928). The Swede, Victor Sjostrom, directed Lillian Gish in *The Scarlet Letter* (1926) and *The Wind* (1928). Griffith had directed the melodrama *Broken Blossoms* with Lillian Gish and Richard Barthelmess in 1919, followed by *Way Down East* (1920), *Orphans of the Storm* (1922) and *America* (1924).

The great comedians, Chaplin and Keaton, helped give screen comedy a new status. Chaplin with *The Gold Rush* (1925) and *The Circus* (1927), and Keaton with *The Navigator* (1924) and *The General* (1927), earned themselves serious attention as creative artists. Douglas Fairbanks achieved huge success with *The Three Musketeers* (1921), *Robin Hood* (1922), *The Thief of Bagdad* (1924) and *The Black Pirate* (1926), which was a very early exercise in colour film.

Fans who liked their stars larger-than-life adored Rudolph Valentino in *The Sheik* (1921), *Blood and Sand* (1922) and *The Eagle* (1924). Alla Nazimova, starring in *Salome* (1922) and *The Redeeming Sin* (1925), tried her utmost to be exotic and other-worldly enough to satisfy the fantasies of millions of men.

Then on 6 October 1927, the première of *The Jazz Singer* took place. Al Jolson was heard speaking one line: 'You ain't heard nothing yet, folks. Listen to this.' The sound film was born and two years later silents were finished.

LEFT

Al Jolson initiated movie sound in The Jazz Singer *(1927).*

RIGHT

Zasu Pitts in Von Stroheim's silent masterpiece, Greed. *Stroheim originally shot fifty reels of film but reduced it to a four-hour running time before an exasperated Irving Thalberg cut it to around 100 minutes.*

THEY DON'T MAKE THEM LIKE THAT ANYMORE!

I N THE HEYDAY of Hollywood each of the major studios resembled a factory. The aim of these factories was to make a product – movies – that could be shown in cinemas all over the world. The studios had to make enough movies to allow for weekly changes of programme and, at various times in cinematic history, for double-feature bills. When 90 million people in the States alone were going to the cinema each week, there seemed to be an unceasing demand for the Hollywood product. To satisfy this demand movies were produced by a mode of production that was close to an assembly line.

Each worker in that assembly line knew exactly what their specific job was. In 1941 a film industry publication calculated that there were 276 separate crafts involved in making a motion picture and most of those crafts formed guilds that protected their members' right to perform their specific tasks. Studio heads, after their initial misguided opposition to these craft guilds, realised this kind of 'demarcation' philosophy suited their purpose, which was to make the product they required to service their cinemas in sufficient quantity and as cheaply as possible.

'If you've seen one, you've seen them all!' is a frequent complaint about the movies, and it is true that movies, certainly in the old days, fell into definite categories, frequently called 'genres'. Genres made sense economically because a studio could re-use the same sets, locations, actors, directors, costumes and even plots to churn out more westerns, musicals, crazy comedies, war movies, horror flicks, swashbucklers, etc., an assembly line approach which produced economies of scale and which also bred a sense of familiarity in the mass audience. Audiences would know what to expect if they paid their money to see a musical, and if you added Gene Kelly or Judy Garland, then they would have two sets of expectations at least – of the genre and the star. Genres, and stars, were a means of product differentiation and a way of

persuading the customer to come back for more. As a way of producing movies relatively cheaply and encouraging customer loyalty, genre films were good news for the studios.

> ♦♦*A cowboy actor needs two changes of expression – hat on and hat off.*♦♦
> **FRED MACMURRAY**

RIGHT
Alan Ladd as the eternal loner Shane in the 1953 western of the same name, directed by George Stevens. Shane is the romantic western of all time.

THE WESTERN

The western is the most cinematic of the genres because no other art form can hope to emulate the cinema's power to represent the myths of the American frontier in such an immediate and all-embracing manner. But why have westerns been so popular with the public in the past and why have they largely disappeared nowadays from our cinema screens? The answer lies in the way westerns deal in mythology. They present a view of America's frontier and agrarian past that feeds the American Dream: the rugged individual striking out for the unknown, Man against raw Nature, the pursuit of an independent way of life, the acquiring of land and wealth, the conquering of hostile elements in the shape of Indians and 'bad' men, and building communities out of the wilderness based on simple values, hard work and Godliness.

As the memories of that trail-blazing past recede, the American public may feel less need for frequent doses of western mythology, hence the drastic drop in the number of westerns produced in the last twenty to thirty years. In addition, perhaps too much reality has broken through the mists of legend to sustain the western myths any longer. For example, most Americans now accept that a form of genocide was practised against the Indian population in order for the white man's civilisation to flourish. In an era where so-called heroes turn out to be mere mortals after all, it is also difficult to suspend our disbelief when watching these larger-than-life western heroes create law-and-order out of chaos. Cinemagoers are more interested in the new heroes, the urban guerillas of Stallone and Schwarzenegger, than the straight-shooting cowboys of yesteryear.

> ♦♦ *An adult western is where the hero still kisses his horse at the end, only now he worries about it.* ♦♦
>
> MILTON BERLE

LEFT
Paul Newman as Butch Cassidy in Butch Cassidy and the Sundance Kid *(1969), which is more a 'buddy movie' than a western, although all westerns are in part buddy movies. The hero of a western also usually meets his 'double' and often the double is his own evil side that he has to destroy.*

THE MUSICAL

The musical is another genre that Hollywood took over and made its own. When sound came to Hollywood, the studios poured out film after film with people singing and dancing rather inexpertly, and audiences seemed to love these happy films. However, soon the public tired of the new phenomenon, the movie musical – perhaps it was the onset of the Depression, perhaps there was just a surfeit of musicals.

It took Astaire and Rogers and Busby Berkeley to seduce the customers back into the cinemas to

ABOVE

A delightful sequence in the snow where Fred and Ginger take turns with 'A Fine Romance' in Swing Time *(1936). The plush sets designed in Art Deco black and white were a feature of Astaire–Rogers musicals. Their 'fairy tale' nature was meant to compensate for the Depression the audiences were enduring back there in reality.*

watch musical extravaganzas. Warner Bros., Berkeley's studio, sensed people needed glamour, hope and extravagance plus an acknowledgement that there were hard times out there, so that's what they served up; Berkeley, using the camera to create his elaborate and rather soulless fantasies, was the ace director and choreographer who delivered the goods. Astaire and Rogers had no such truck with reality in their RKO musicals, however; Astaire was debonair and usually rich, Rogers was Rogers. The black-and-white Art Deco sets, the sumptuous costumes, the vision of society life, the exotic locations – all these elements combined to create pure escapist fantasies for the masses who were struggling with the realities of unemployment and poverty.

Musicals are inherently 'Utopian'; they concoct an alternative vision of reality that panders to our dreams. The search for love and popularity, for success and wealth, is always celebrated in them. Love leads to marriage, putting on a show leads to massive popularity and success, the coupling of boy-and-girl strengthens the community and reinforces role models and orthodoxy. All movie genres are conservative in the values they espouse and none more so than the musical. In the forties and fifties, the heyday of the MGM musical, some more adult elements were introduced to the storylines, but the resolution was always the same: Kelly would win Garland or Charisse or Caron, Astaire would woo Hepburn, Vera-Ellen or Hayworth and be showered with not only success in love but worldly success as well. Love and success went hand-in-hand in the world of musicals.

Musicals were among the first genres to be discarded with the break-up of the studio system in the fifties. They were expensive to make, required a large body of permanent employees to produce, and were deemed commercially risky if written specially for the screen. From the mid-fifties on, the only musicals made, by and large,

were film versions of Broadway hits. Since the heyday of musicals, there have been talented individuals such as Bob Fosse and Barbra Streisand working in the genre, but there has been no group of people to match the greats of the MGM musical years. The dancing MGM musical vanished with the demise of the studio as a major movie-producing factory.

> ❝*I don't dig this brooding analytic stuff. I just dance and I just act.*❞
>
> FRED ASTAIRE

> ❝*My style is strong, wide-open, bravura. Fred's is intimate, cool and easy.*❞
>
> GENE KELLY

GANGSTER MOVIES

Edward G. Robinson was only a little guy but he packed menace into every pound, as he shows here in Little Caesar *(1930). An interesting sidelight on movie gangster heroes is that so many of them were played by small men – Robinson, Cagney and Bogart. Gangster films as fantasy vehicles for the little guys in the audience?*

Between the years 1930 and 1932 Hollywood produced a number of gangster movies that were genuinely more radical in spirit than those of other genres. The three best known are *Little Caesar* (1930), *The Public Enemy* (1931) and *Scarface* (1932). They are morality tales, a kind of Horatio Alger success story but turned upside down and viewed from the point of view of the dispossessed of society, who have to steal and murder their way to the top because all other 'normal' avenues are cut off for them. The authorities were disturbed by the social undertones of these films and forced the studios to attach moral homilies to the movies: *Little Caesar* ends with titling on the screen saying, 'Rico's career had been a skyrocket, starting in the gutter and ending there'. Soon, the Hays Office, set up by the movie moguls themselves to stave off external censorship and to answer increasing protests about the moral depravity of movies, was clamping down on the manner in which gangsters were portrayed on film. Criminals were to be represented as psychopathic and isolated individuals, whom all decent citizens should despise and help the authorities to destroy.

The public loved the exploits of Cagney, Muni, Bogart and Raft on the screen, and all these actors became major stars, largely through their impersonations of real-life gangsters such as Al Capone and John Dillinger. The gangster genre has never been as popular again as it was in the thirties, but since then it has produced some of Hollywood's best movies: *The Asphalt Jungle* (1950), in which a character pronounces that 'Crime is merely a left-handed form of human endeavour', *Bonnie and Clyde* (1967), a glamorising and myth-making treatment of the story of thirties gangsters, and *The Godfather* and *The Godfather Part II* (1972 and 1974). All these four films seem to imply that society is hypocritical in its attitude to crime and that the boundaries between 'respectable' business, the forces of law and order, and organised and 'disorganised' crime are very thin indeed. In the eighties movies such as *Scarface* and *Once Upon a Time in America* reflect the continuing fascination with gangsterdom and what criminals tell us about the society we live in.

British gangster films never had the resonance of their Hollywood counterparts though recent British attempts at the genre have shown a tougher approach: *Get Carter*, *Villain* and *The Krays*. The French have always found Hollywood gangsters irresistible, and movies such as *Rififi*, *The Samurai* and *La Balance* show their debt to the Hollywood originals.

Humphrey Bogart as Philip Marlowe in The Big Sleep *(1946). Howard Hawks's movie has such a complicated plot that no one has ever truly understood it, including, it seems, Raymond Chandler, the author of the original novel.*

ADVENTURE MOVIES

Adventure movies, or 'action films', come in various guises but inevitably involve a resourceful hero, and occasionally a heroine, up against incredible odds and winning through in the last reel. Under adventure we could classify the wild fantasies of the James Bond movies, the swashbucklers, historical extravaganzas, 'jungle' and 'desert' epics, and a whole range of 'actioners' including disaster movies. Universal, when it was still a minnow studio in the forties and fifties, produced a series of adventures supposedly set in exotic desert locations but actually shot in local sandpits; these movies were irreverently known as 'tits and sand' in the trade, because of the opportunity it gave for the studio to put its glamorous stars in skimpy costumes and to shoot cheaply on the back lot.

Just as weepies were intended to appeal predominantly to a female audience, so action films were perceived as appealing to men, hence the creation of major male stars who stood for adventure in the public mind: Douglas Fairbanks Senior and Junior, Clark Gable, Errol Flynn, Tyrone Power, Gary Cooper, Stewart Granger, Charlton Heston, Alan Ladd, Sabu, Cornel Wilde, John Payne, Sean Connery, John Wayne and Harrison Ford. Women inevitably played second

fiddle to the male stars in these movies, but names such as Yvonne De Carlo, Rhonda Fleming, Paulette Goddard, Susan Hayward, Dorothy Lamour, Maureen O'Sullivan and Maria Montez would appear above the title in many a routine actioner.

If particular stars were associated with action movies, so were individual directors who acquired a reputation for being able to keep the action moving and providing enough thrills and spills to please audiences. Among these were Irwin Allen (*The Lost World, The Poseidon Adventure, The Towering Inferno*), Cecil B. De Mille (*Reap the Wild Wind, Unconquered, Northwest Mounted Police*), Henry Hathaway (*Lives of a Bengal Lancer, Prince Valiant, North to Alaska*), Howard Hawks (*Only Angels Have Wings, Hatari, The Big Sky*), John Huston (*Moby Dick, The Treasure of The Sierra Madre, The African Queen*), Zoltan Korda (*Sanders of the River, Elephant Boy, The Four Feathers, The Thief of Bagdad*) and Raoul Walsh (*They Drive by Night, They Died with Their Boots On, Gentleman Jim, Captain Horatio Hornblower*).

Sub-genres under the umbrella of action films would also include boxing movies, motor racing films and movies adapted from novels by John Buchan and Rider Haggard.

Things are looking tough for Ernest Borgnine, Stella Stevens and Gene Hackman (amongst others) in this scene from The Poseidon Adventure *(1972). Why were disaster movies so popular during the seventies? Were they a metaphor for Western unease, a symbol of the ground giving way under our feet? I blame President Nixon!*

BELOW LEFT
'So what do we do now, Dad?' asks kid Harrison Ford of pop, Sean Connery, in the last Indiana Jones adventure, Indiana Jones and the Last Crusade *(1988).*

The Hollywood actioner could always be relied on to throw up some absurd casting, such as Alan Ladd as a knight of the Round Table (*The Black Knight*) or Tony Curtis as an Arab in a tale of Arabian adventure (*Son of Ali Baba*) or as a Viking (*The Vikings*). Saturday morning serials were basically actioners stretched thinly over countless episodes (*The Perils of Pauline, Flash Gordon, Captain Marvel* and *Batman*). Each episode would leave the hero or heroine in some dreadful predicament from which no apparent escape was possible. The *Raiders of the Lost Ark* series was Spielberg's affectionate tribute to the good old days of Saturday morning cinema when you cheered the goodies and hissed the baddies.

> ♦♦ *Any little success I have had was because I was one of the mob and catered to the mob.* ♦♦
>
> **MACK SENNETT**

COMEDIES

Abbott and Costello, Laurel and Hardy, the great comedians of the silents, Martin and Lewis, The Three Stooges, Fernandel, Bob Hope, Sid Field, the *Carry On* series, the *Doctor* series, the *Pink Panther* series, screwball comedy, Red Skelton, Hepburn and Tracy comedies, Preston Sturges, Ealing comedies, Mel Brooks, Woody Allen, W.C. Fields, Danny Kaye, Ernst Lubitsch, the Marx Brothers, Neil Simon, Frank Tashlin, Billy Wilder, Gene Wilder: all these and many, many more make up some kind of Hall of Fame for cinematic comedy.

Comedy divides opinion like no other type of movie. Woody Allen is the funniest man alive for some people; for others his angst-ridden attempts to provoke laughter leave them entirely unmoved. Many people still laugh at Abbott and Costello when their movies are shown on television, while many other people wonder what anyone could have ever seen in the little fat guy and his straight-man partner, though at their peak in the forties they were No. 1 box-office stars in America.

The fact is that nothing dates as fast as comedy and often what people cling on to when watching old comedies again is the memory of their youth and what made them laugh in the good old days. Try telling a contemporary young person why you think Danny Kaye movies are funny and watch the incredulous look appear on their face. And how to explain the awful fascination that Three Stooges movies can have with

> ♦♦*First picture I've ever seen in which the male lead has bigger tits than the female.*♦♦
>
> GROUCHO MARX ON 'SAMSON AND DELILAH'
> STARRING HEDY LAMARR AND VICTOR MATURE

their nose-twisting, ear-pulling, thumb-wrenching sadism? Did we really find that funny in those days? Was Jerry Lewis always as inane? Did anyone, anywhere, ever find Red Skelton funny? Yes, obviously they did, because Skelton was big box-office for a time in the forties. There's no accounting for taste in comedy.

For example, I have tried to appreciate the comic genius that Preston Sturges is supposed to have poured into comedies such as *The Great McGinty*, *Sullivan's Travels* and *Hail the Conquering Hero* – but, for the life of me, I just can't see it. The *Carry On* series leaves me absolutely cold and leaves, I suspect, the rest of the world outside Britain the same way, but every time those comic epics crop up on television they get decent audiences, so somebody out there *must* like them. My own favourite type of Hollywood comedy, the screwball variety, is a taste that many people do not share. But for me, movies such as *Bringing Up Baby*, *His Girl Friday*, *Ball of Fire*, *I was a Male War Bride*, *Monkey Business*, *Twentieth Century*, *Love Crazy* and numerous others had an anarchic tone and a paciness to them that made them the most enduring of screen comedies. I admire some Ealing comedies such as *The Lady Killers* and *The Man in the White Suit*, but generally find the view of British life represented in the majority of these films too cosy and self-congratulatory. Many, many would disagree.

Only a small proportion of films survive the passing of years to impress future generations with the same impact as when they were first released. But for comedies, the job is even harder. In 2020, will Peter Sellers as Inspector Clouseau seem funny to people for whom Sellers is just a vague name from the past? Is Woody Allen's appeal a particularly contemporary one, relevant only to the eighties and nineties? Will anyone still be watching The Three Stooges in 2020? Perhaps we should leave these questions to the academics and just enjoy what we enjoy when we enjoy it.

ABOVE
The crude, the exaggerated, the subtle and the cruel – Police Academy, The Greatest Show on Earth, Radio Days *and* Laurel and Hardy.

EPICS

BELOW

*Robert Taylor as a Roman
general in the 1954*
Quo Vadis.

The cinema has always tried to provide spectacle for mass audiences. The camera can go anywhere and record scenes of enormous vistas and detail. The technological and material resources of cinema can recreate any period of history, any imaginary world, any vision of writers and directors. Movies have tried ever since they became a mass entertainment to provide spectacles that no other art or entertainment medium can rival in their size, opulence and authenticity.

Birth of a Nation was the cinema's first great spectacle and from then on many producers and directors have attempted to impress us with the

ROBERT TAYLOR
in
"QUO VADIS"

Kirk Douglas as Spartacus in the 1960 film of the same name. One of the most literate of movie epics, Spartacus was directed by Stanley Kubrick, and also starred Laurence Olivier, Charles Laughton, Jean Simmons and Tony Curtis.

"An epic is the easiest type of picture to make badly."

CHARLTON HESTON

grandness of their designs, the extravagance of their concepts, their devotion to reproducing a historical period and to rewriting history itself.

Unfortunately, along the way, authenticity was often the first casualty, so we saw such errors of taste as John Wayne as a Roman centurion at the foot of the Cross mouthing 'Truly, this was the son of Gawd'. Tony Curtis, complete with Brooklyn accent, would play Roman slaves, and Victor Mature would wrestle with stuffed lions. Epics would become the excuse for excessive religiosity in Cecil B. De Mille's spectacles or for viewing female stars in skimpy costumes as with Lana Turner in *The Prodigal*. Somehow scripts tended to be more leaden for epics; as Howard Hawks said about the dreadful *Land of the Pharaohs*, which he directed, 'I never knew how a Pharaoh talked.' How *does* Moses talk, how does a Roman slave leading a rebellion against the Roman Empire talk? Indeed, does Ben Hur need to talk?

Only a handful of epics stand up to any test of real quality; the vast majority are best enjoyed as cinema at its most ostentatious and its most vulgar. You do not go to an epic to be educated about a historical period or learn how people lived in past times. You go to an epic to be impressed by the sheer size of things and to wonder at the effort that went into the whole enterprise.

"'Ben Hur'. Loved Ben, hated Hur."

ANONYMOUS REVIEW

Cinemascope meant directors had to fill the wide screen with spectacle, making every dollar of the production budget show up there on the screen. This is a shot from the 1955 Helen of Troy, which, like many other epics of the period, was shot in Europe to take advantage of cheap local labour, tax concessions and money the American studios had had 'frozen' in Europe.

FILM NOIR

Strictly speaking, film noir is not a genre. It is a body of films that emerged from Hollywood between 1941 and 1958 that shared stylistic and thematic concerns. The term was first used by French critics when they noticed the 'blackness' of look and theme common to the American movies released in France after the Liberation. Perhaps because they had been cut off for four years from American films, these critics remarked on how different these movies were from the standard Hollywood product with its glossy, high-key lighting and upbeat reassuring message. These films noirs were bleak social documents, turning a disenchanted eye on the contemporary American scene and uncovering a society full of anxieties and divisions.

The filmmakers who made the films noirs were perhaps influenced by German Expressionism and Italian Neo-realism. Expatriate European directors such as Wilder, Preminger, Ophuls, Siodmak and Curtiz made some of the best-known noirs with their determinedly shadowy images and nihilistic view of human nature.

RIGHT
John Garfield falls for Lana Turner in the 1946 version of The Postman Always Rings Twice. *Adapted from a James Cain pulp novel, this would be remade in 1981 by director Bob Rafaelson with Jack Nicholson and Jessica Lange co-starring.*

BELOW
'Goodbye, baby,' as Walter Neff (Fred MacMurray) could be saying to Phyllis Dietrichson (Barbara Stanwyck) in the 1944 Double Indemnity, *another adaptation from a James Cain novel. Billy Wilder and Raymond Chandler had an uneasy working relationship while co-writing the screenplay, which Wilder eventually directed himself.*

Very often a film noir is about a male protagonist encountering a *femme fatale*, who uses her sexual attractiveness to manipulate him into murder. She then double-crosses the sap until order is restored by the destruction of this powerful female figure, often at the cost of the hero's life. Film noir is misogynist in its general representation of women: the women are beautiful but duplicitous, predatory and promiscuous. This trend in wartime and post-war American movies may have had something to do with the uncertain relationship between the sexes due to wartime dislocations and suspicions about what had gone on while the boys had been away at war. Additionally, millions of women had had their first opportunity to work during the war years, and this had fed male paranoia that women were breaking out and refusing to play their 'correct' roles in society as mothers and wives.

Film noir was often the product of the 'B' picture system, whereby low-budget films were produced by the studios to fill the lower half of double bills. As a result these 'B' pictures were not given the same scrutiny as the 'A' pictures, which allowed creative directors and writers the freedom to experiment and handle themes that would have been out of bounds on more expensive products.

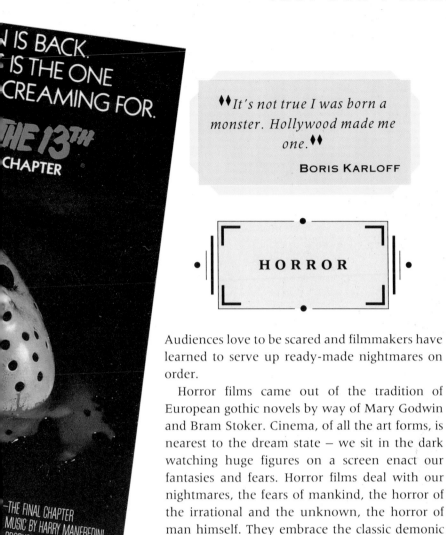

❖❖It's not true I was born a monster. Hollywood made me one.❖❖

BORIS KARLOFF

HORROR

Audiences love to be scared and filmmakers have learned to serve up ready-made nightmares on order.

Horror films came out of the tradition of European gothic novels by way of Mary Godwin and Bram Stoker. Cinema, of all the art forms, is nearest to the dream state – we sit in the dark watching huge figures on a screen enact our fantasies and fears. Horror films deal with our nightmares, the fears of mankind, the horror of the irrational and the unknown, the horror of man himself. They embrace the classic demonic myths of Frankenstein and Dracula, the concept of Nature that turns abnormal, the horror of human personality. Horror is the Creature, the blood-sucking vampire, the fiendish scientist, the ghoul, or Freddie with the murderous, nightmarish nails. Horror is all around us in the everyday world: it is a shadow on the walls of a deserted swimming-pool (*Cat People*), it is a hesitant, shy and psychopathic young man in a motel (*Psycho*), it is a man with 'Love' and 'Hate' tattooed on the back of his right and left hands (*Night of the Hunter*).

Some observers see the horror film as an expression of our subconscious wish to smash the norms that oppress us. For example, many horror films are located in the family situation. In horror films the underside of normality is exposed and the irrational chaos beneath respectability and convention explodes and threatens to engulf society. As in all genres, however, the monstrous has to be defeated and the norms restored. We have been able to indulge our rebellious instincts for a while before the status quo wins through. While watching the horror movie, we half-long for the forces of chaos to win, but fear at the same time what that chaos will reveal about ourselves.

LEFT
A scene from the Roger Corman 1971 movie Murders in the Rue Morgue.

CENTRE LEFT
I've heard of bad phone connections but this is ridiculous! Heather Langenkamp takes a call from Freddy Krueger in Wes Craven's Nightmare on Elm Street *(1984).*

ABOVE LEFT
Your wildest fantasies of murder and mayhem in yet another Friday the 13th *movie.*

FAR LEFT
'Look, let's face it, I don't think it's worked out. What do you think?' Boris Karloff has doubts in the 1931 Frankenstein.

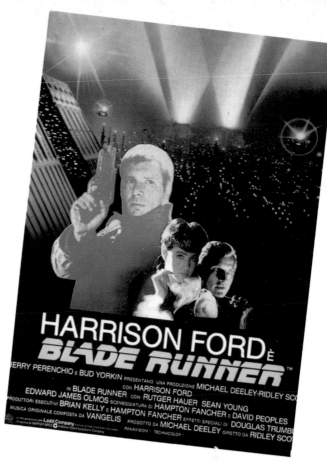

Bug-eyed monsters. Aliens with incredibly high IQs. Invaders that act suspiciously like Commies. Insubstantial jelly-like creatures that mean no harm to us earthlings. ET. All these are cinematic manifestations of our dreams about space and those unknown creatures that may or may not inhabit it. In the fifties, aliens, whether invading the earth or encountered when Man ventured into space, were invariably hostile and subversive; this view of extra-terrestrials suited the politics of the Cold War where anybody thought to be 'Un-American' was suspected of Communism and subversion. SF films in the fifties were employed as parables for their times: to warn against alien beings taking over the minds and territory of Americans, or as a reminder of the dangers of conformity and paranoia.

By the seventies and eighties, with the Cold War receding, aliens could be seen as benevolent. Conversely, in Spielberg's movies, the individual well-meaning citizen has to ward off the attentions of the sinister powers of the state to make real contact with the aliens (*Close Encounters of the Third Kind, ET*). Now that old enemies have become new friends and the Cold War is officially dead, how will future cinematic aliens be represented, and who will they stand for in our dreams about the vast, unknowable reaches of space?

ABOVE

In 1982 Ridley Scott directed Blade Runner, *a nightmarish vision of Los Angeles in the distant future.*

LEFT

Sigourney Weaver as Ripley saves the prettiest male among the crew in Aliens *(1987). The part of Ripley was originally written for a man but Weaver took over the role and showed that women could be just as resilient and gritty as male screen heroes.*

FAR LEFT

George Lucas's Star Wars *was popular enough to spawn two sequals, winning audiences everywhere with pyrotechnic effects and engaging extra-terrestrials.*

LOVE STORIES

By 'love stories' or 'romantic movies', one usually means movies where the main interest is in the romantic involvement of the two leads. Some people, on that basis, would argue that *Gone with the Wind* is a love story about Scarlett O'Hara and Rhett Butler rather than a civil war epic. Similarly, *Casablanca* is about the tragic love between Bogart and Bergman rather than a thriller involving the Nazis, Claude Rains as a Vichy policeman and the Resistance. Some love stories are located in specific periods and are enacted amidst important events, such as *The Way We Were*, which deals with the McCarthyite period in Hollywood but is more about the on-off romance between Streisand and Redford. Who remembers very much about the Spanish Civil War from *For Whom the Bell Tolls*? But everybody remembers the Gary Cooper-Ingrid Bergman love affair.

The British have made their share of romantic movies, but until the sixties they were usually of the tight-lipped, blouse-buttoned variety, such as the most famous of them, *Brief Encounter*, where Celia Johnson is appalled when Trevor Howard arranges for them to borrow a friend's flat for some adulterous love-making. Oh, the shame of it all! Indeed, lovers had to be very discreet in the movies right until the early sixties when the Production Code that ruled what you could and could not show in movies began to break down. British movies such as *Room at the Top*, *The Girl with Green Eyes* and all those movies about

Social realism Hollywood-style in George Stevens's 1952 A Place in the Sun. *Montgomery Clift plays a poor boy who wants rich girl Elizabeth Taylor, but Shelley Winters as the factory girl Clift makes pregnant gets in the way. Adapted from Theodore Dreiser's novel* An American Tragedy, *the movie is hugely romantic and dedicated to the concept of a love that transcends all.*

In Above and Beyond (1952), Robert Taylor plays the pilot who carried out the mission to bomb Nagasaki and Hiroshima. Movie-goers had somehow to be distracted from that horrible reality and a love story was concocted to make it palatable.

Rachmaninov on the sound-track, post-war austerity as the keynote, Celia Johnson's clipped vowels, Trevor Howard's decency – what more could you want for a good old wallow in sentimental nostalgia? David Lean directed this ever-so-British love story from a Noel Coward script in 1948.

❖❖ *The great art of films does not consist of descriptive movements of face and body, but in the moments of thought and soul transmitted in a kind of intense isolation.* ❖❖

LOUISE BROOKS

Swinging London swept most of the restrictions aside. But romance was not about sex and bedroom scenes, it was about Katharine Hepburn being swept off her feet by Rossano Brazzi in *Summer Madness*, it was about Montgomery Clift and Elizabeth Taylor in *A Place in the Sun*, it was Jennifer Jones waiting on a windy hill for the return of William Holden in *Love is a Many-Splendoured Thing*, it was Joan Fontaine in *Rebecca* and *Letter from an Unknown Woman* expiring of love for Laurence Olivier and Louis Jourdan.

Lately, there have been few movies that are straight romances. There have been a few that portray gay or lesbian love affairs, but they have generally failed to attract a wider audience. Perhaps the relationships between men and women are too fraught at this time for conventional romantic movies to be popular. There is a continuing obsession with sex in the movies, but even sex is shown to be a dangerous and potentially destructive instinct when indulged (*Fatal Attraction*, *Jagged Edge*, *The Morning After*). One eighties love story, *Falling in Love*, with De Niro and Meryl Streep as the lovers, failed disastrously at the box-office. In many ways, the movie was a throwback to the days of the great movie love story with two of the biggest contemporary stars playing opposite one another, but it failed to click with the general public. The time may be out of joint for the hankie-sodden love story.

LEFT
Broderick Crawford as the gangster and William Holden as the tutor who compete for the favours of Judy Holliday in the romantic comedy Born Yesterday *(1950).*

ABOVE
In Rebecca *Laurence Olivier played the aristocratic owner of a country estate where he takes his new bride, timorous Joan Fontaine. The story revolves round whether or not Olivier had killed his former wife. But love wins out in the end . . .*

MELODRAMAS, WEEPIES OR WOMEN'S PICTURES

Hollywood took over melodrama from the 'penny dreadfuls' and theatre of the nineteenth century. Melodrama has always been looked upon as the poor relation of tragedy and realism, but important novelists such as Dickens and Dostoevsky are full of melodramatic incident and climaxes. Silent movies lent themselves to melodramatic excess; when only the image and gesture communicated meaning, then actors and directors had to hook into the melodramatic tradition to tell their stories and express feeling.

Hollywood producers thought largely in stereotypes when considering audiences, so it was to the female audience that most melodramas were directed because of the appeal that the subject-matter was thought to have for women. Thus, these movies came to be known as 'women's pictures' or 'weepies' because of the excessive emotion they supposedly provoked in the largely female audience. However, these movies also gave the opportunity for the representation of powerful women on the screen, and some independently minded stars were created by the genre: Davis, Crawford, De Havilland, Stanwyck.

There were sub-genres within the genre of melodrama: the maternal melodrama in which a mother figure was variously scorned, neglected or sacrificed for her children, or the family melodrama in which the institution of the family was put under strain and finally reinforced. There were the melodramas of romantic love in which the female protagonist would be wooed, abandoned, tricked or seduced but usually end up with the man of her choice. The ideological purpose was to reinforce female roles, but, by making women the pivotal figures in the story, these movies raised questions about what women should do with their lives, and created powerful role models for millions of cinemagoers. Katharine Hepburn, Bette Davis and Barbara Stanwyck were early versions of the liberated women we see on our screens today.

All Quiet on the Western Front *(1930), directed by Lewis Milestone, presented a picture of the First World War from the German soldiers' point of view.*

American soldiers destroy a Vietnamese village in Michael Cimino's The Deer Hunter *(1978). The film aroused controversy because it avoided making any condemnation of the American involvement in Vietnam and portrayed the Vietcong exclusively as the perpetrators of atrocities.*

WAR MOVIES

All major movie-producing nations have made war movies to attract a mass audience who either perceive them as a kind of adventure yarn or as an authentic attempt to reproduce the experience of war on the screen. They have been used as propaganda by all nations, especially in times of war, or the aftermath of wars, when morale has to be kept high or national pride and mythology have to be celebrated. As a result, too many war movies in the past have been exercises in jingoism or self-congratulation, too few have represented war authentically. Fifty years after World War II and with the reality of the horrors of the 'television' war in Vietnam still fresh in our minds, it is now more difficult for film-makers to pass off war as a variant of the boys' own adventure, though some still try to do so.

'War is hell!' is a plea that both jingoistic and anti-war movies make. Very few films actually glory unreservedly in the gore and destruction, though some John Wayne epics such as *The Green Berets* come very close to doing so. Many

Willem Dafoe tries to get at the sadistic Tom Berenger in Oliver Stone's movie about 'grunts', Platoon *(1986).*

Charlie Sheen (back left) plays a sensitive grunt who learns the horrors of Vietnam service the hard way.

jingoistic movies, whilst pointing to the horror of war, simultaneously indulge in the most dishonest heroic posturings and simplification of the issues and who the good and bad guys are. Such films are westerns under a different guise and it is not surprising that Wayne was such a big star in both genres. A Wayne war movie was not that different from a Wayne western. The main difference was that the bad guys in the former were 'nips' or 'krauts' or 'commies' in general.

If the American cinema had the mythology of the opening of the western frontier to feed off and add to, the British cinema seemed to find its central myths in the Second World War when Britain stood alone against the power of Germany and Japan. Postwar British cinema was obsessed with recreating the 'finest hour' and reinforcing the myths surrounding 'the Dunkirk spirit', the Battle of Britain, the struggle on the home front, the battle at sea and the defence of the British Empire by its loyal subjects. A large proportion of British films in the forties and fifties seemed to star John Mills, Jack Hawkins, Richard Attenborough, Bryan Forbes, Peter Finch, John Gregson, Donald Sinden, Anthony Steel *et al.* in a variety of uniforms showing the world and themselves how Britain did it. It was as though British filmmakers were stuck in a time warp and were drawn irresistibly to the tales of POW escapes ('My turn for the tunnel, sir'), submarine warfare (Richard Attenborough turning yellow below the waves), dog-fights in the air ('I bagged a couple of gerries, Flight!') or espionage behind the enemy lines ('Your job is to convince those krauts the Normandy landings are going to take place in Spain').

RIGHT
British war films tended to glorify the officer class and show decent chaps keeping stiff upper lips in awfully difficult circumstances.

FAR RIGHT
Elliott Gould as Hawkeye in Robert Altman's M*A*S*H (1970). The film that spawned a long-running television series, M*A*S*H undercut the myths of wartime heroics and devotion to duty.

BELOW
Platoon *was a picture of the Vietnam war from the 'grunts' point of view. Basing it on his own experience as an infantryman in Vietnam, Oliver Stone directed the 1986 movie and won an Academy Award for his efforts.*

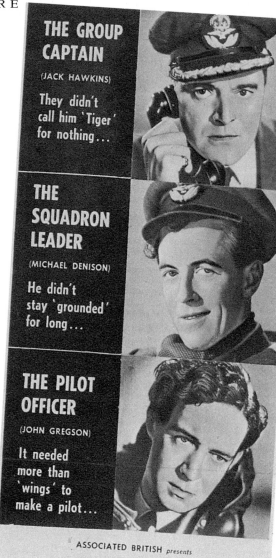

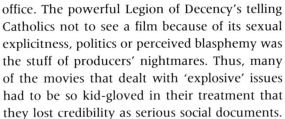

SOCIAL PROBLEM MOVIES

Every so often the cinema deals with a 'social problem' such as racial prejudice, political unrest, alcoholism, drugs, poverty and unemployment, sexual inequality and violence towards women, or mental illness. The movies are meant to appeal to a mass audience, but because of this need to attract millions of people the tendency has been to emphasise the personal problems of the characters at the expense of the general social issue that ostensibly is being represented. In the heyday of the studio era, Hollywood was careful not to alienate sections of public opinion, and thereby endanger box-office returns; studios had to contend with multifarious pressure groups such as the Catholic Legion of Decency, the American Legion, the Daughters of the Revolution and frequently bigoted local censorship boards, all of which might put a seal of disapproval on a film, a move that could have a major impact on how well it did at the box-

office. The powerful Legion of Decency's telling Catholics not to see a film because of its sexual explicitness, politics or perceived blasphemy was the stuff of producers' nightmares. Thus, many of the movies that dealt with 'explosive' issues had to be so kid-gloved in their treatment that they lost credibility as serious social documents.

In the thirties through to the fifties, the Production Code Administration, or Hays Office, which had the job of imposing censorship on all movies that aspired to being shown in American cinemas was a very conservative organisation which saw its function as the defence of 'Americanism' and the American Way of Life. Any movie that implied, for example, that racial prejudice was rife in the States would be frowned on, so producers and writers learned to portray such manifestations as isolated examples rather than the rule. For example, in the film noir *Crossfire*, one of the themes is anti-semitism in post-war American society, but the film had to imply that the anti-semitism portrayed was merely a prejudice of one psychotic individual, played by Robert Ryan, rather than a widespread social phenomenon. When Ryan is shot dead at the end of the film, the implication is that the problem disappears with him. Another forties film, *Gentleman's Agreement*, again deals with anti-semitism, but instead of showing a Jewish person coming up against actual prejudice, audiences saw Gregory Peck as a journalist pretending to be a Jew to find out the extent of anti-semitism in America. The film manages to be reassuring and self-congratulatory by individualising the issue and suggesting simplistic solutions.

The movies nowadays deal more authentically and frankly with social problems, although the tendency to exonerate societies and institutions by showing the occasional sinner being punished for his transgressions is still prevalent. In *Wall Street*, Gecko, the character played by Michael Douglas, is shopped by his former disciple and the implication is that he will go to jail for his illegal junk bond dealing; Wall Street is shown to be capable of cleaning itself up, that all it takes is for one good individual to stand up for morality for things to change. Most Hollywood films dealing with social issues are melodramatic and fairly simplistic; the narrative almost inevitably seeks an ending that resolves the problem in favour of a consensus solution. Even social problem movies have to have happy endings.

Michael Douglas as Gordon Gecko in Wall Street *(1988). Gecko is the villain of the eighties, a corrupt, ruthless bond dealer who makes a religion out of greed. He's trapped at the end of Oliver Stone's movie, which seduces the audience into thinking the system is subject to control in the final analysis.*

LEFT

Jack Nicholson becomes a demented psychopath while holed up for the winter with his family in a Colorado hotel in Stanley Kubrick's The Shining *(1980).*

LEFT

Harrison Ford starred with Emmanuelle Seigneur in the 1988 thriller Frantic, *directed by Roman Polanski. Ford plays an American surgeon whose wife is kidnapped in Paris and who becomes embroiled in a scenario of nuclear devices, Middle-Eastern terrorism and Parisian low life.*

Suspense thrillers were standard products for the Hollywood studios – murder mysteries, chase thrillers, women-in-peril movies, private eye yarns. The thriller format was often used by writers and directors to explore aspects of society and human psychology within a recognisable formula of unravelling a mystery or situating the main protagonist in danger and mayhem. Some thrillers can be classed as film noir but film noir crossed generic frontiers and many thrillers had no discernible noirish elements at all.

The acknowledged master of the thriller was Alfred Hitchcock. He used the genre to manipulate his audience by means of suspense while exploring his personal obsessions about guilt and punishment, sexuality and voyeurism, and the darker sides of human nature. For Hitchcock, plots were the means of hooking an audience which he then manipulated to feel as he wanted them to feel, to switch allegiances and sympathy for the characters as he wished them to do and, generally, to react on cue according to the stimuli that he as the filmmaker controlled through the images on screen.

There have been many imitations of Hitchcock's films, but few have achieved the same mastery of audience manipulation as he did. Most cinema is manipulative in the sense that most films seek to draw you, the viewer, into their representation of reality so that you suspend your disbelief. Thrillers depend on that suspension and on suspense as well; if you are, metaphorically, to be on the edge of your seat, you have to believe that the heroine is genuinely going to fall off the cliff or that the hero has been fatally wounded and will not recover. You have to feel the danger the protagonists are feeling, you have to want desperately for them to escape and for the villains to be defeated. To enjoy a thriller fully, your fears have to be engaged, you have to care, you have to go through agonies and suspense before relief is granted. If you are detached from the action on the screen, you might be able to admire clinically how the formula is constructed but you are unlikely to gain much more from the experience.

Dennis Quaid corners Ellen Barkin in the 1986 thriller set in New Orleans, The Big Easy.

Vertigo *(1958) is one of Hitchcock's most resonant thrillers. James Stewart plays an ex-cop who becomes* obsessed with recreating a woman he once loved and lost. Kim Novak is his fantasy.

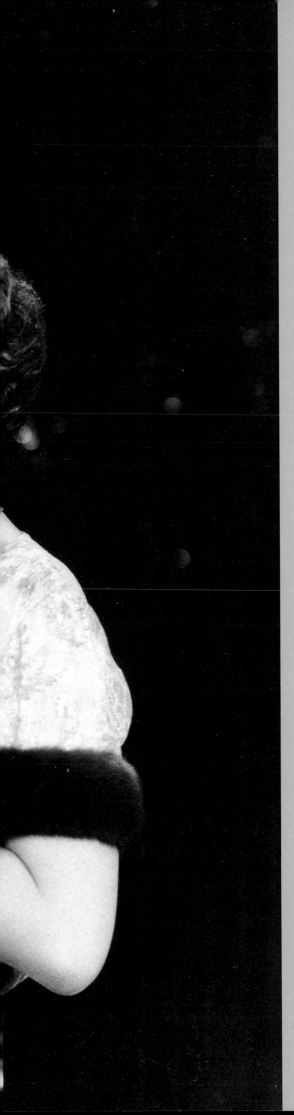

Hollywood Congratulates Itself: The Oscars

IN 1927 THE Hollywood film industry set up the Academy of Motion Picture Arts and Sciences ostensibly to 'raise the cultural, educational and scientific standards' of movies. In reality, studio moguls like Louis B. Mayer of MGM hoped the Academy would suffice as a kind of bosses' union and stifle the spread of Hollywood craft unions among studio workers. That did not work, but the Academy became the symbol of how Hollywood would like its corporate identity to be perceived. In its pursuit of excellence, the members decided to make awards to themselves and so the annual orgy of self-congratulation known as the Oscars began on the night of 16 May 1929. The famous gilt statuettes were called Oscars, either by Margaret Herrick, then librarian to the Academy, because she said they resembled her Uncle Oscar, or because Bette Davis named them after her first husband, Oscar Nelson Jnr. You pays your money, you pick your Hollywood legend.

LEFT

Norma Shearer receives her 1929 Oscar for best actress in The Divorcee.

235

There have been highlights and low points on Oscar nights since that first ceremony – deserved and wholly undeserved winners, tears and embarrassments, and loads of laughs and sheer vulgarity. Here is a selection of some from all of these:

'30s

1929/30: Oscars for *All Quiet on the Western Front* and Lewis Milestone who directed it.

1931/32: MGM's *Grand Hotel* gets the Best Picture award, while Fredric March (for *Dr Jekyll and Mr Hyde*) and Wallace Beery (for *The Champ*) tie for Best Actor.

1932/33: Ham is officially blessed as Charles Laughton wins for *The Private Life of Henry VIII*. Katharine Hepburn gushes her way to the Best Actress award for *Morning Glory*.

1934: Columbia's *It Happened One Night* wins all four major awards: Best Picture, Best Actor (Clark Gable), Best Actress (Claudette Colbert) and Best Director (Frank Capra).

1938: Actors playing priests, nuns or deaf mutes are always in with a chance at Oscar time, and so it proved this year with Spencer Tracy getting the award for his 'tough guy' priest in *Boys' Town*. As a contrast Bette Davis won hers for *Jezebel*.

1939: Premiered in December 1939, *Gone with the Wind* won Best Picture award, whilst Vivien Leigh 'fiddle-de-deed' her way to the Best Actress Oscar as Scarlett O'Hara.

'40s

1942: Wartime propaganda, so *Mrs Miniver*, a cloying, glossy piece of MGM nonsense, won Best Picture, while James Cagney's brash and rather dislikeable portrayal of George M. Cohan in *Yankee Doodle Dandy* won Best Actor. Best Actress? Why, Greer Garson as Mrs Miniver, of course.

1944: Priest time again: Bing Crosby for *Going My Way*.

1945: The opposite! Ray Milland playing an alcoholic in *The Lost Weekend*, which also won Best Picture.

BELOW

Clark Gable gets the Oscar in 1934 for his performance in the previous year's comedy hit It Happened One Night. *The film cleaned up with five Oscars, including those for best film and best director (Frank Capra).*

BELOW

Walt Disney accepts a Special Oscar at the hands of Shirley Temple for Snow White and the Seven Dwarfs *during the 1938 awards.*

ABOVE

Greer Garson and Walter Pidgeon in the 1942 Oscar-winner Mrs Miniver.

RIGHT

Ray Milland won an Oscar for his performance in The Lost Weekend *(1945).*

1946: Tinsel Town reveals a heart when it gives war amputee Harold Russell, a non-professional actor, the Best Supporting Actor Oscar for *The Best Years of Our Lives*.

1948: Culture Goes Over Big In Tinsel Town! Olivier's *Hamlet* wins Best Picture and Best Actor awards.

'50s

1951: A musical *An American in Paris* wins Best Picture. Special Oscar for Gene Kelly for his achievements in screen choreography.

1954: Brando's year with *On the Waterfront*, also voted Best Picture and Best Direction (Elia Kazan).

1956: If Mike Todd's *Around the World in Eighty Days* was the best picture of the year, then what were the rest like?

1959: Hollywood follows the box-office and *Ben Hur* wins. Charlton Heston wins Best Actor Oscar. They had to be kidding!

RIGHT

Oscars are often awarded to movies that won out at the box-office, rather than for their intrinsic merits as movies. A case in point is the 1956 Around the World in Eighty Days, *Mike Todd's lumbering and rather tedious version of the Jules Verne tale.*

ABOVE

*The Best Film of 1965?
Well, both the Academy and
the box office reckoned it was
The Sound of Music, so
who would disagree?
Certainly not Julie
Andrews, who also picked
up the award for Best
Actress.*

'60s

1960: Billy Wilder wins Best Direction Oscar for *The Apartment*, Burt Lancaster Best Actor for *Elmer Gantry* and, unbelievably, Elizabeth Taylor Best Actress for *Butterfield 8*.

1962: *Lawrence of Arabia* wins it by a camel's length and Greg Peck gets it for sincerity in *To Kill a Mockingbird*.

1963: Britain again wins with *Tom Jones*, with Tony Richardson as Best Director.

1965: Best Picture? Wait for it! *The Sound of Music*! The Hollywood hills are alive with the sound of cash registers . . .

1969: Sentiment alone, or perhaps Richard Nixon, could have been behind giving John Wayne the Best Actor award for *True Grit*. Maggie Smith went over-the-top in *The Prime of Miss Jean Brodie* but won an Oscar for it. *Midnight Cowboy* won the Best Film Oscar.

RIGHT

Peter O'Toole in Lawrence of Arabia, *the Oscar-winning film of 1962.*

'70s

1970: George C. Scott refused the Oscar for his role in *Patton*, saying that he thought actors were not in competition with one another. Mutes do well again as John Mills gets Best Supporting Actor for pulling grotesque faces in *Ryan's Daughter*.

1972: *The Godfather* year for Best Picture, while Marlon Brando, winner for his performance as Don Corleone, sent Sacheen Littlefeather, an American Indian, to read a letter from him, refusing the award and drawing the audience's attention to Hollywood's history of misrepresenting American Indians on the screen.

1975: *One Flew over the Cuckoo's Nest* swept the board of the four major awards, including Best Actor for Jack Nicholson.

1977: Woody Allen wins for his direction of *Annie Hall* but chooses to play jazz in Michael's Bar in New York rather than picking up the Oscar; co-star Diane Keaton does turn up to collect her Best Actress award.

1978: Michael Cimino, Best Director for *The Deer Hunter*, which also won Best Picture.

'80s

1980: Robert De Niro is rewarded for his professional fanaticism in adding 60 pounds to his frame for his role as Jake La Motta in *Raging Bull*. Robert Redford gets an Oscar for directing *Ordinary People*.

1981: Colin Welland, screenwriter of the British winner *Chariots of Fire*, shouts 'The British are coming!' and embarrasses most people with his crass jingoism and boasting. Jane Fonda accepts dying father Henry's Oscar for *On Golden Pond*. Warren Beatty comes good with his Oscar for his direction of *Reds*.

1982: The British did come with *Gandhi*, and perhaps the Academy regretted their choice because they had to listen to a speech of acceptance from Richard Attenborough.

1983: Linda Hunt wins Best Supporting Actress Oscar for her role as a male photographer in *The Year of Living Dangerously*.

1984: A wonderful year for fans of Oscar embarrassments. Sally Field, accepting her Oscar for *Places in the Heart*, emotes, 'You like me! You like me!' to a bemused audience and wins herself an additional honorary Oscar for the most over-the-top acceptance speech of all time. Nonprofessional Cambodian Haing S. Ngor wins Best Supporting Actor for his role in *The Killing Fields*.

1988: *Rain Man* wins four major awards, including best actor for Dustin Hoffman. Best Actress goes to Jody Foster for her strong performance in *The Accused*.

1989: Plenty of films to tug at the heart strings this year. Jessica Tandy becomes the oldest Oscar winner for her role in *Driving Miss Daisy*. Daniel Day Lewis wins Best Actor for *My Left Foot*.

1992: Clint Eastwood, after 39 years in the industry, wins Best Director for *Unforgiven*, which also won Best Picture. Al Pacino, after six nominations throughout his career, finally wins Best Actor for *Scent of a Woman*. Three awards go to *Howard's End*, including Best Actress for Emma Thompson.

1993: Steven Spielberg finally wins Best Director for *Schindler's List*, which also deservedly wins Best Picture. It's certainly political correctness time in Tinsel Town as Tom Hanks wins Oscar for playing an AIDS victim in *Philadelphia* (Bruce Springsteen wins Best Song which he wrote for the same movie).

1994: Tom Hanks wins his second successive Oscar for playing *Forrest Gump*, Jessica Lange wins Best Actress for *Blue Skies*, and Tarantino wins Best Screenwriter for *Pulp Fiction*. Elton John follows in Springsteen's footsteps, picking up Best Song for his contribution to *The Lion King*.

ABOVE
Reds *won the Best Director Oscar for actor Warren Beatty, who also produced, co-wrote and starred in the movie.*

BELOW
Forrest Gump *(1994) was a hugely successful movie that particularly appealed to Americans looking back to an age of conservative values and forgotten innocence.*

'90s

1990: *Dances with Wolves* swept the board with seven Oscars although best actor for director/star Kevin Costner wasn't one of them. That award went to Jeremy Irons for *Reversal of Fortune*.

1991: Cannibalism and serial killers are big business at the box office and popular with the critics – *Silence of the Lambs* wins all five main awards. *Beauty and the Beast* became the first animated film to be nominated for Best Picture.

HOLLYWOOD SCANDALS AND TRAGEDIES

IT IS A hoary old cliché that Hollywood, and show-business in general, extracts a heavy price for its prizes of stardom and fame, but the history of the American film industry *does* seem to be littered with the dead bodies and ruined reputations of many of its most famous personalities. It may be that the movie industry extracts no higher price for success than, say, the profession of accountancy does, but suicides and murders among movie stars tend to reach the front pages rather more often. Another matter of debate is how much these unfortunate stars were victims of an uncaring, exploitative system and how much they contributed to their own downfall through their own self-destructive natures. What is undoubtedly true is that people living under the glare of the Hollywood spotlights are at high risk of succumbing to egomania, self-destructive patterns, delusions, feelings of unworthiness and sundry other unhappy syndromes. Ah, well, as the man said, if you have the fame, you have to take the heartaches that go with it . . .

THE FATTY ARBUCKLE AFFAIR

In the very early days of Hollywood, Roscoe 'Fatty' Arbuckle became a famous Mack Sennett slapstick comedian. He was a great box-office attraction with a salary to match, until events in 1921 put paid to his meteoric career.

At a weekend-long party organised by Arbuckle in the St Francis Hotel in San Francisco, a young starlet, Virginia Rappe, was severely injured, injuries that led to her death five days later from peritonitis. How she came to be seriously hurt was never finally established, but Arbuckle had been in a bedroom alone with her just before she was discovered in a state of severe pain and with her clothing torn.

Arbuckle was charged with rape and murder. The scandal rocked Hollywood, and the nation's moral guardians, eager to attack the film colony, labelled it a modern-day Sodom and Gomorrah. Rumours spread that Arbuckle had used a Coca-Cola bottle on Rappe in an attempt at unnatural penetration. Three trials ensued and, after two hung juries (one opting for acquittal, the other for conviction), the third jury cleared Arbuckle of all charges. But his film career was over. Despite his acquittal, his erstwhile friends and the film studios turned their backs on him. He became an alcoholic and died at the age of 46 in 1933.

BELOW
Fatty Arbuckle was a major star before his encounter with Virginia Rappe at a Hollywood party.

PAUL BERN
AND
JEAN HARLOW

Paul Bern was a top MGM executive in the thirties. He was a small, unattractive man, hardly the type to be thought of as a likely husband for blonde star, Jean Harlow, whose screen persona was brassy and promiscuous. However, Harlow had married Bern in July 1932. Perhaps she believed that a top executive such as Bern would help and protect her career at MGM; perhaps Bern, twenty-two years her senior, represented some kind of father figure for her.

Two months after the marriage Bern was found shot dead in their home. A suicide note was left in his handwriting, referring to his 'abject humiliation' and a reference to the pre-vious night as 'only a comedy'. It seemed that Bern was so ashamed of his inability to make love to his screen goddess wife that he took his own life. Louis B. Mayer and Irving Thalberg, who ran MGM at that time, were on the scene before the police, giving rise to the rumour that some kind of cover-up had been put into opera-tion. Harlow was then a very 'hot' property for the studio. It was stated that Harlow had been staying with her mother at the time of Bern's death. But was there more to this affair than met the eye? Could the suicide note have been forced out of Bern to make it look like suicide? Was Harlow actually there in the house at the time? Whatever the real facts, Harlow herself did not survive her husband that long; by 1937 she too had died, from uremic poisoning.

LEFT
Jean Harlow was the epitome of sexual allure for thirties' audiences, so it was odd that insignificant-looking Paul Bern, an MGM executive, should be the man to marry her.

ERROL FLYNN

Errol Flynn was a renowned womaniser on and off the screen, but his promiscuous ways landed him in deep trouble in 1942 when he was charged with statutory rape under a Californian law that made it illegal to have sex with anyone under the age of eighteen. At the Grand Jury hearing, Flynn was acquitted because the girls involved told conflicting stories. However, the authorities pursued the case and Flynn had to stand trial.

Jerry Geisler, top-notch criminal lawyer, defended Flynn and managed to tear the girls' stories to shreds. Flynn was again acquitted. The real puzzle was, who or what was behind this campaign to get Flynn? A whole can of worms involving Warner Bros. and Flynn's studio paying kickbacks to politicians and the police could have been opened, if anyone had spilled the beans. As it was, Flynn's reputation as a lover and star was only enhanced by the trials. But, even after his death in 1959, they were still trying to pin something on old Errol: he has been variously accused of being a Nazi spy and an IRA supporter. Perhaps Flynn wasn't the only one who had difficulty in telling the difference between reality and the movies.

LEFT

Errol Flynn was sold as the epitome of male sexuality, and he seemed to have done his best to live up to his own legend. That legend includes rumours that Flynn was an IRA supporter, a Nazi agent, and a freedom fighter for Castro – a busy guy!

FRANCES FARMER

The story of Frances Farmer raises the issue of responsibility: was her steep fall from Hollywood grace largely self-inflicted, was she the victim of a vindictive system, or was it six of one and half-a-dozen of the other?

Like other Hollywood luminaries such as John Garfield and Elia Kazan, Farmer had emerged from New York's Group Theatre, which had a reputation for being left-wing and challenging in theatrical terms. She was signed up by Paramount, but was used largely in extremely mediocre movies. Along the way she married a Hollywood actor, Leif Erickson, who, according to her, beat her up regularly. In 1943 she had a couple of dust-ups with the Los Angeles Police Department over traffic violations and the subsequent breaking of her parole. At her trial, she threw an ink-pot at the judge and slugged a police officer. She was put in a straitjacket, served some time in jail and a private sanatorium, then was committed for ten years to a state asylum where she was systematically abused and humiliated. Finally, she had a lobotomy, which left her stable but unrecognisable. When she was released from the asylum she even fronted a television show for a while. Her story was filmed in 1983 with Jessica Lange playing her.

Farmer was undoubtedly a strong-minded, independent woman with left-wing sympathies. This combination probably accounts in part for the horrific treatment that was doled out to her. Had she been a star in Hollywood in the sixties rather than in the thirties, her form of

spirited independence might have been accommodated. As it was, in the forties when her real troubles began, the powers-that-be were unaccustomed to dealing with young women who didn't take any shit and were not over-grateful for getting trashy parts in tenth-rate movies.

LEFT
Frances Farmer in a pose from the 1937 Ebb Tide.

LANA TURNER
AND
THE HOOD

In 1958, Lana Turner's daughter Cheryl stabbed to death her mother's lover Johnny Stompanato, in her mother's bedroom in the Beverly Hills mansion that the three of them shared. Stompanato, a psychopath with gangland connections, had repeatedly threatened Turner during the course of their relatively brief relationship. Cheryl, fourteen at the time of the killing, had overheard the 'gigolo-type' Stompanato threatening to cut her mother up: she had then taken a long kitchen knife and plunged it into his stomach.

At the subsequent trial Turner reputedly gave one of her best performances – as the distraught and contrite mother fighting for her daughter. The jury returned a verdict of justifiable homicide. However, the details of

Turner's private life were splashed over every front page in America. Her love letters to Stompanato were released by some vindictive people to the press. The irony is that, after all this bad publicity, Turner's career had an upsurge and she continued to make films, one of which, *Imitation of Life*, was her greatest success. The connections between Hollywood and organised crime have always been known about but hushed up; the Turner-Stompanato affair brought some of those tawdry connections to light.

RIGHT

Lana Turner. The scandal surrounding her lover's murder did nothing to harm her career

GEORGE CUKOR AND *GONE WITH THE WIND*

In 1939 George Cukor was assigned to direct *Gone with the Wind* by producer David Selznick. It was a dream assignment because even before it came in front of the cameras *GWTW* was the most talked-about movie ever. Cukor, one of Hollywood's most discreet homosexuals, had made his reputation by directing female stars (Hepburn, Garbo and Crawford) in *Dinner at Eight*, *Little Women*, *Sylvia Scarlett*,

Shortly after filming commenced, Selznick replaced Cukor with Victor Fleming, a journeyman MGM director. Seemingly, Clark Gable, Rhett Butler in the film, had insisted that Cukor be replaced because the star felt that Cukor was too much of a woman's director and was giving undue attention to Vivièn Leigh in her role as Scarlett O'Hara, and too little to Gable and the male side of the story.

Near the end of his life, however, Cukor gave a quite different explanation for his replacement. According to this, before he had become a star, Gable had been an up-market rent-boy for Hollywood's homosexual colony. Gable was aware that Cukor knew this sordid detail about him and could not bear to be directed by the man. Thus, he insisted Cukor be given the push. By the time Cukor made these allegations, Gable, of course, had been dead nearly thirty years.

LEFT

Clark Gable in his most famous role as Rhett Butler. Could the most masculine of Hollywood stars really have had a spell as a rent-boy, as director George Cukor claimed?

Alfred Hitchcock frequently fell for his leading ladies, none of whom seemed to have requited his passion. Tipi Hedren, seen here in Marnie *(and mother of current star, Melanie Griffiths), was no exception.*

THE STRANGE OBSESSIONS OF ALFRED HITCHCOCK

Hitchcock's obsession with cool, blonde women was well-known, but the extent to which he carried this neurotic attachment with one of his stars, Tippi Hedren, was disturbing to say the least. Hedren starred in two of Hitchcock's movies, *Marnie* and *The Birds*, the latter being about the sudden inexplicable onslaught by our feathered friends on a small fishing village.

For some of the scenes, Hitchcock insisted that real birds be used to peck away at Hedren while she was pinned down by invisible bonds. After a week-long shooting of a particular scene, things got wildly out of hand. Hedren was reduced to hysteria after remorseless attacks by crazed birds and she also suffered a severe injury to one of her eyes.

Hitchcock undoubtedly was strongly sexually attracted to her, a feeling that was not reciprocated. The director clearly represented his anger at being repulsed by the actress in these elongated scenes of ornithological assault. It seems that Hitchcock was eaten up with self-loathing because of his obesity and took it out on blonde actresses who aroused his hopeless passions.

GIG YOUNG

No screen persona belied the reality of an actor's life more than that adopted by Gig Young. Young had a long movie career as a light comedian, playing the hero's best friend, the charming rival of the star and the second lead who never seemed to get the girl, in movies such as *Old Acquaintance*, *Young at Heart*, *Desk Set*, *Ask Any Girl*, *That Touch of Mink* and *Strange Bedfellows*. In real life Young was an alcoholic and in the latter part of his life suffered from skin cancer.

In 1978 at the age of 64, Young married a woman of 31. Three weeks later both of them were found dead in his New York apartment. Young was clutching a revolver. The obvious conclusion was that Young had first shot his wife in the head, then turned the gun on himself. Whether she was party to a suicide pact or not remains in doubt.

The carefree actor in some of Hollywood's lightest confections had faced up to the desperation of his own life and put an end to it, taking his new wife with him. Movies create illusions – about ourselves, about the stars we see on the screen, about what is perceived as reality. In the case of Gig Young, the escape he found in the illusions of the screen was no longer enough of a safety net. He ended those illusions with a bullet to his head.

RIGHT

Gig Young in this studio pose is the debonair actor the world saw on screen, but behind that carefree air was a deeply insecure man. When the ageing process caught up with him, he could not face his life any more.

THE LOVING MOTHER

In 1977 Christina Crawford, Joan Crawford's adopted daughter, wrote a memoir about her mother entitled *Mommie Dearest*. It chronicled a story of the Crawford family life as vicious and uncaring. Up there on the silver screen Joan Crawford so often played the sacrificial mother fighting her way to the top to give the good things of life to her children. In real life, Crawford seemingly acquired her two adopted children because it would help her image as a caring star and hence her film career, which had gone into decline. She imposed severe discipline on the kids, beating them with coathangers amongst other things, and expecting absurd levels of obedience and regimentation.

Crawford had always worked hard at her career, seeking sugar daddies in her younger years who were in a position to land her the small parts that were essential if she was to climb the stairway to stardom. Eventually, by sheer determination rather than talent, she became a featured player, then an MGM star. Stories abound in Hollywood about her legendary bitchiness, especially to other female stars such as Norma Shearer, Garbo and Bette Davis. When she could no longer play ambitious secretaries, she turned to playing suffering matrons. All her career she pandered to the fan magazines and in public played the role of the star to the hilt.

RIGHT

A publicity still showing the 'loving' Joan Crawford with her adopted daughter Christina. A biography written after Crawford's death alleged that the reality of home life was very different.

Crawford's adopted children were forced to pose with her for loving family publicity pics, which disguised the hell they were living through. The final straw for daughter Christina was when her mother took over her role in a television soap opera when she (Christina) was lying ill in hospital. Seeing her mother play a part, her part, that was meant for an actress forty years younger probably finally prompted Christina to write *Mommie Dearest*. It was filmed in 1981 with Faye Dunaway playing Crawford. As someone who courted fame and publicity assiduously all her life, Crawford might not have been too unhappy at this late burst of fame. In 1938 she had been one of the stars whom an ad, placed by exhibitors in *Hollywood Reporter*, had dubbed 'box-office poison'. She fought her way back from that nadir and she would have clawed her way back after *Mommie Dearest*, had she not died in 1977.

Endquotes

♦♦*Hollywood is a place where people from Iowa mistake each other for stars.*♦♦

FRED ALLEN

♦♦*I believe that God felt sorry for actors, so he created Hollywood to give them a place in the sun and a swimming pool.*♦♦

SIR CEDRIC HARDWICKE

♦♦*Los Angeles is a city with the personality of a paper cup.*♦♦

RAYMOND CHANDLER

♦♦*You can take Hollywood for granted like I did, or you can dismiss it with the contempt we reserve for what we don't understand. It can be understood too, but only dimly and in flashes.*♦♦

SCOTT FITZGERALD

♦♦*The cinema in the hands of the Soviet power represents a great and priceless force.*♦♦

JOSEPH STALIN

♦♦*All those years at MGM I hid a black terror behind a cheerful face.*♦♦

ROBERT YOUNG

♦♦*People needed a dream world to get away from the awfulness of the reality around them – breadlines and all that. And boy, did we know how to give them dreams!*♦♦

DONALD OGDEN STEWART

♦♦*Gary Cooper and Greta Garbo are the same person. After all, have you ever seen them in a movie together?*♦♦

ERNST LUBITSCH

♦♦*You need to be a bit of a bastard to be a star.*♦♦

LAURENCE OLIVIER

RIGHT
Robert Young.

FAR RIGHT
Laurence Olivier in A Bridge Too Far.

❞America is a happy-ending nation.❞

DORE SCHARY

❞Now I can retire from politics after having had 'Happy Birthday' sung to me by such a sweet, wholesome girl as Marilyn Monroe.❞

JOHN F. KENNEDY

❞Look at that bunch of pants-pressers in Hollywood making themselves millions.❞

JOSEPH KENNEDY

❞The making of a blockbuster is the newest art form of the twentieth century.❞

ROBERT EVANS

❞Who wants to see me do 'Hamlet'? Very few. But millions want to see me as Frankenstein so that's the one I do.❞

PETER CUSHING

❞She's got talent and personality. Give me two years and I'll make her an overnight star.❞

HARRY COHN

❞Every MGM picture is a good one. Some pictures are better than others, but there are really no bad pictures – at any rate there are no bad MGM pictures.❞

LOUIS B. MAYER

❞The lunatics have taken charge of the asylum.❞ (He said this on hearing that Pickford, Fairbanks, Chaplin and Griffith had formed their own studio, United Artists.)

RICHARD ROWLAND

FAR LEFT
Marlon Brando.

LEFT
Peter Cushing.

INDEX